COMPUTERS, TEACHING, AND LEARNING
An Introduction to Computers in Education

Jerry W. Willis
D. LaMont Johnson
Paul N. Dixon

dilithium Press
Beaverton, Oregon

©Copyright 1983 by dilithium Press. All rights reserved.

No part of this book may be reproduced in any form or by any means, electronic or mechanical, including photocopying, recording or by any information storage and retrieval system without permission in writing from the publisher, with the following two exceptions: any material may be copied or transcribed for the non-profit use of the purchaser, and material (not to exceed 300 words and one figure) may be quoted in published reviews of this book.

10   9   8   7   6   5   4   3   2   1

Library of Congress Cataloging in Publication Data

Willis, Jerry.
  Computers, teaching, and learning.

  Bibliography: p.
  Includes index.
  1. Computer-assisted instruction. 2. Computer managed instruction. 3. Microcomputers.
I. Johnson, D. LaMont, 1939-   . II. Dixon, Paul N., 1944-   . III. Title.
LB1028.46.W54   1983   371.3'9445   82-23549
ISBN 0-88056-065-7

Printed in the United States of America

dilithium Press
P.O. Box 606
Beaverton, Oregon 97075

To Professor Robert Anderson

Preface

Writing this book was like trying to hit a moving target on a carnival midway. Our topic, the use of computers in education, was constantly changing and evolving. The eighties are not a time to sit back and ponder; the time calls for action, for doing and changing. We have thus tried to present an action oriented book that focuses on the issues, concepts, and facts relevant to the educator who wants to consider using computers to accomplish learning objectives. The book is intended as an action guide, but it is not simply a technical manual for plugging your computer into the wall and announcing that "computer literacy" has arrived. There are important decisions to be made, there are competing ideologies that urge us to move in different directions, and there are serious questions to be considered.

We need to think and plan carefully before rushing headlong into a future of classrooms filled with blinking cursors and whirring disk drives. Uncritical acceptance of computers may do more harm to the cause of educational computing than uncritical rejection. The demands on education today are greater than at any other time in history, and they are growing. Educational computing, as it exists today, is a poor means of accomplishing some educational objectives; it is a good alternative for others; and an excellent, cost efficient means of reaching some. Educational computing may have an important, even crucial, role in the classroom of tomorrow. In this book we have tried to point out the difference between current realities and future possibilities. Educational computing is good now; its future will depend on the ability of professional educators such as yourself. We hope this book provides you with a foundation for thoughtfully and carefully developing expertise in educational computing.

We would like to thank a number of our colleagues for reviewing different versions of this manuscript. Dr. Larry Hovey read the entire manuscript and offered many useful criticisms as did graduate student Sondra Cosby who also lent us her considerable expertise as a photographer. Other graduate students at Texas Tech University who provided useful critiques of the manuscript include Mary Ann Speck, Melanie White, and Hugh Smith.

We would also like to thank Dean Robert Anderson for his support, guidance, and leadership. This book was completed by three faculty in the College of Education at Texas Tech University during Dr. Anderson's last year as Dean before retirement. His leadership, and his support for the development of an educational computing graduate program at Texas Tech, were important factors in making this book possible. We therefore dedicate this book to Dean Anderson.

Jerry W. Willis
D. LaMont Johnson
Paul N. Dixon

Contents

Section One	INTRODUCTION	1
Chapter One	**The Computer, The School, and The Revolution?**	1
	What This Book Covers	8
	A Short History of Computers	9
	Educational Precursors of the Computer	23
	The Teaching Machine	23
	Programmed Instruction	25
	The Computer's Roles in Education	26
Chapter Two	**Current Applications**	29
	Minnesota Educational Computing Consortium (MECC)	33
	Educational Computing in Ireland	35
	Bellingham High School	37
	Institute for Child and Family Studies	38
	Professor of Education	43
	Common Usage Patterns in Schools	45
Chapter Three	**Selecting Educational Computers**	53
	Step One. Identify Major Uses	54
	Step Two. Software Considerations	55

	Step Three. Specify Minimum Requirements and Preferred Key Features	57
	Step Four. Identify Likely Secondary Uses and Desirable Machine Features	71
	Step Five. Decide How Much You Can Spend—Now and Later	71
	Step Six. Try it Out	73
	Step Seven. Survey Sources	74
	Step Eight. Buy it	75
	Potentially Important Features . . .	75
Section Two	**COMPUTER LANGUAGES**	85
Chapter Four	**BASIC**	85
	Computer Languages	86
	BASIC	88
	Getting Started	90
	Structure	90
	A Program	92
	Analysis of Program 4.1	95
	Summary of Program 4.1	96
	Input and Output	96
	You as a Programmer	97
	Remarks Statements (REM)	98
	Some Essential Statements	98
	Analysis of Program 4.3	99
	A Little More Sophistication	104
	Analysis of Program 4.4	105
	Working With Strings and Arrays .	106
	Some New Skills	108
	Analysis of Program 4.5	111
	Where to Go From Here	114
	How to Use What You Have Learned	114
	Saving Your Program	115
Chapter Five	**PILOT**	**117**
	Advantages	118
	What It's Like	120
	Getting Started	122

Chapter Six	Logo	137
	Piaget and Child Development	138
	Piaget Applied to Education	142
	The Logo Language	144
Section Three	**TYPES OF EDUCATIONAL APPLICATIONS**	**159**
Chapter Seven	**Computer-Assisted Instruction** .	**159**
	Computer-Assisted Instruction ...	160
Chapter Eight	**Computer-Managed Instruction**	**185**
	CMI Today	187
	Issues in CMI..................	194
	Administrative Issues	199
	Where Is CMI Appropriate?	199
	An Extension of CMI: Career Counseling.....................	200
Chapter Nine	**Applications in Assessment and Evaluation**	**203**
	State of the Art.................	204
	Dealing With the Objections	205
	Enhancing the Relationship Between Testing and Teaching ...	207
	Some Specific Applications.......	210
	What the Future Holds	223
Section Four	**SOURCES OF INFORMATION** .	**225**
Chapter Ten	**Sources of Information**	**225**
	Periodicals	225
	Sources of Educational Software and Software Information	238
	Commercial Software Distributors	244
	Book Publishers	246
	Organizations	248
	Databases and Indexes of Interest .	249
	Computer Databases............	250
	Summary	252
Index	....	**253**

Section One

INTRODUCTION

1

The Computer, The School, and The Revolution?

Technology has played a role in education ever since some enterprising teacher used a handy stick to draw pictures in the dirt for an eager student. This book was written to introduce you to a relatively new technology that holds considerable promise for educators. Two of the primary purposes of this book are, 1) to describe and explain the range of roles computers can play in education, and 2) to teach you how to select, buy, and use an educational computer.

True, the field of education has not been exactly an eager consumer of new technology, whether it was slates, blackboards, filmstrips, television, or computers. On the other hand, technology has not been all that dependable when asked to fulfill the promises made on its behalf.

It is an unfortunate fact that many, if not most, educational innovations take more of a teacher's time than expected and produce far fewer gains than promised. We feel that the fault, however, lies not with the technology but with some of the enthusiastic missionaries of technology who allow their enthusiasm to overwhelm their sensibilities. Proponents of new technologies have often seen their particular approach as something that would replace rather than coexist with existing technology and methods. It is therefore important to differentiate between the new technology itself and advocates of the new technology. New technology is sometimes poorly served by its advocates.

Even the lowly blackboard can be an amazing piece of technology in the hands of a skilled teacher. It is not useful in every class and it won't replace the teacher, but it does have a place—it is useful technology.

From our perspective, computers are much like blackboards. Computers are not final answers to the pressing problems of education and they are not likely to displace teachers in the schools of the future (although they may change the job of a teacher considerably). In the hands of a talented and well-trained teacher computers can be used to teach many subjects more quickly, more effectively, or more economically than other methods. Few schools today are without aids such as blackboards, 16mm projectors, videotape machines, and so on. The schools of the future will also have computers—in classrooms, in learning centers, in libraries, and in their offices. The effectiveness of these computers, and their role in the school, will be determined by the educators who use them.

Figure 1.1 The Educational Computing Center in a high school.

Although the concept of a machine that works like a computer is well over a hundred years old, the computer as a real piece of equipment has a short history of around forty years. Computers have been used in education for just over twenty years. (They were, of course, a topic of study themselves as soon as they were developed.) Pioneering projects such as Suppes' work at Stanford University, however, used large, expensive computers which could not be placed in individual classrooms or resource centers. Instead, keyboard/printer devices called *terminals* were placed in the schools and connected to the computer by phone. This method was the only option available twenty years ago, and it is still a major means of getting computer-based learning into the classroom. In those days the computers were big, expensive, and difficult to use. Programming and operating a computer required extensive training, often a bachelor's or graduate degree in computer science. Twenty years ago, a computer could cost as much as constructing a small elementary school building and might require the school system to design special, costly rooms for the computer and employ high-priced professionals to run it. Even with the tremendous expense, early computers were not very reliable; maintenance and repair costs were high.

Figure 1.2 A modern mainframe computer center.

In spite of the limitations and the expense of computers in the sixties and seventies, many pioneering school systems did experiment with educational applications of computers. In a typical system, one large or *mainframe* computer located in the central administrative building would be connected over phone lines to terminals in classrooms or computer centers in the schools. Children typed in responses on the terminal's keyboard and waited for the computer to answer by either printing a message on a video screen or on a printer. Having one large computer serve many children at one time (called

4 • Computers, Teaching and Learning

Figure 1.3 A modern mainframe computer center.

time sharing) is still a popular approach. Several large corporations now offer comprehensive systems of computer-assisted instruction using the time-sharing method. Control Data's PLATO system and the work of the Curriculum Development Corporation are two very good examples.

Figure 1.4 A modem is necessary to connect computers by phone. *Photo courtesy Novation Inc.*

In spite of the history of large computers as learning machines, we feel that the future of educational computing lies in the increased use of small computers. They are less expensive, easier to use, more reliable, and easier to install in a school. When faced with the choice of buying one large computer or 100 small computers school districts are now frequently electing to buy small computers such as the TRS-80 Model III, Atari 400 or 800, the Apple II, the Texas Instruments 99/4A, and the Commodore 64.

Why are schools leaning toward desktop computers? Cost is one reason. The small computers often cost far less than the price of one terminal for a larger system. Dependability is probably the second major reason. To use a time-sharing system requires a terminal that is working, a phone line that is reasonably clear of interference, and a remotely located computer (sometimes several hundred miles away) that is not only working but has the time to respond quickly to the student at the terminal. If any one of the elements in the chain isn't working, the entire system will not work, and a scheduled learning period in the classroom is lost. The logistics involved in using small computers are much less complicated, and therefore more reliable. One distinguished computer educator with experience in both time sharing and small computer applications made the point very clearly:

Figure 1.5 A small desktop computer in an elementary school.
Photo courtesy Texas Instruments

The inexpensive microcomputer, more than any other event, has made school-based computer education a possibility. The development of small time-sharing systems about ten years ago brought hardware costs per student terminal down to about $10,000 — a major breakthrough, but still far too costly for most schools. Worse yet, time-sharing systems lack robustness against hardware failure: 97% uptime is achievable and sounds good, but it means that there is no computer one day per month, and no computer class. The new personal computers have brought the cost down to from $1,000 to $2,000 and have increased robustness dramatically: 97% uptime for personal computers means that out of a collection of ten machines, nine are working all the time and all ten are working most of the time. Class goes on. (A. Leuhrmann, "Computer Illiteracy — A National Crisis and a Solution for It," *Byte*, July, 1980, 98-102).

Figure 1.6 The Apple II personal computer is very popular in schools. *Photo courtesy Apple Computer Inc.*

Figure 1.7 The Commodore line of small computers is frequently found in schools. *Photo courtesy Commodore Business Machines, Inc.*

There is one final reason for the shift to small computers. Recent technological advances allow a school to develop time-sharing systems which are based on microcomputers rather than more expensive mini or mainframe computers. Several products, for example, permit Apple, Atari, Commodore, and Radio Shack computers to share expensive peripherals such as disk drives and printers. This process is often called *networking*. More expensive microcomputers, such as the Godbout CompuPro and the Model 16 from Radio Shack, can be used with terminals, thus allowing more than one student to use them at once. Since the computer is in the same building as the terminals, there is no need for phone line connections (less expense, more reliability).

Because we believe the small, inexpensive computers will be a major force in the future of educational computing they will be the focus of this book. The large computer did play a crucial role in the development of educational applications and it is certainly not headed toward educational extinction,

Figure 1.8 The Network 3 allows up to sixteen Radio Shack Model III computers to share one set of disk drives and a printer. *Photo courtesy Tandy Radio Shack.*

but it will play a more limited role than it did in the past. Thus, while the focus of the book is on the smaller computers we will also frequently mention their larger brethren as well.

WHAT THIS BOOK COVERS

This book is divided into four sections. Chapters 1 through 3, which make up the first section, contain introductory material that sets the stage for future chapters. The final segment of Chapter 1 is a short history of computers with the emphasis on microcomputers and their use in education. Chapter 2, Current Applications, gives the reader a more detailed look at some representative applications in preschool, elementary, high school, and college settings. Chapter 3, Selecting Educational Computers, is the last one in the introductory section. It covers the essentials of selecting the best computer or computers for your applications and offers some suggestions on how to go about purchasing equipment. Software selection is also discussed.

Section Two, Computer Languages, is an introduction to three of the computer languages used most often in schools. Each chapter describes the general characteristics of the language and then begins a tutorial on that language. You won't be an expert on BASIC when you finish Chapter 4, but you will be able to use that computer language to write simple programs, and you will be able to read and understand many educational programs which are written in BASIC. Chapter 5 covers PILOT while Chapter 6 deals with Logo.

Section Three, Types of Educational Applications, introduces, explains, and provides examples of the major ways in which computers are used in educational settings. Chapter 7 focuses on CAI, or Computer-Assisted Instruction. In CAI, the computer is actually programmed to provide practice or training for the student. Chapter 8 covers CMI or Computer-Managed Instruction. With CMI the computer is not actually used to provide instruction, instead it keeps track of student progress and may administer and score tests for students as they work through assignments. Chapter 9, Applications in Assessment and Evaluation, covers a relatively new and underdeveloped area of computer use. Computers are now being used to help teachers, special educators, and psychologists develop individualized learning plans for students with special difficulties. Chapter 9 reviews work in areas related to evaluation and individual program planning.

The fourth and final section of the book, Sources of Information, contains only one chapter. It describes other information sources including books, magazines and journals, and computer databases.

A SHORT HISTORY OF COMPUTERS

One of the earliest ancestors of electronic computers is the music box. The sound from a music box is created by a slowly rotating drum with small metal pins protruding from it. As the drum revolves, the pins catch on extensions from the box's sound board and then flip back as the drum continues rotating. This relatively simple process can be used to create music boxes that play very complex, very beautiful compositions. The important point to remember is that the music box builder had only two options in creating the pattern of pins on the drum. He or she could either place or not place a pin in a given location. When you have only two choices (i.e., put a pin there or don't put one there) you have the essentials of a "binary" number system. The binary number system has only two digits, 1 and 0, and it uses those two digits to build larger numbers. The music box builder converts binary 1's and 0's into pins on a drum (i.e., 1=pin, 0=no pin) while the computer designer converts binary numbers into electrical signals (1="on", 0="off"). The principle is essentially the same. Both systems build complicated patterns from simple ones. There were other precursors to the computer besides the music box. The abacus was one of the most successful of the early mechanical calculating aids.

During the seventeenth to the nineteenth centuries several scientists, including John Napier, Blaise Pascal, Gottfried Leibnitz, and Charles Babbage invented mechanical aids for solving simple mathematical problems. The devices of Pascal, Leibnitz, and Babbage all used intermeshed gears to represent the basic mathematical operations of adding, subtracting, multiplying, and dividing. On these machines, adding 56 and 34 involved turning some gears (which in turn, caused other gears to rotate). The answer to the problem was then read from indicators which were attached to the gears. The most ambitious of these devices, the Difference Engine of Charles Babbage, was so complex that it required gears more precise than could be produced in the nineteenth century.

The early, gear-driven calculating devices are most accurately considered as direct ancestors of modern adding machines and calculators rather than computers. This is true because these machines performed one type of task, computing, in a specified pattern. Computers, on the other hand, can be *programmed* or given instructions to perform many different types of tasks. In spite of his difficulties in actually building the Difference Engine, the English mathematician Charles Babbage is generally called the Father of Computing because he also developed the Analytical Engine, a device that can be programmed or instructed to perform a variety of computational tasks. Unfortunately, like the Difference Engine, it was never successfully constructed, although the concepts upon which it was based were sound. Babbage intended to use cards with holes punched in them to tell the Analytical Engine what to do. He borrowed the idea from a

French silk weaver, Joseph Jacquard, who had invented a weaving machine that created very complex tapestries by following instructions on stiff cards with holes in them. Different patterns of holes produced different patterns on the tapestry. The cards with holes in them are a link back to our music boxes, and a link with the punched cards of the modern electronic computer. All of these use a binary number system; the codes created by different binary patterns are used to provide instructions to a machine. Thus, the music box, the loom, the Analytical Engine, and the multimillion dollar computer, are all based on the same concept. Different results are produced by different instructions. These machines can all be programmed.

The reason that computers are relatively young, therefore, is not the complexity of the concepts used to create them. It was the problem of manufacturing them that held back earlier efforts. Babbage's Analytical Engine was to be a huge assemblage of metal rods, wheels, and gears, run by a steam engine. The precision possible at that time was simply not good enough to allow the design to work properly. Charles Babbage died in 1871, and in 1876 an American engineer named George Grant demonstrated a Difference Engine that worked. Grant, in fact, actually sold a number of machines that he called rack and pinion calculators. As the nineteenth century ended, the precision required to produce reliable mechanical calculators became available. It was also at this time that American technology began to equal, even exceed, European technology. An American named Herman Hollerith developed a machine which greatly simplified the work on the 1890 census. Hollerith used a system that punched holes in cards to represent different types of census information. Hollerith's approach is a direct ancestor of the IBM punch card (remember "Do not fold, bend, spindle, or mutilate"?). Hollerith's Tabulating Machine Company eventually became IBM. Another American, Dorr E. Felt, developed a machine called the Comptometer which was still in use as late as the early sixties in many companies. A major competitor to the Comptometer was the calculating machine designed by another American, William Burroughs.

In the first half of the twentieth century several scientists and engineers added pieces to the puzzle that would become the modern computer. By 1930, mechanical adding machines were common in businesses, offices, and factories. They were not computers since they could not be programmed, and generally performed only simple mathematical operations. Babbage's general purpose Analytical Engine was conceptually a computer, but it could not be manufactured because of the precision required. Some twentieth century scientists continued to work on a mechanical computer; others decided to explore the possibilities of an electronic computer.

Vannevar Bush, a professor at MIT, built and demonstrated a differential analyzer in 1930. It was large, and had many gears, but it used electric motors. It worked, and could be reconfigured (programmed) to perform many different types of calculating work. Bush's machine was also the first to use electricity not only to turn the gears, but to indicate quantities. His machine could store numbers or quantities as electricity in one part of the sytem. This ability led some to name Bush the Father of the Electronic Computer.

The day of the gear driven computer was almost over, however. Konrad Zuse, a German engineer, and Howard Aiken, a Harvard math professor, both built hybrid (part mechanical, part electronic) machines in the period between 1930 and 1950. Both used binary arithmetic (1's and 0's were the only digits) and both used electric relays to perform math operations. Aiken's machine was dubbed the Harvard Mark I. But the future belonged to the fully electronic rather than the mechanical computer. Although there is some controversy over the title, many consider the still secret British computer called the Colossus, the first electronic digital computer. The term digital means that the computer deals with discrete quantities rather than analogue values. A mercury thermometer is an analogue device since, as the mercury moves up the tube, it can represent thousands, even millions of temperatures. One temperature blends into another, there is no dividing line between locations of the mercury (although we try to simulate them by adding marks on the glass tube). In contrast, a digital thermometer will register 98.65 and then register 98.66 as the temperature increases. There is no way of indicating anything between 98.5 and 98.6 (e.g., 98.5434). Analogue systems are like ramps into a building, digital systems are like stairs. It is much easier to build computers using digital or discrete quantities.

Colossus was built and used by the British to crack German communication codes during the war. Colossus was built to do one specific job, crack codes. An American computer called ENIAC was the beginning of the general purpose electronic, digital computer.

ENIAC or Electronic Numerical Integrator and Calculator, was developed by J. P. Eckert and J. W. Mauchly at the University of Pennsylvania during World War II. It was a huge machine with thousands of vacuum tubes that were only moderately reliable, but ENIAC set the stage for greater things to come. The initial idea was to develop a device that could both determine missile trajectories and predict the weather. Within a few years the machine was being used for a variety of business and government applications. By 1952 it was predicting election outcomes, and a now famous company, International Business Machines, had entered the field. Over the next two decades a number of developments helped bring us from boxcar sized computers to computers the size of a portable typewriter. The first of these developments was the transistor.

The invention of the transistor in 1948 made modern computers practical because of its dependability, small size, and low power requirements. Transistors replaced vacuum tubes as the building blocks of computers, and the computer age was underway. Since then several major advances in semiconductor technology have produced smaller and smaller components that do more and more. In the late fifties and early sixties the integrated circuit or IC was developed. An IC contains several transistors, resistors, and capacitors in a circuit that is enclosed in a single small case or chip. Large Scale Integrated (LSI) circuits followed soon afterward with hundreds, then thousands of components packed into a single chip. It may be somewhat misleading to say that there are components inside an IC. Actually there is generally one wafer of material such as silicon on which several different layers of other types of material have been deposited. The pattern of these layers creates the effect of transistors, resistors, and capacitors without the necessity of manufacturing individual components and then installing them in a circuit.

In 1970, the first *microprocessor* IC was produced. These computers on a chip are what made personal computers possible. A single chip today contains the same amount of computing power that took tons of equipment twenty years ago. ENIAC occupied 3,000 cubic feet of space, took 140,000 watts of power, weighed 30 tons, and had 18,000 tubes, 70,000 resistors and 10,000 capacitors. Today the VIC computer from Commodore weighs only a pound or so and can be carried under your arm. Yet it is more powerful than ENIAC and does its work much faster. The VIC is also about 10,000 times more reliable and costs under $200.

Since the fifties computers have steadily become smaller and cheaper, and this pattern has produced a corresponding change in the type of people who use them. Early computers were within the financial reach of only a few large companies, universities, and government agencies such as the military. As the price of computers decreased, they became cost effective for more and more companies, especially those with large amounts of routine numerical operations to be done. Almost every bank today, for example, uses a computer to maintain accounts. As the technology of producing semiconductor integrated circuits advanced, a new type of computer—the minicomputer—emerged. Instead of occupying entire rooms like the giants of the fifties, the mini is closer to the size of a large office desk. Digital Equipment Corporation sold thousands of their PDP-8 minicomputer to businesses that did not need a large computer. Steel fabricators developed programs for the PDP-8 that allowed them to control precisely the manufacturing process by computer. Scientists used minicomputers to control experiments in the laboratory without tying up a large computer, and trucking companies used them to arrange routings, compute charges, and do paperwork.

The minicomputer brought the power of the computer to some small businesses, but not to individuals or to individual teachers in a classroom. Although the cost of a mini has dropped considerably in the past few years, a typical business system still costs over $20,000, much more than most individuals can afford and more than most schools are willing to spend on equipment for one classroom.

An honest-to-goodness computer revolution occurred in 1971, when Intel Corporation produced the first microprocessor or computer on a chip, the 4004. It was a crude, expensive device that was used primarily in commercial settings. In 1972 Intel introduced the 8008, a more sophisticated microprocessor chip that was cheap enough to be attractive to individuals interested in computers. However, its use was limited by a shortage of the support chips needed to create a working 8008 computer system and by the fact that few people knew exactly what to do with a computer on a chip. Intel marketed the 8080 in 1973, and it has become the foundation for a whole new industry—personal computing. Although it cost several hundred dollars in 1974, the 8080 can be purchased for less than $5 today. Its position of preeminence has been challenged successfully by other chips such as the Z-80 from Zilog and the 6502 from Commodore/MOS.

At about the same time that Intel was busy creating microcomputer hardware, another important ingredient in the personal computing movement was emerging. Hardware, the actual computer and its accessories, is only half the computer system. In order to do anything useful, the computer must be given a set of instructions that tell it exactly what to do. These instructions are called *programs* or *software*, and they are at least as important as the nuts and bolts of a system. Until the early seventies not many programs existed that would be of interest to educators or individual computer users. Few of us, for example, need to know where a 60mm shell would land if fired from a particular artillery piece at a 30 degree angle in a ten-mile-an-hour crosswind, nor do we have a use for a program that will calculate the load capacity of a 30 foot steel beam.

In the early days of computing the instructions (or software) were written in a way that was easy for computers to understand but not so easy for people. Programming was thus a specialized task that required sophisticated training. In 1963, however, a simple computer language called BASIC, Beginners All-purpose Symbolic Instruction Code, was developed by John Kemeny and Thomas Kurtz at Dartmouth College. BASIC is easy to learn, yet it is a powerful way of talking to the computer in a language that is similar to English. The creation of BASIC made computers easily accessible to thousands of people who had no previous contact with them. People like Bob Albrecht, then with Digital Equipment Corporation (DEC) spread the gospel of BASIC through workshops, introductory books, and general enthusiasm. David Ahl, another DEC employee, was also a preacher of the BASIC gospel. Between them, Ahl and Albrecht helped to create a collection of recreational programs written in BASIC that made computers interesting and available to thousands. Believers, often educators, then taught others how to use minicomputers to play games, draw pictures, and provide instruction. Albrecht, Ahl, and their followers are still active in the personal computing movement. Today, however, most of their work is on microcomputers rather than minicomputers.

Although Ahl and Albrecht were excited about the personal computing market their employer, DEC, had about as much as it could handle from its traditional customers and made little effort to build smaller, less expensive equipment that would be within reach of individuals. Yet DEC support for BASIC and its encouragement of the development of recreational uses of minicomputers helped to create a small army of knowledgeable computer users who wanted more—at a price they could afford.

In 1974 the market created by Ahl, Albrecht, and others was tapped. Several groups offered computer kits that could be assembled by users. The result was an inexpensive microcomputer system that, at least theoretically, would do many of the things the PDP-8 minicomputer would do. By taking advantage of technological advances in large scale integration several companies were able to offer a working computer that was about the same size as a home stereo system. The best known of these early kits was the Mark-8 which used an Intel 8008 microprocessor chip. Over 1,200 people ordered the Mark-8 kit after it was described in a 1974 Popular Electronics article. The kits offered during this period were, unfortunately, financial failures. Assembling and operating one of these early kits still required a fair level of sophistication in electronics and computer logic to make them work. These qualifications severely limited the market for the first microcomputer kits, yet they were the leading edge.

The market and the product both changed in late 1974 when an obscure company with the unlikely name of Micro Instrumentation and Telemetry System (MITS) produced its first microcomputer. MITS was founded in 1969 by H. Edward Roberts to produce electronic systems for model rocketeers. With about $10,000 in equipment and a $400 investment by four partners, Roberts moved from model rockets to calculators and began selling a low-cost programmable calculator in 1971 for $199. Comparable units from Hewlett Packard cost $6,000. Their success in the calculator market led MITS into the handheld calculator field at a time when giants like Texas Instruments were about to settle down to a serious price war. MITS was an early casualty in that war and borrowed heavily to avoid closing down permanently. Roberts decided that his next venture would be in the personal computing market, and in 1974 a MITS microcomputer kit was featured on the cover of Popular Electronics. Although some employees had suggested names like Little Brother, Leslie Solomon, the technical editor of Popular Electronics, convinced Roberts to look for other names. Solomon's daughter suggested the name Altair (from the television series Star Trek.) The name stuck and the orders rolled in. MITS expected 800 orders in 1975; they shipped 1500 units in the first two months at $398 each. Many of these units went to high schools and colleges where eager teachers and students assembled them and put computers to work in the classroom.

The Altair was the first commercially successful microcomputer, but as demands for it increased, the time between placing an order and receiving a kit also increased. These long delays at MITS created openings for several companies such as IMSAI, Southwest Technical Products Corporation, Processor Technology, and Digital Group. Between 1975 and 1977 these companies also began offering microcomputers and accessories to a growing market which began to include people from nearly all walks of life. Competition since 1974 has been tough and with the exception of Southwest Technical Products, all of these pioneering companies are gone.

The computers offered by MITS, Altair, Processor Technology, and others can be considered second-generation machines with the Mark-8 being first generation. The Altairs and their competitors were available in assembled as well as kit form, could usually be programmed in BASIC, and could be connected to a variety of accessories (e.g., printers, video monitors) with a moderate amount of technical effort. Many second-generation machines could be purchased assembled, but they still required the user to know quite a bit about computers to be able to use them effectively.

Second-generation machines were still being refined and improved when a third generation emerged. During 1977-78 several large manufacturers and retailers brought mass merchandising to personal computing. Radio Shack, Commodore (the calculator company), and Apple (a bootstrap computer company that survived and prospered), all offered third-generation microcomputers designed specifically for the beginner in personal computing; people with neither the electronics background nor the knowledge of computers that characterized many of those who bought second generation machines. The Radio Shack computers, the Apple II, and the Commodore PET all come assembled. All were designed so that the buyer can unpack a system, plug it in, and begin operating immediately. BASIC is usually built-in so that the operator can use English-like words to talk to the computer. Third generation systems are not essentially improvements over second generation systems, but reflections of a change in design emphasis. The third-generation machines are still on the market and are still excellent machines. Most school systems with active educational computing programs use third-generation machines, particularly the Apple II and the TRS-80 Model I or III.

Some writers have referred to third-generation computers as appliance computers since there is little more hassle in installing them than there is in installing any other major appliance. These computers are being sold as appliances in mass market outlets such as Sears and Montgomery Wards.

Third-generation computers bring us to the beginning of 1983. The market seems to be moving in three directions at present. First, new models in the tradition of third-generation machines are appearing regularly and in some instances, gaining a substantial share of a rapidly growing market. For example, the ATARI 800 and ATARI 400 computers are technologically superior computers designed to compete directly with computers such as the Apple II and TRS-80 Model III. Several Japanese manufacturers, including Sharp, Canon, Hitachi, and NEC, also offer current models that take advantage of the latest technology. Advances in technology are allowing all manufacturers to build computers that are faster, have more memory, and larger capacity storage systems.

By design, third-generation computers have usually been general-purpose computers. That is, they would do many things adequately. The TRS-80 can run many types of game

Figure 1.9 The ATARI 800 computer.

Figure 1.10 The Radio Shack TRS-80 Model III.

software, but it will also run accounting software, word processing programs, and home/health programs. It is not ideal for some of these applications, but it can do them all. There are indications some manufacturers may be ready to move away from general purpose personal computers in order to make their new models particularly suited to specific applications. Two Japanese manufacturers, Epson and Sharp, market small portable computers that meet the needs of a particular group of computer users, although these computers are not general-purpose machines.

In another area of the market, both IBM and Xerox announced personal computers near the end of 1981. Whereas Atari moved up into the computer market from an established position in consumer electronics (i.e., video games), IBM and Xerox both came down to this market from markets oriented toward the business community. Their computers display that heritage. Both the IBM and Xerox computers are particularly suited to the applications which are important to professional and business oriented users.

Figure 1.11 The IBM PC with accessories from Percom. *Photo courtesy Percom.*

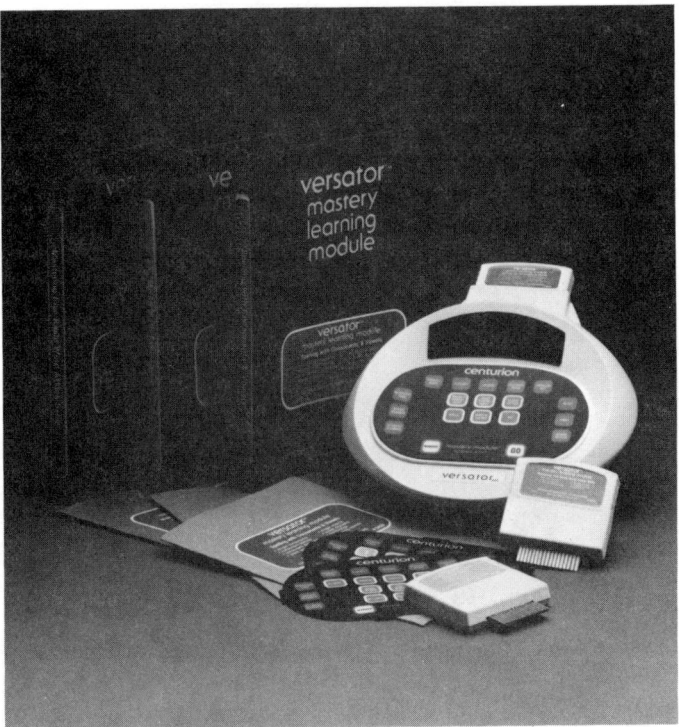

Figure 1.12 An educational computer from Centurion Industries.

Thus far there have been few serious attempts to market a special computer oriented toward the educational marketplace, but five companies—Atari, Texas Instruments, Commodore, Radio Shack, and Apple (along with its educational partner Bell and Howell) have invested considerable effort in tapping that market. During the decade of the eighties, specialization in the educational market is most likely to come in the form of educational software. That is, companies such as Texas Instruments, Apple, and Atari may form cooperative relationships with educational publishers and software developers with the idea of making their computers more attractive to schools by offering a large and comprehensive list of educational software to go with them. The result is likely to be a wealth of educational programs available in the future compared to the shortage we are experiencing today.

22 • Computers, Teaching and Learning

Figure 1.13 The Centurion system in action.

One developing technology that is likely to influence educational computing in the next decade is a procedure called networking. Almost all of the first, second, and third-generation small computers were designed to be used by one person at a time. Each computer was independent of any other computers in the room and thus required its own set of accessories. In contrast, large mainframe and minicomputers generally allow more than one person to use the computer at a time. A typical time-sharing computer can attend to the needs of 30 to 300 different users at once. This simultaneous sharing of computer resources by many users is often an economical approach if overhead costs are small and reliability problems can be kept to a minimum. It appears likely that small, desktop computers with time-sharing features are likely to become popular. These systems will probably cost less than $10,000 (in 1983 dollars), and allow 6 to 50 students to use them simultaneously (each would work at a "terminal" that would cost $250 to $700). Whether these small time-sharing systems will become the dominant type of computer in schools is unclear. If the cost of standard, stand-alone computers continues to drop, time-sharing systems may still be relatively more expensive.

EDUCATIONAL PRECURSORS OF THE COMPUTER

The ancestral family tree of computers as educational tools has a long history. We could justifiably include quill pens, lead pencils, blackboards, and the slate in our catalog of educational ancestors of the computer since all these innovations are tools which enabled teachers to do a more efficient or effective job in the classroom.

The invention of the printing press was a technological development that revolutionized education and made widespread dissemination of knowledge an obtainable goal. Virtually every area of education today relies heavily on the printed word for learning.

In the twentieth century, teachers also profited from emerging technologies in the audio-visual field. Textbooks were joined by films, filmstrips, slides, audio tapes, transparencies, television, videotapes, and videodisks. Today students can not only read Hamlet, they can watch an excellent presentation of the play and then listen to a review or critical analysis of it from an expert.

In spite of their contributions to education, all of the twentieth century technologies mentioned thus far suffer from the same limitations—they are passive learning systems. There is usually little opportunity for the learner to intervene or participate other than by stopping or starting the device. It is up to the teacher to arrange for student involvement through discussion or some other procedure. Passive learning experiences are not necessarily ineffective, but there is a need for more active learning experiences in the classroom. Two other twentieth century innovations, the teaching machine and programmed instruction, represent efforts to provide the student with a more active role in learning.

THE TEACHING MACHINE

The teaching machine began as a testing machine. In the 1920s Sidney Pressey, a psychologist at Ohio State University, designed machines that would automatically administer classroom tests. Pressey's machines required the student to push buttons corresponding to multiple choice answers to test items. If the answer was correct the machine presented the next question. Incorrect answers caused the machine to record the error and ask the student for another answer. Since the student knew immediately whether an answer was correct or not, Pressey felt the machine taught through the feedback it provided. Students probably did learn more from taking one of Pressey's automated tests than they did from a test that was scored by hand and given back days later, but most of the learning was still accomplished through traditional methods.

Another well known psychologist, B.F. Skinner, also worked on the development of teaching machines after visiting his daughter's elementary school classroom. As he observed the methods used to teach basic information and skills, Skinner decided that there were better ways than the traditional group lecture/demonstration method. During the forties, Skinner began developing a learning machine that actually taught as well as tested. In a typical application the machine presents very small segments of information to the student. After a few segments have been presented the student must answer one or more questions which test for understanding of the material. If the student responds correctly, more material is presented. If some answers are incorrect, the student may be required to review the material or the program may branch to remedial material that gives the student extra help.

The modern teaching machine does have some advantages over other audio-visual methods. Foremost is its ability to involve the learner actively in the learning process. In addition, the responses made by a student can be used to determine what to do next (i.e., present new material or provide remedial work), and the regular testing provides the student with feedback which may be helpful. In spite of this, teaching machines have never been popular in American education. Only a tiny percentage of the student population ever uses a teaching machine, and an even smaller number uses teaching machines regularly. That contrasts with the relatively large number of students who use audio-visual aids in learning. A teaching machine is no more costly than a 16mm projector. Then why does virtually every teacher have access to projectors while few have access to teaching machines? The answer lies, at least partially, in the strengths and weaknesses of each. Films and filmstrips are relatively passive learning tools, but they bring some of the world into the classroom in living color and sound. Teachers can compensate for the passive nature of the technology by the way they use audio-visual aids. In contrast, the teaching machine does provide for learner participation, but much of the material for teaching machines is rather dry, boring, colorless material that holds little interest. Teachers cannot compensate for that.

There are also other drawbacks to teaching machines, many of which are also characteristic of another closely related innovation, programmed instruction.

PROGRAMMED INSTRUCTION

Programmed instruction has been described as a teaching machine without the machine. There are, indeed, many similarities between the programmed instruction text and the programs used in teaching machines. Both tend to break material down into small steps, often called frames, and both provide for regular testing and feedback to the student. There are thousands of programmed texts available today which cover topics from prereading skills to college-level math. These texts are used in more classrooms than are teaching machines, but they still represent a tiny fraction of the texts used in classrooms today. There are significant problems which limit the usefulness of the programmed text.

Programmed instruction comes in two basic types—linear and branched. Linear programs divide the material to be taught into small, digestible bits called frames. Using a linear text involves reading through the text sequentially from the first frame to the last. The learner proceeds through a learning sequence which has been predetermined by the person who designed the program. Authors of linear programs try to write frames that can be understood by the great majority of students who are to use the text, since errors are not easy to handle in linear programs. The result is often a program written for the lowest common denominator rather than for average or above average students. With the exception of allowing students to learn at their own speed, programmed instruction, particularly linear programs, is difficult to adapt to different learning needs.

The other type of programmed instruction, branching, does try to deal with different learning patterns. Instead of breaking the material into hundreds or thousands of frames, branching programs teach larger chunks of information before testing the student. Then, if a student makes an error on the test, he or she is branched to other material that deals with the particular mistake. Thus, a student who answers most of the test questions correctly may never read most of a branching program since much of the material is read only by students who did not understand the initial presentation. Branching texts are extremely difficult to write because the writer must anticipate the types of errors a student is likely to make, and provide appropriate instructional assistance. Also, since the student does not proceed through the text in a set order, the branching text is often unwieldy to use, requiring constant page flipping. A student may begin on page ten, branch to page forty-three, go back to ten, then proceed to page fifty-five, and so on. Good branching programs are effective learning tools, but there are not many good programs available in spite of several decades of work.

At this point a logical question might center around the possibility of combining audio-visual technology with the technology of teaching machines and programmed instruction. Could an interesting method of teaching be developed which allows for active learner participation, regular testing, and feedback? Today there are a number of research and development projects underway which attempt to combine videotape, videodisk, and film media with programmed instruction and/or teaching machines. The videodisk, in particular, seems to have a bright future since some models provide for random access to each of thousands of frames on the disk (in contrast to films which must be run sequentially).

The focus of this book is on another method of marrying audio-visual technology and teaching machines—the small computer. Computers can generate both visual and auditory information, they can be programmed to run linear or branching material, they can control tape recorders and videotape/disk machines, and they have the ability to serve as learning aids in ways which are not possible with traditional programmed instruction or audio-visual aids. The final section of this chapter will introduce the computer as a learning aid and set the stage for the chapters which follow.

THE COMPUTER'S ROLES IN EDUCATION

In his book *The Computer in Education: Tutor, Tool, and Tutee*, Robert Taylor divided the educational roles of the computer into three broad categories—tutor, tool, tutee. That seems to be a very good framework and will be used in this section.

The Computer as Tutor

The computer is being used daily in many schools to teach students. Its role as tutor is accomplished in many different ways, but the term Computer-Aided Learning (CAL) is often used to describe this tutorial role. CAL can also be divided into two smaller categories: Computer-Managed Instruction (CMI) and Computer-Assisted Instruction (CAI). Computer-Managed Instruction involves the use of computers to manage the learning process, usually through administering tests to students and making lesson assignments. In CMI the actual instruction is provided through traditional means such as textbooks, library assignments, laboratory exercises, and lectures. The computer shoulders much of the responsibility for the clerical work involved in a typical classroom. Chapter 8 deals with CMI.

In CAI or Computer-Assisted Instruction the computer is responsible for at least some of the teaching. A high school student might take a course in intermediate algebra or trigonometry on the computer. The computer could provide most of the instruction, keep track of each student's progress, note problem areas for the teacher, and provide recommended grades at the end of the course. The teacher's role in such a class might be one of supervising the learning rather than directly teaching. Most of the teacher's class time is spent troubleshooting the problems of individual students rather than providing lectures. Chapter 7 deals with CAI.

The Computer as a Tool

In most schools today, computers are used primarily as tools. They are there because they perform tasks efficiently in the same way as a typewriter, calculator, or telephone perform useful functions. As in most organizations, there are records to be kept, payrolls to be met, and bills to be paid. The great majority of medium and large-sized school districts use computers for the traditional accounting procedures such as accounts payable, accounts receivable, general ledger, inventory, and payroll. Such uses of the computer differ little from the applications found in many businesses today.

Schools may also use computers to schedule classes, keep track of student records, provide grade reports, keep attendance records, analyze grading patterns, and score tests. Again, such applications are very similar to the record keeping and data gathering functions of computers in business applications.

Computers are also beginning to be used in schools not only for scoring multiple choice tests, but for gathering and synthesizing diagnostic information which can be used to provide students with more appropriate educational experiences. This function is dealt with in Chapter 9.

At the classroom level, teachers may use computers to score their classroom tests, keep grade records for the semester, and compute grades. Small computers are also used by students in math classes, science classes, and in business education programs. Small computers can do complex math, solve equations, test formulas, and serve as word processors. In each instance, the computer is a tool used by the teacher or student in much the same way a slide rule, calculator, or typewriter would be used.

The Computer as Tutee

Several pioneers in educational computing, particularly Arthur Luehrmann and Seymour Papert, have argued that a major educational application for computers will be as machines that can be taught rather than as machines which teach. Students who learn to teach the computer to do interesting things may not only learn how to use computers in their daily lives, they may learn better problem solving skills and may develop or improve their cognitive abilities in the process. This concept of computers in education is considered in more detail in Chapter 6.

It would be difficult to predict which of the roles discussed above will flourish in the coming years. All show promise today. Their future will depend in part on you and other educators who will investigate their possibilities and consider applying them in the classroom.

2

Current Applications

The eighties may well be the decade of the computer in education. Alfred Bork, a pioneer in computer-based learning, put it this way:
   We are at the onset of a major revolution in education, a revolution unparalleled since the invention of the printing press. The computer will be the instrument of this revolution.... By the year 2000 the *major* way of learning at all levels, and in almost all subject areas will be through the interactive use of computers. ("Interactive Learning," *American Journal of Physics*, 47 (1), Jan, 1979.)

While we might consider Bork's view at least slightly optimistic, the fact remains that there are thousands of computers in schools where, only a year or two ago, there were no computers, and not even any serious consideration of using computers. A study titled *Microcomputers in Education* produced by Creative Strategies International, a California market research and consulting firm, predicted the educational market for computers between 1980 and 1985 will exceed one billion dollars. The report predicts drastically increased use of computers at all levels of education including elementary schools, trade and technical institutes, and universities. A survey conducted by Chambers and Bork (1980) indicated that 13% of the school districts in the U.S. used computers for instructional applications in 1970 while 74% were using computers for instruction in 1980. Based on responses from school superintendents, Chambers and Bork predicted that 87% of the school districts would use computers for at least some instruction by 1985. Usage was concentrated in secondary schools, with math departments reporting the heaviest usage followed by the natural sciences, business education, and language arts. (Chambers, J.A., and Bork, A. "Computer Assisted Learning in U.S. Secondary/Elementary Schools," paper in *Topics: Computer Education for Elementary and Secondary Schools*. New York: Association for Computing Machinery, 1981, pp. 10-11, #812810.)

A recent survey from the National Center for Educational Statistics (1981), titled *Student Use of Computers in Schools* also found increased use of computers but identified lack of appropriate software as a major roadblock to rapid acceptance of computers in educational settings. The study estimated there were 52,000 microcomputers and computer terminals in American elementary and secondary schools in 1981. If the goal advocated by Arthur Melmed (1981, Information Technology for the Schools and Nation, unpublished paper) of thirty minutes of computer-aided learning a day for the average school child is to be reached by 1990, the nation will have to place approximately five million additional computers in the schools. If we extrapolate from Melmed's thirty minutes a day in 1990 to Bork's vision of the year 2000 with computers serving as the major way we learn, it is easy to conclude that we will either be a society awash with computers by 2000 or a society significantly short of the goals set by enthusiastic advocates of computers in education.

Even if the United States were to fulfill Melmed's 1990 goal by only 25%, we would still be faced with a substantially increased demand for computer equipment, educational programs, and educators who are experienced computer users. Some reports cite the lack of good quality software as a major factor limiting the growth of educational computing. In our view, even with huge amounts of software, the growth of computer usage will be slower than necessary because we have not prepared teachers to use computers in their classrooms or to teach students about the use of computers.

The Elementary and Secondary Schools Subcommittee of the Association for Computing Machinery, led by David Moursund, has also expressed concern about the preparation of educators for the computer revolution. A task group on

Figure 2.1 Computer Learning Centers may be common in schools of the future. *Photo courtesy Softworks, Inc.*

Teacher Education has identified three sets of competencies required by teachers. (Jim Poirot, Robert Taylor, and Jim Powell, "Teacher Education," a report in *Topics: Computer Education for Elementary and Secondary Schools*. New York: Association for Computing Machinery, 1981, p. 18-27, #812810). The first set consists of competencies that the task group feels should be universal; every educator should have these skills. They require the ability to read and write simple computer programs, experience or training in using computers in education as well as an awareness of the capacity and limitations of computers, a working knowledge of computer terminology and the history of computer applications, and a basic understanding of the ethical and social implications of using computers. While all that may sound like an extensive list, it is only the foundation, the competencies that every teacher should have.

The second set of competencies relates to the skills required of an educator who teaches about computers. These competencies call for a high level of skills in areas such as writing and documenting programs, understanding the components of computer systems and how they operate, as well as the broad knowledge required to organize and teach effective courses on computers. Educators who serve as consultants or resource persons for their school or district require additional competencies.

The third set of competencies consists of subject-specific skills which enable teachers to use computers effectively in their particular subject specialties. This third set would thus depend on the area of specialization of each teacher.

Although the efforts of educators such as Poirot, Taylor, Powell, and Moursund have laid the groundwork for teacher education programs in computer usage, the fact remains that very few colleges of education currently offer training programs in educational computing. In fact, the great majority do not even familiarize undergraduate education majors with the use of computers in education. There are exceptions, of course. Stanford, Columbia, University of Oregon, North Texas State University, Lehigh University, State University of New York at Stony Brook, University of Florida, University of South Florida, Texas Tech University, Arizona State, University of Illinois, Lesley College in Massachusetts, and several others have graduate and/or undergraduate programs for teachers. If computers are to play a major role in the future of education it will be necessary to provide hundreds of thousands of teachers with the training they will need to work comfortably with computers. Some of this training will involve preservice experiences, often through courses which carry college credit. For teachers already in the field, the necessary skills may be obtained through inservice training programs, graduate courses on computer usage, independent study, or on-the-job training. Indeed, in a few years, you may find yourself providing some of that training.

Up to this point, we have dealt primarily with the future and the problems likely to impede the growth of educational computing. But what about the present? What is going on now? There are many innovative, effective, and promising programs already in operation. In the next section of this chapter, we will describe a few of the many good educational computing projects currently in operation. Although they vary in size, goals, and operation, all of these projects provide us with a vision of what things may be like in thousands of schools in the future. And on a hopeful note, these programs are only a tiny sample of the many excellent efforts already underway.

MINNESOTA EDUCATIONAL COMPUTING CONSORTIUM (MECC)

MECC is probably the best known and also one of the oldest statewide projects in educational computing. MECC began in 1973 and was funded by an appropriation from the state legislature. Its job is to encourage and coordinate efforts to provide educational computing services in the state's public schools, colleges, and universities. MECC does many things. It reviews plans for services, buys equipment and software, provides training, develops educational programs, and arranges for maintenance on equipment in Minnesota schools and colleges.

In the early days MECC provided schools with educational computing on a time-sharing basis. It has a large Control Data Corporation CYBER 73 computer which can handle 420 terminals at once. MECC serves hundreds of schools scattered throughout the state with an extensive telecommunications network that allows a school to connect its terminals to the main computer in St. Paul. Many educational programs, as well as programs for administrative applications (e.g., pupil records, accounting), can be used by any school with a terminal.

When microcomputers appeared a few years ago, MECC established a state level task force to select both a microcomputer and a vendor for the state. The Apple II, to be purchased directly from Apple Computer Incorporated, was selected. Minnesota schools have purchased over 2,000 Apple computers under the state contract. The Apples are used at all levels, from elementary schools where students get drill and practice in basic skills, to high school where many students take computer literacy and computer programming classes or use the computer in science or business education classes. Although used less intensively in colleges and universities, Apples provide training for future teachers in several colleges of education. In 1981, when the MECC contract was bid again, Atari Incorporated won and will provide computers for the next few years.

MECC has been an active participant in the growth of microcomputer applications in schools. MECC employs ten Instructional Coordinators who spend their time providing courses and workshops to educators across the state. In many instances the MECC courses are attended by local administrators and consultants who in turn provide their own training to local teachers. MECC's Instructional Coordinators also personally deliver the first microcomputer ordered by a school and provide assistance in setting it up.

In addition to an active training program for teachers, MECC developed a large library of educational programs which can be used with the Apple II (many will now be converted to the Atari computers as well). MECC now has many good programs which are being marketed nationally. Over 95% of the educational systems in Minnesota use a computer for at least some instructional purposes. The state and MECC are models which many seek to emulate. You can get more information on MECC by writing to MECC, 2520 Broadway Drive, St. Paul, Minnesota 55113.

One area where the pioneering steps of MECC are being followed is the Province of British Columbia on the Pacific coast of Canada. British Columbia has two major urban centers, Victoria and Vancouver, and a large number of smaller communities, many of which are relatively isolated. Victoria is located on a large island which can only be reached by ferry or by plane. In the late seventies BC schools, like many others, began to use microcomputers. Unfortunately there was little coordination of uses and little funding. In many schools students learned to use a computer on equipment purchased by a teacher. In September of 1980, the province began a pilot project which involved the purchase of 100 Apple II computers to be placed in fifty schools across the province. Using MECC software, commercial programs, and programs developed in BC, the project is designed to be a springboard from which to launch an effort to put computers within reach of all the half million students in BC schools.

The project is funded by the provincial government and coordinated by the University of Victoria through JEM Research, a research institute located on the campus. The initial target areas for the BC project are the eighth through tenth grade science curriculum, kindergarten through seventh grade language arts, eighth through twelfth grade music, and kindergarten through twelfth grade mathematics. Although the project is in the initial stages it has already had an impact on BC education. For more information write JEM Research, Discovery Park, University of Victoria, P.O. Box 1700, Victoria, BC V8W 2Y2.

EDUCATIONAL COMPUTING IN IRELAND

Although most of us would prefer to work in a state or province where the government supports educational computing with both rhetoric and resources, the unfortunate fact is that most of us probably meet with as much resistance as appropriations. A few determined Irish educators have shown that progress can be made even in the face of stiff resistance. Our description of the history of Irish educational computing is taken from an article by Michael Moynihan ("Computing in Irish Second Level Schools," *T.H.E. Journal*, January, 1981, 8, 1, 42-43).

The Republic of Ireland, because it has a very favorable tax system for new industry and a large supply of workers, has attracted a large number of computer related businesses in the last two decades. They now export over a billion dollars worth of electronic products each year, with a significant portion of that total being computers or computer peripherals.

In spite of the general slowness in the Irish economy, and a relatively high unemployment rate, the computer industry in Ireland has been unable to hire qualified workers for many of its jobs. Michael Moynihan, Chairman of the Computer Education Society of Ireland, places part of the blame for the shortage on the Irish Department of Education which exercises strict control of schools throughout the republic. While the European Computing Services Association has recommended that all students in European schools receive at least one course in computer literacy, there has been considerable resistance to the idea of computer courses in elementary and secondary schools in many European countries, including Ireland.

Until 1980, computers were not on the approved list of subjects to be taught in Irish schools. This meant that teachers could not be paid to teach computer courses, and computer courses could not conflict with any approved course. Thus most of the courses on computers were taught after regular hours (often conflicting with extracurricular activities) or were taught surreptitiously under another course name. Interest in computers was stimulated in the early seventies when the Irish Department of Education provided one-week courses taught by a professor from England. Teachers learned to run FORTRAN programs (FORTRAN is a popular computer language) on the IBM computer at University College, Galway. These courses led, in part, to the organization of the Computer Education Group in 1973 which worked with the Department of Education to develop a policy on computer courses in schools. Several members of the Computer Education Group attended courses on computers in England and began offering week long courses for Irish teachers in 1974 which were funded by the Department of Education. Unfortunately the Department cut funding in 1975 and the courses ended. The Computer Education Group (which became the Computer Education Society of Ireland) decided to run courses independent of the government education agency and, since 1975, has regularly offered training to teachers who are interested in providing computer courses in secondary schools. The Department of Education has provided some funding since 1975, but it has always been inadequate.

Until 1978 schools which offered courses on computers were forced to seek the assistance of local firms who had computers. There were no funds to buy computers for schools. Since the advent of the microcomputer, several Irish secondary schools have purchased computers for classroom use. In July of 1979 there were fifty computers in Irish schools. In July of 1980 there were over 400, the great majority of which were Apple IIs along with some Commodore PETs.

The rapid acceptance of microcomputers in Irish schools, and the pressure provided by the Computer Education Society of Ireland, helped convince the Department of Education to give official recognition to Computer Studies in 1980. It is now an optional extra in the mathematics curriculum of the senior year. Although many teachers of computer courses objected to the linking of their subject matter to another area—mathematics—they accepted the decision as a step toward recognizing computer studies as a regular part of the secondary curriculum. The Department of Education also set up an advisory committee which will make recommendations for the future. At the same time the Computer Education Society of Ireland had 300 educators in its 1980 courses, up from 50 in 1979.

BELLINGHAM HIGH SCHOOL

Bellingham, Washington is a small city located about a hundred miles north of Seattle and about thirty-five miles from the Canadian border. Like many small cities there is one central high school which serves the town and the rural area surrounding Bellingham. Unlike most cities, however, Bellingham's high school has a very active computer education program run by Julian Pietras. The high school has two computers and one printer.

The high school offers the following courses:

Computer Awareness Mini-Course. A two week course which all ninth graders take. It serves as a beginning step toward computer literacy.

Computer Concepts Course. This course lasts one quarter and covers the basic concepts of computer usage.

Programming. This course deals with the fundamentals of writing and using programs written in BASIC.

Projects. After the programming course students can receive one quarter of credit by studying advanced programming topics in languages such as BASIC, PILOT, or Pascal.

Teacher Workshops. The staff at Bellingham High School offers a twenty to thirty hour course for other educators in the district. Participants receive credit for the course from the district and study a variety of topics from BASIC and PILOT to using CAI.

Business Workshops. The staff also offers a thirty hour course on computer applications to adults interested in learning to use a computer in their business.

Administrative Workshops. Finally, there is a twenty to thirty hour workshop for school administrators.

If you would like more information on the work at BHS write to Julian Pietras, Bellingham High School, 2020 Cornwall Avenue, Bellingham, Washington 98225.

INSTITUTE FOR CHILD AND FAMILY STUDIES

Although we have concentrated on the use of computers in the classroom so far, it would be inappropriate to totally ignore the many uses of computers in the business and administrative offices of schools and school systems. Texas Tech University's Institute of Child and Family Studies, directed by Dr. Mary Tom Riley, uses small computers to handle many of the routine, time consuming tasks of the Institute. A description of the Institute's use of computers is given below. It was provided by Dr. Deborrah Smithy-Willis, Manager of Educational Research and Computer Support Services for the Institute.

The Institute for Child and Family Studies provides support services for Head Start in Texas and adjacent states. Institute personnel train teachers, teacher's aides, parents, and administrators in effective ways of interacting with children aged three to five years. This training includes a wide variety of topics from classroom management to nutrition to managerial styles and motivation. In addition to training, the Institute staff also develops workbooks, films, and "hands on" activities to support workshop programs. Yet this is just the beginning of the various tasks the Institute is responsible for within the five state region. There is an inventory of all equipment, a mailing list of all Head Start programs in Texas as well as all directors in the region, federal reports which must go out on a regular basis, accurate financial records which must be maintained for both university and federal inspection, and many other tasks which require reams of paper and thousands of hours of typing, editing, and preparation. Thus, it was suggested that a microcomputer be purchased to handle the clerical aspects of these activities. Little did we realize that a year later eight computers would be an integral part of the Institute's daily operation.

In September 1980, the Institute bought a TRS-80 Model II with one external drive and an NEC Spinwriter letter quality printer. Software purchased at the same time included: *Magic Wand* (a word processing program), and Radio Shack's *Inventory Management*, *Mailing List*, and *Profile II*. Since that time Model II *Scripsit*, another word processing program has been added, making the merging of letters on a word processor and a mailing list on *Profile II* an incredible time saver. With this system, names and addresses from *Profile II* are interfaced with material on the word processor so that the correct name is printed at the top of each individual letter. This function makes each letter appear to be an original with the personal touch of name and address without the time investment.

At first, there was reluctance among the office staff to accept the computer. The first person to be converted was the secretary who regularly typed a 500 name mailing list. The *Mailing List* program allows the user to enter name, address, city, state, zip code, and up to six other descriptors by which an individual (or group of individuals) can be located. Our list, for example, can be printed by region of Texas (North, South, East, West), state (Louisiana, Arkansas, Texas, New Mexico), business title (director, community representative, etc.), or the basic name and address information. Thus we can get mailing labels for our entire list, or for any particular subsection of the list. Once the names were entered and the first list came majestically from the printer, it was the beginning of a beautiful relationship.

Figure 2.2 One of the Institute's computers.

In addition to the mailing list, the Institute uses the Model II for several other functions:
- word processing
- report writing
- inventory maintenance
- terminal mode
- bookkeeping

Word Processing

The addition of a word processor to the Institute has made it possible to use one part-time employee, rather than a full-time secretary, to handle much of our complicated typing. The development and editing of manuscripts is much easier with a word processor than through traditional methods of typing and retyping. Our Management Skills Manual, written by two Institute staff members, was developed on the computer, as were the training manuals used by consultants.

Report Writing

As a federally funded project, the Institute has several reports which must be submitted at various intervals. Using commerically available software, templates have been set up so that each report is ready to be printed with new information added as necessary. For example, reports on Training and Technical Assistance (TTA) are handled by the computer.

Figure 2.3 Report writing is much easier on a computer.

Requests for services are reported, confirmation data are stored, and evaluation of TTA are kept for federal reports. This method eliminates the need to retype text that remains the same in each report.

Inventory Management

While Texas Tech maintains an inventory of campus materials, it has sometimes been necessary to discover the whereabouts of equipment quickly. With our own inventory program, it is possible to tell at a glance the number of typewriters, desks, computer peripherals, etc., and where they are located. This service has probably been most beneficial to a unit of the Institute known as the Materials Lending Library. Their toys, books, and equipment are listed and checked from time to time against the materials in stock for items that need to be replaced.

Terminal Mode

With the microcomputer in the terminal mode, communication with other computers is possible. This has allowed the use of the the DIALOG data base system (ERIC, Psychological Abstracts, Medline, etc.) for literature searches. Direct communication with the system in Palo Alto is possible which reduces the time, cost, and potential errors of computer-based searches.

In addition to communicating across the country, the microcomputer can talk with the mainframe system at the Texas Tech Computer Center. This allows data entry, editing, and instructions to be transmitted directly from our Model II without trips to the Computer Center.

Bookkeeping

Because of the minute by minute change in finances at the Institute (hiring consultants, flying/driving to workshops, travel costs, etc.), accurate record keeping is critical. The University provides ledger sheets, but they are often a month or so behind and are not very helpful when information is needed on the spur of the moment. With a commercial bookkeeping package, our administrative assistant can report within seconds the status of each of our major accounts.

The Model II is now viewed as a necessary component in the Institute's daily activities. The success with this machine has led us to seek other applications that might be helpful to our target populations—preschool children and those who care for them. For example, the Institute, in conjunction with the Texas Tech College of Education, has developed a letter discrimination program for preschoolers.

Classroom Applications

Recently five Apple II+ computers were purchased to be placed in Head Start centers in the West Texas area. Research programs are planned that use both the color and graphics capabilities of the Apple II+. In time, it is hoped that a voice synthesizer will be added to the basic system so that work with vision and speech impaired children will begin.

Figure 2.4 Working on the computer can be a group activity.

Although somewhat unfamiliar with computers, the staff at the Institute for Child and Family Studies has come to rely on microprocessor technology for relief from clerical duties. The Institute is now searching for ways to facilitate the social and educational growth of disadvantaged preschool children through the use of computers in the classroom.

PROFESSOR OF EDUCATION

Up to this point we have presented summaries of computer applications in schools, states, and countries. However, many educators are buying computers for their personal use. Small computers can do many jobs for an educator. This final section describes the work of a university professor who made the decision to buy a computer for his own personal use. Dr. Gene Rooze, a Professor of Elementary Education, provided the material below:

"You bought a microcomputer! Why did you do that?" was the question a friend asked me. Most people viewed my purchase as something, not necessarily weird, but perhaps a bit bizarre. "You really have a microcomputer at home?"

After my recent divorce I found myself without a typewriter, a basic tool of my trade. Besides teaching courses in elementary education, I write for professional journals and publish textbooks. I really needed a typewriter. As I shopped for a full size machine, I found that typewriters which met my list of specifications sold for $1,000 to $1,500. That seemed like a lot of money for a single purpose machine. Since I had received some training in word processing, I began to reconsider my specifications.

Word processing seemed to be a good answer to my problem. I had a microcomputer and a letter quality printer available to me on a shared basis at the College of Education at Texas Tech University. After a few aborted attempts I found the shared-user arrangement seldom met the needs of my creative temperament. I needed ready access to equipment in a quiet environment where I would not be interrupted. It is hard to schedule creative periods so that they match the availability schedule of a heavily used word processor!

Figure 2.5 Dr. Rooze at work.

Word processing was not all that intrigued me. I also had the desire to create educational programs. No typewriter has that capability. Testing students during class time has always seemed wasteful to me. Like most professors, I believe that there is so much information and so many experiences that students need before they enter the working world that I'm always looking for some way to increase my time with students; always trying to find ways of getting routine tasks, such as testing, done more effectively. Learning to design CMI materials interests me.

I also despise repetitive lectures. I have convinced myself that a small-group interactive environment is a better use of time in the courses I teach. Providing myself with the time to do this type of instruction means I must find some way of providing initial instruction in concepts and skills in other ways. My experience and the literature on educational computing convinces me that the microcomputer can help here too.

To answer my apprehensive friends and interested readers—I purchased my TRS-80 Model III microcomputer for several reasons. First, to provide myself with a useful word processor (I'm writing this section with it). Second, to develop skills in the preparation of CMI materials, both for my own use and the use of others in teacher education. Third, I'd like to experiment with preparing CAI materials.

I've encountered problems learning to operate the dumb machine (that's both a common term and an acceptable expletive; both are intended). I needed a lot of training time. Learning the word processing package, *Scripsit*, has taken me about 40 hours. This package now allows me to prepare a manuscript (an eight-page journal article, for example) in about three days, and I'm getting faster. I'm certainly not an expert—eight months after beginning I have produced two articles, three eighteen page reports, and three substantive proposals. These all required tables and charts which I produced on the TRS-80. I learn something new each time I try another task, and I'm able to help other neophytes which is very good for my self concept. That pleases me and astonishes my skeptical friends.

A second task I've undertaken is the learning of BASIC for my Model III. I tried learning BASIC without my own computer. I wasn't too successful. The book *Getting Started with TRS-80 BASIC* has helped me learn the language. I've spent approximately twenty-five machine hours on this task and I produced my first substantive program totally unassisted.

Looking ahead, I see several roles for myself in working with my microcomputer. I'm going to continue my word processor, adding enhancements to my present package. I've found word processing to be delightful and much easier than preparing manuscripts on a typewriter.

I've also begun learning about programs available for elementary school children. Learning about present programs is helping me to learn more about several types of educational applications. Since my goals were initially to learn word processing and to develop skills in both CMI and CAI, I feel that my microcomputer has filled my needs well and provided me with some interesting new horizons which I intend to explore.

COMMON USAGE PATTERNS IN SCHOOLS

One problem with the educational computer is the fact that it *is* so versatile. It can be used in virtually any area of the school, in any subject, by any student. That does not mean every student in a school with computers is equally likely to spend some time with the school's computers. Here are a few of the more common usage patterns:

Elite, Select Few Model

Often one or two computers are purchased by the school and allocated to a particular department, frequently math or science. The computers then become the property of that department and because they are a scarce commodity access is limited to a few of the brightest, most enthusiastic students who eagerly jump into the world of computers. In schools with this usage pattern a few students often become known as the "computer freaks." They have knowledge about a mysterious machine that no one else possesses. Students with little or no exposure to computers may thus learn that computers are tools to be used only by the elite—those with special talents and training. The gap between computers and the average student is thus widened rather than closed by the use of computers in the school.

In an era when computer literacy (knowledge about computers) is a required skill for more and more occupations, it is becoming increasingly difficult to defend the elite model of usage. Certainly students with special talents and interests should be given access to computers, but the trend is toward the use of computers by people who have not been trained as computer programmers or engineers. The lawyer, the factory foreman, the small business owner, the health care professional, the minister, and others will increasingly find computers useful, perhaps essential, in their work. Many of these people will not be the math or science students who will spend their entire school day at the computer if permitted. Schools need to take that fact into consideration when establishing usage patterns for their computer facilities.

Brief Encounter

At the opposite end of the continuum from the elite model is the brief encounter model. This model generally assumes that computers will be such an important part of most people's lives that *every* student should be exposed to computers, how they work, what they do, and the societal implications of computers.

The brief encounter may be as short as a four or five-hour block of time spread across several weeks. A few schools re-

Figure 2.6 Computers are common in high school science classes. *Photo courtesy Hewlett Packard.*

quire a semester long course on computer literacy, and a very few even include a full year of computer coursework as a requirement for graduation from high school. It would be unfair and inaccurate to label semester-long courses as brief encounters simply because they are required of all students. Yet the fact is that only a tiny percentage of American public schools have such requirements. A more typical pattern involves a much briefer exposure with limited instructional goals or no contact with computers at all.

Is it appropriate to monopolize limited computer resources with round after round of brief encounters? Shouldn't the emphasis be placed on students who are considering a career in computer science? There are conflicting opinions. We believe that the brief encounter model may be more appropriate than the elite model because computer usage patterns are changing quickly. Computers are no longer the sole province of specially trained experts who serve as interfaces between the general public and the computer. In the future the general public will have its own computers. This shift in usage patterns will require a computer literate public. Thus we would rank literacy for every student higher on the list of priorities than intense training for a few students. Ideally, of course, it would be nice to have enough resources to do both.

Scheduled Assignments

Another common usage pattern puts the computer to work in a particular class or course. There are several ways this is accomplished:

Remedial Work. Computers are frequently used to provide remedial training in basic academic skills. There are two reasons for this. First, remedial programs using traditional methods are notoriously ineffective. The ones that do succeed tend to be labor intensive. That is, they require a great deal of time from well trained, experienced educators. It is expensive to provide good remedial programs. It is generally cheaper to provide remedial education through a computer than by traditional methods as long as the project is of sufficient size to warrant the initial investment in equipment and programs.

The second reason for using computers in remedial education is simple. There are several good packages of material designed for remedial programs and many others that are easily adapted. Many good, computer-based remedial programs provide intensive diagnostic testing, make precise and detailed assignments based on the test results, provide feedback and explanations when the student makes an error, and adjust assignments depending on the student's progress. All of these factors contribute to the success of computer-based remedial projects. In schools where large numbers of students fail to reach even minimally acceptable levels of academic achievement, the use of computers in remedial programs may be both cost efficient and timely.

Figure 2.7 A "room full of computers" in Abernathy, Texas.

Routine Classwork. Many of the features that make computer-based learning attractive in remedial education programs are also helpful in routine or regular classes. Many schools use computers in regular classes because they are economical alternatives to other methods. In small schools where a few teachers are often expected to teach many different subjects computers can be used in areas where demand is low but the course is considered important enough to be taught. Or the computer can be used to teach courses taken by many students, thus freeing up teacher time for other courses.

Figure 2.8 Computers allow one teacher to supervise students studying many different subjects. *Photo courtesy Softworks.*

In some small schools one teacher with some experience and training in educational computing can supervise a classroom of twenty students who are actually working on many different courses!

Reward. Another common usage pattern involves a contingency arrangement. Students are told that those who finish other assignments satisfactorily (and often within a certain time limit) will be permitted to use the computers. Those who do not complete their work are not allowed access.

We have mixed feelings about this model. Since computers can be set up to run all sorts of video games that interest students, it is easy to make the computer a reward for other, less interesting work. Our preference would be to make the other work more interesting. If that is not possible, explore the possibility of teaching the skills by computer. The reward model limits access to the computer. That is a problem. And if the computer is only used to play games, it gives students an inaccurate image of the power and usefulness of computers.

There are probably a few settings where the use of the computer as a reward is justified. The emphasis should be on the word "few." If we are serious about developing computer literacy in all students, this model is one of the least acceptable for educational computing.

Handicapped Applications

A graduate student at Texas Tech University, David Craig, is working with a bright eleven-year-old boy named Scotty as part of his dissertation research. Scotty has cerebral palsy and cannot speak. He is confined to a wheel chair and has only limited use of his hands. While Scotty can understand what is said to him, it is very difficult for him to communicate with others. Until recently, the only way he could carry on a conversation was through the use of a communications board, a device with squares on it that contain the letters of the alphabet, numbers, and a few words or phrases. To communicate it was necessary for Scotty to place his hand over each letter of the word he wanted to indicate. This was a slow, difficult process for him since he has limited motor skills. Thus, many of the bright, witty things Scotty had to say were never said. They remained locked in his head because he had no efficient means of communicating with others.

That has changed now. Scotty uses a device called an Autocom which has a microcomputer in it. The Autocom is about three feet wide and two feet long. It is attached to Scotty's wheel chair. Like the communications board, it contains squares with letters, numbers, and phrases on them. To communicate, Scotty moves a small magnet attached to his hand across the surface of the board. As he pauses on a square, the letter or phrase in that square is displayed on a small screen attached to the front of the Autocom. As he builds a sentence it is displayed on the screen. There is also a printer which can provide a permanent copy of what Scotty is saying. In addition, Scotty can compose short paragraphs and store them in the memory of the Autocom. By putting the magnet on one or two squares of the board, his message appears automatically on the screen. It is much faster than the old method.

David Craig is working with Scotty to interface his Autocom to a small computer. Scotty's Autocom board has become a large keyboard through which he can talk to the computer. Scotty is now very good at playing several of the games available for his computer, he uses a word processor to write his school assignments (something that was not possible before), and he is rapidly learning to program the computer in BASIC. Craig hopes to be able to design a system that will allow Scotty to control his environment via the Autocom board (e.g., turn off lights, change the room's temperature), and to enable Scotty to communicate with other handicapped children with similar systems over the phone. All this is possible with equipment that costs less than $7,000. In the future, individuals with handicaps are likely to be able to use a wide range of computer-based devices to enable them to live more normal lives. Many physical disabilities may cease to be the barriers to full, productive lives that they have been in the past.

The usage patterns described so far are only a few of the patterns found in schools today. They should, however, give you an idea of the options. Today, you will find computers in

Figure 2.9 A second-grader and his Apple. *Photo courtesy Softworks.*

the back of self-contained classrooms, in libraries, in learning centers, on mobile carts that travel from room to room, and even in mobile vans that travel from school to school. There is really no preferred pattern of placement today, perhaps because there is no single, dominant usage pattern. In the future we may see computers in all areas of the school, from the high school physics lab to the kindergarten classroom.

3
Selecting Educational Computers

This chapter is in the introductory section because it deals with an issue that is frequently a top priority in the early stages of developing a program. Logically, the selection of a computer for your school is something to do after you have had an opportunity to get some experience. Unfortunately, that is not the way things are always done. Often you must select the computer before you can get the experience. If you are faced with that task you may find several other books from dilithium Press useful. *Computers for Everybody* is a short book (about 272 pages) written by Jerry Willis and Merl Miller for the beginner. It covers the basics of computer equipment (teaches you what all those words like RAM and ROM mean) and explains what computer software is. An important feature of the book is a chapter that reviews and compares most of the popular models of computers. Another book, *Peanut Butter and Jelly Guide to Computers*, by Jerry Willis and Deborrah Smithy-Willis, is a more technical introduction to computer equipment (called hardware by the computer fraternity). It may be particularly useful when you are required to write a detailed bid specification for equipment.

By the time an educator begins shopping for a computer, he or she is probably already looking ahead to the many things that the computer can do. The eagerness to get started sometimes leads to hasty and unfortunate decisions about which computers to buy. Although most of the small computers available today can be used as learning aids, there are features which are more important in a learning environment than in other settings. In this chapter, we will deal with the problem of selecting a computer by recommending a plan of action for buying a computer and by identifying features which may be important in your applications.

STEP ONE. IDENTIFY MAJOR USES

It may seem obvious to say that you need to decide just what you want the computer to do. Yet you would probably be surprised at the number of people who buy a computer with only a vague notion of its intended uses. Will the computer be used in elementary school classes to teach basic math skills, in a junior high science class, in a high school algebra program, in the business education department to teach accounting and word processing? Each of these applications calls for a somewhat different set of features. Thus the computer that may be ideal for the businesss education department may not be the best computer for your elementary math basic skills project.

Figure 3.1 A Texas Instruments TI 99/4A is popular for preschool and early elementary school applications. *Photo courtesy Texas Instruments.*

Selecting Educational Computers • 55

Figure 3.2 The Commodore SuperPET 9000 is a popular machine in university-level computer science programs. *Photo courtesy Commodore.*

The first step is the most important. Decide what your major uses will be. Once that's clear, it will be easier to identify the computer systems capable of doing the work that you want done.

STEP TWO. SOFTWARE CONSIDERATIONS

A computer will not do anything until it has a program (a set of instructions) to follow. Computer programs or software can be obtained in two ways. You can write your own programs or you can buy canned programs that run on your computer. A science teacher, for example, may buy several programs for use in chemistry and physics classes and write some special programs that deal with science topics which receive special emphasis locally. If you plan to write your own programs, it will be important to look carefully at the *languages* spoken by any computer you are considering. Most small computers can be programmed in BASIC, a very popular language today.

Other languages such as PILOT are available for some, but not all, personal computers. Section 2 deals with the languages used most frequently in educational settings: BASIC, PILOT, and Logo.

If you don't know how to program a computer and want to learn, pay careful attention to the teaching aids available with each computer. Are the manuals easy to understand and clear, can you get teaching aids such as computer assisted instruction programs that help you learn the computer language you will use, and do you have a choice of languages? Such features will also be important if the computer will be used in computer literacy or programming classes.

Although learning to program a computer can be both interesting and useful, a large percentage of the educators who use computers in their classrooms will probably spend very little time writing programs. Most teachers do not write the textbooks they use; writing programs is just as difficult a task. If you plan to use programs written by others, be sure there are programs to buy for the machine that you select. A few models have gained such wide acceptance that many different companies sell all sorts of programs for them. Since without software a computer is just a bunch of parts, the variety and quality of software available for a particular computer becomes an important point to consider when buying a system.

Figure 3.3 There are hundreds, perhaps thousands, of educational programs available for the Apple II computer. *Photo courtesy Apple Computer Corporation.*

With most of the popular small computers you will probably be able to buy at least one or two programs in each of the major applications areas. Newer computers, and those from less popular manufacturers, have not attracted as much interest from independent programmers, and there is no guarantee that a large number of suitable programs will be available. Unfortunately the newer machines tend to be the ones with the most sophisticated features. The buyer may be caught in a dilemma that pits an older model with plenty of software against a newer model with many desirable hardware features but less available software. Fortunately the manufacturers of new models are beginning to recognize this problem. Atari has invested a considerable amount of corporate energy and money into software development projects for their computers. Other manufacturers also seem to be aware of the important role software plays in the acceptance of their computers. Most computers aimed at the educational market today have at least a minimum of educational software available. Be sure there is software for your applications before buying a particular computer.

STEP THREE. SPECIFY MINIMUM REQUIREMENTS AND PREFERRED KEY FEATURES

Once you clearly specify the major uses, you will need to identify the hardware features a computer must have to do those jobs. For instance, computers used in business education to teach word processing must have a standard size keyboard that permits fast touch typing. This is just the first of a number of minimum requirements for word procesing.

Of course, there must be a good word processing program available for the computer. It would be nice to have a video display that can put 24 lines of 80 characters on the screen at one time. This is a nice feature, but one that can increase your cost. You can do acceptable work with a display of 24 lines of 40 characters or 16 lines of 64 characters (but not with 22 lines of 23 characters). Several computers with the 24 by 40 or 16 by 64 format are available at an affordable price. None of the requirements noted for word processing are essential, and perhaps they are not even desirable, in a computer that is to be used in a junior high school science department. Instead you may want to consider characteristics such as whether the

58 • Computers, Teaching and Learning

Figure 3.4 The Radio Shack Color Computer has many desirable features, but its keyboard makes it unsuitable for word processing. *Photo courtesy Tandy/Radio Shack.*

Figure 3.5 The Commodore 8032 has a standard keyboard and 25 by 80 display, both desirable features for teaching word processing. *Photo courtesy Commodore.*

computer has a color display, high quality graphics, and a programming language that is easy for students to use and understand. Color graphics make computer assisted lessons more interesting and more effective. A program called SCRAM is a very realistic simulation of a nuclear power generating plant which can teach students about the operation of such plants, the dangers they pose, and the safeguards used. SCRAM was written for Atari computers and takes full advantage of the color graphics capability of that computer.

The final section of this chapter discusses a number of other potentially important characteristics of computers. Few people will find all of them equally important. Your intended uses will determine which features are crucial, which are important, and which are of little importance. When you finish Step 3 you should have a list of minimum requirements that a computer should have before you consider buying it. Before going on to Step 4, we will discuss some features which are particularly important in educational settings.

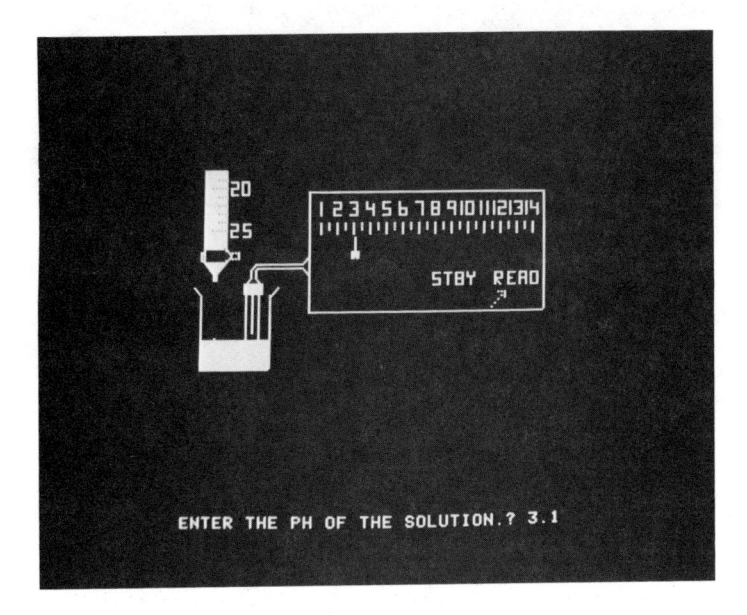

Figure 3.6 Screen displaying a chemistry lesson on an Apple II. *Photo courtesy High Technology.*

Figure 3.7 Some computers and printers are capable of creating very good quality graphics. *Photo courtesy Macrotronics.*

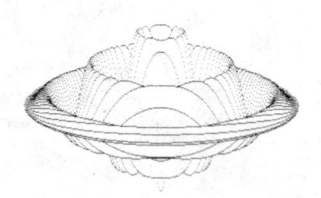

Figure 3.8 A printed copy of graphics from a Commodore PET computer. *Photo courtesy Skyles Electronics.*

Selecting Educational Computers • 61

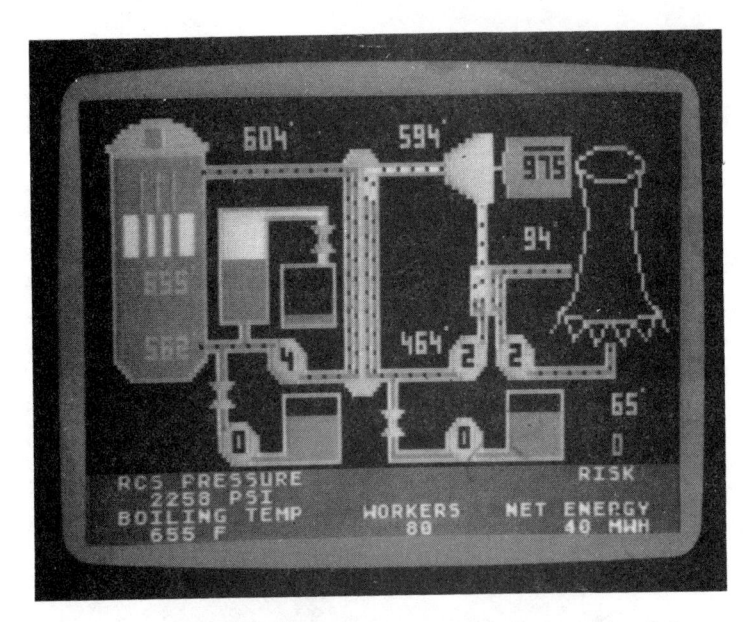

Figure 3.9 Screen display of SCRAM. *Photo courtesy Atari, Inc.*

Figure 3.10 DEC's GIGI computer terminal produces very high quality graphics displays. *Photo courtesy Digital Equipment Corporation.*

Is User Training Easy?

Computers in schools are used by many different students and by many different teachers as well. If there is too much *learning overhead*, that is, if the computer is so complicated to use that it takes each user five or ten hours to learn to turn the machine on, load a program and begin using it, the system is not suitable for educational applications.

Computers designed primarily for business applications often require a one to five day training program for primary operators. A business can afford such a time investment if there are only a few people who will use the computer, and there is not a high staff turnover rate. Since there is a new crop of students periodically the educational computer must be relatively easy to learn to use.

Figure 3.11 SRA's Computer Discovery (tm) package is available for several computers. It provides junior and senior high school students (and teachers) with a comprehensive computer literacy course. *Photo courtesy Tandy/Radio Shack.*

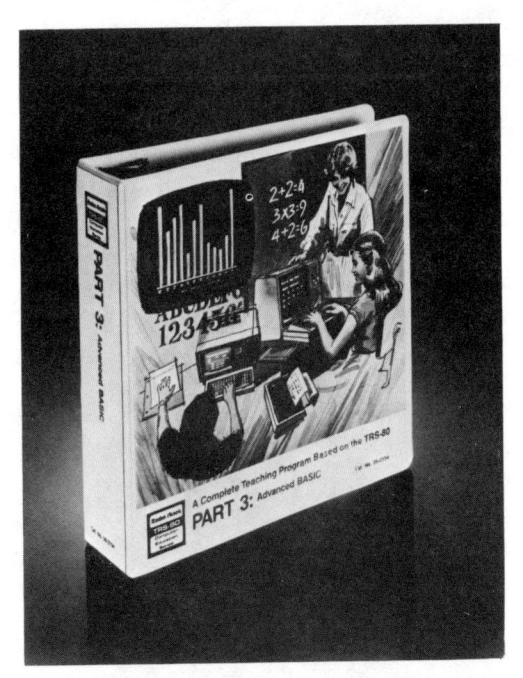

Figure 3.12 Radio Shack offers several computer programs that teach you how to use and program the computer. *Photo courtesy Tandy/Radio Shack.*

Is the Computer *Friendly*?

Many people approach a computer with considerable trepidation and anxiety. Even if the the computer is relatively easy to use, the anxious operator who expects difficulty will find it. The design of the computer should be such that a new operator feels comfortable using it. An attractive case, a simple but functional keyboard, the use of color coding, and the absence of any *doomsday* keys all contribute to a friendly computer. A doomsday key is a key that, when pressed by accident, will destroy the program in the computer's memory. There are few things worse for a first time computer user than being told *Whatever you do, don't hit this key; if you do it will destroy everything in memory!* The anxious learner often spends more time trying to stay away from that key than in learning to use the computer (and it is, of course, the first key the curious learner pushes).

The Atari 800 is a good example of what you should look for; protection from a doomsday key. It has a key labeled SYSTEM RESET. It is a handy key when you want to erase the computer's memory and start over. However, when accidentally pressed in the middle of some programs, its effect can be disconcerting. Atari placed that key well away from the other keys, made it a different color, and placed a plastic guard around it. It is almost impossible to press it without intending to.

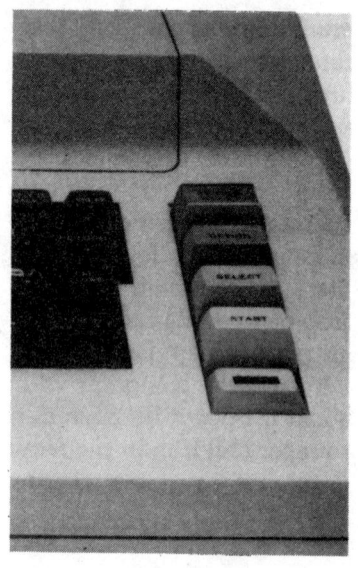

Figure 3.13 The system reset key is protected on the ATARI 800. *Photo courtesy Atari, Inc.*

Computer programs can also have doomsday instructions in them. Some word processing programs have instructions that delete everything you have typed into the computer's memory. A student who has just spent six hours of hard work typing in a term paper will be understandably upset if he or she inadvertently hits a key that erases everything before it is printed. A friendly word processing program will make it difficult to erase large amounts of material (i.e., require pressing several keys at once rather than one or two). One word processor asks ARE YOU SURE? before doing something drastic.

Can the Computer be Networked?

When several computers are to be housed in one location such as a computer learning center, there are several advantages to being able to buy less expensive models and interconnect them so that they share expensive peripherals. Disk drives and printers, for example, often cost the same, or are more expensive than the computer itself. Computers such as the Apple II, the Commodore PET series, and the Radio Shack Model III can be networked or *interfaced* so that computers that do not have disk drives and printers use common or shared disks and printers. In addition, networking allows a teacher to put a program in one computer and then transfer that program to all the other computers in the network.

If you plan to have several computers in one location, be sure to check on the possibility of networking.

What Kind of Input Options Are Available?

Some computers only permit the user to talk to them through the keyboard. That is convenient for some purposes and inefficient for others. Educational programs can often take advantage of other input options such as joysticks and light pens.

A light pen is a small device shaped much like a ball point pen. When placed against the television screen the computer can read its signal and determine where it is located. An educational program that involves multiple choice items, for example, could use a light pen instead of the keyboard for input. When choosing an answer the student only has to put the tip of the light pen beside the answer selected. Your applications may not call for such fancy input options, but they are useful for some types of educational programs. Look for a computer that offers the option to add them if you decide that they are needed.

What Kind of Output Options Are Available?

Virtually any computer will display letters and numbers on its video screen. All of the computers used in schools can be

66 • Computers, Teaching and Learning

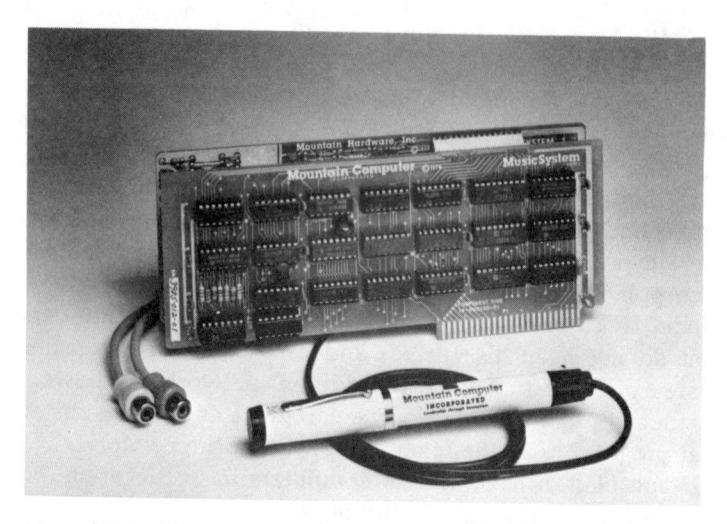

Figure 3.14 The music synthesizer system for the Apple II computer (from Mountain Hardware) is used by a number of high school and university music departments. Input is via the keyboard and light pen. *Photo courtesy Mountain Hardware.*

Figure 3.15 With Mountain Hardware's Supertalker and an Apple II students can answer the computer verbally and it will respond audibly. *Photo courtesy Mountain Hardware.*

Selecting Educational Computers • 67

Figure 3.16 The "BIT Pad" permits a user to select answers or draw figures by moving a pen across a specially designed pad attached to a computer. *Photo courtesy Summagraphics Corporation.*

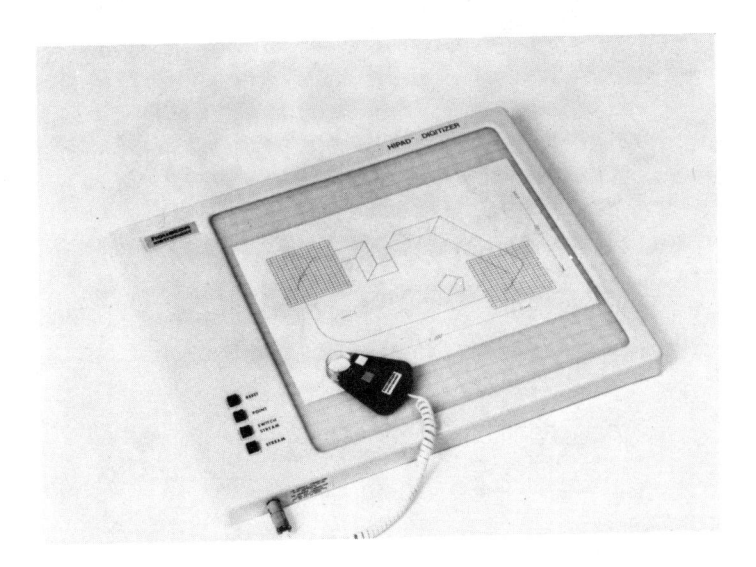

Figure 3.17 The "HIPAD" is another device that allows you to draw complex figures to be input to the computer and displayed later on the screen. *Photo courtesy Bausch and Lomb, Houston Instrument Division.*

connected to a printer which can create a permanent copy of lessons, tests, documents, and tables. Some are capable of generating complicated sound output and very sophisticated color graphics as well as letters and numbers. Interest in educational programs is enhanced by sound and good color graphics. Students not only read about how a nuclear reactor works, they can watch an animated model of a reactor appear on the screen and go through each of its cycles. This type of display is more interesting and it can actually teach many concepts far better than a simple textbook.

Although many educational programs make frequent use of the sound features available on many computers today, there is another, often overlooked, method of using sound in educational computers. Some models use a dual track tape recorder. One track is used for recording the computer program while the other track is used for audio. Several educational programs use the audio track to provide instructions and explanations while displaying text and illustrations on the screen.

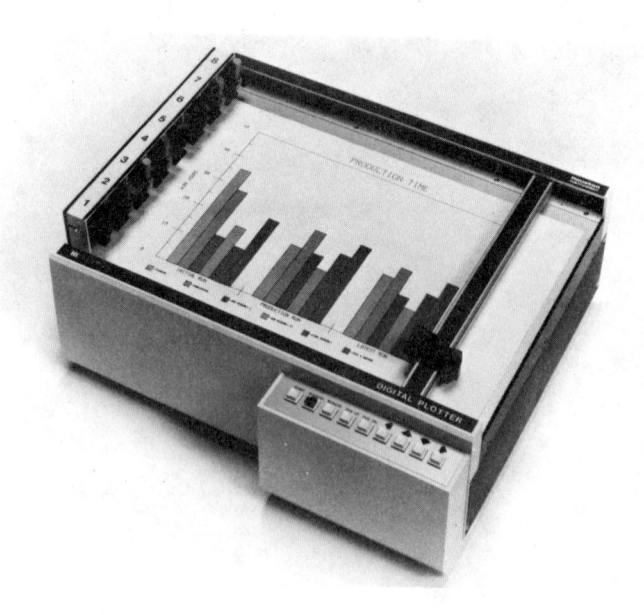

Figure 3.18 Plotters such as this one from Houston Instruments, when used with a computer, can create many different types of figures, tables, and illustrations. *Photo courtesy Bausch and Lomb, Houston Instruments Division.*

Selecting Educational Computers • 69

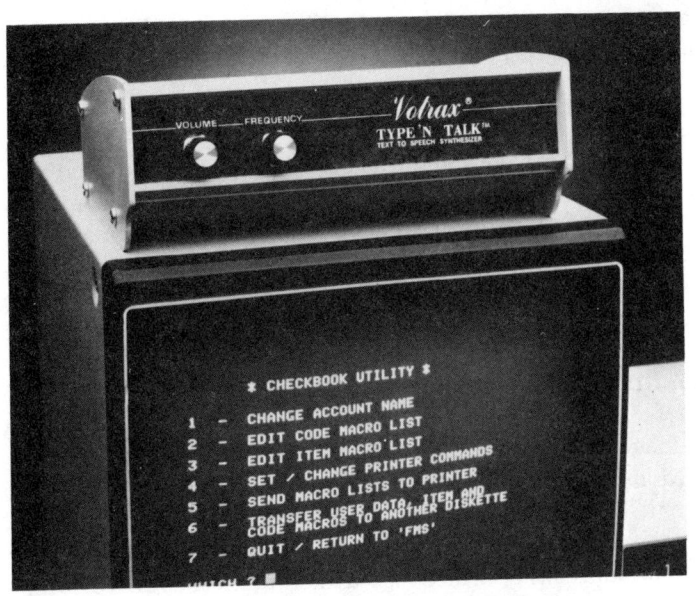

Figure 3.19 You can give the gift of speech to most computers with the "Type and Talk" synthesizer. *Photo courtesy Votrax.*

Since the computer can control the tape recorder it is possible to print a French word or phrase on the screen, and then let the student hear a correct pronunciation of it as well. In another application, the audio track can help young children use the computer even if they cannot read and cannot understand written instructions. The audio track can be used in many educational programs to provide directions, instructions, and test items. In the near future most computers may be able to speak and understand spoken responses. The Texas Instruments computer and one of the Radio Shack computers already offer accessories that provide a limited amount of speech synthesis (the computer speaks) and/or speech recognition (the computer understands spoken language).

In addition, the Texas Instruments computer can use a specially designed bar code reader like the ones used in stores to read the universal product codes (those little lines of varying thickness). TI also markets specially designed early reading books that have a code just below the words to be read. If the child gets stuck, he or she can run the bar code reader across the code on the page and the computer will read the material aloud! That capability is likely to make the TI computer very attractive in the elementary grades as well as in the homes of parents with young children.

Is it Kid Proof?

No electronic equipment is completely immune from prying hands and inquisitive minds, but an educational computer should be designed so that a child cannot easily damage it or be damaged by it. Recently we saw an electronic cash register destroyed in a cafeteria when a customer accidentally spilled a large cup of coffee onto the keyboard while reaching for change in his pocket. The cash register's keyboard was a standard open type with a circuit board located just under the keys. The coffee shorted out the machine and did so much damage the cash register had to be junked.

Many computers have keyboards with circuits just under them. They are more likely to be damaged by a liquid spilled on the keyboard than computers like the Atari 400 and the Commodore Max which use a membrane keyboard. Membrane keyboards are usually made of one piece of embossed plastic that does not allow anything to get between the keys and into the computer itself.

Some computers also present a significant hazard to children because high voltages are present at locations which are easily accessible. Several popular systems with removable tops or cases, for example, have a potentially lethal 120 volts at several unprotected locations. An educational computer should not be too easy to disassemble. If using the computer requires removal of part of the cover or case, access should not expose the user to lethal voltages.

Another aspect of kid proofing is the way accessories are connected to the computer. Connectors should be clearly labeled, and there should be little or no likelihood of connecting something to the wrong plug. Some computers use the same type of connector for the power cord and the accessories. Accidentally plugging the power cord into the wrong socket can produce a variety of unwanted fireworks.

Is There a Special Pricing Arrangement?
What Kind of Service is Available?

Several computer manufacturers, recognizing the importance of educational computing, offer schools a special price discount. Commodore, Radio Shack and Atari all offer some form of discount to schools. Virtually all the major companies are involved in at least a few demonstration projects.

Service, always important, is particularly important in educational settings. Class meets whether the computer is working or not, making dependability and service very important. The method of providing repair service varies from company to company. Although some manufacturers use their dealers for warranty repair service, the trend is toward regional repair centers which specialize in repair work. Radio Shack has an extensive system of repair centers and Commodore has an agreement with TRW which allows Commodore computers to be repaired at TRW repair centers. Check on the repair and service facilities available for a computer before buying it.

STEP FOUR. IDENTIFY LIKELY SECONDARY USES AND DESIRABLE MACHINE FEATURES

Our experience in educational computing suggests that few schools use a computer for a single application. The computer in the first grade classroom may be used in math, reading, music, and art classes, for example. The business education computer in a high school may be used in business math, typing, and accounting classes, and it may also be used to arrange class schedules and keep track of where students are during the school day. When buying a computer, keep possible secondary applications in mind. If those secondary uses would require additional or different features try to select a computer that is great for your primary application and at least good for your secondary applications.

STEP FIVE. DECIDE HOW MUCH YOU CAN SPEND— NOW AND LATER

Now comes the crunch. School budgets today are not likely to have large amounts of excess cash just waiting for your request to buy $20,000 worth of computer equipment. Federal money is no longer readily available for special projects. In many districts the purchase of even one computer will be difficult.

The strategy used to obtain computers in your school or district will depend on local conditions. Can the board be persuaded to set aside money to buy them? Will a supervisor, principal, or assistant superintendent take money from his or her budget and buy computers as part of a demonstration project? Are there funds available at the state level to fund exemplary or demonstration projects? Is there a civic organization in the community interested in helping the school acquire computers? In some schools the math or science club has raised money to buy computers by holding car washes and bake sales. In others local computer dealers have loaned schools one or more systems for a year or for a summer project in hopes of generating interest (and sales) in the future.

Regardless of the source of funds you will probably have less money than you really need. You must decide how to fit your request for $10,000 into the $3,000 you actually have to buy equipment. Decisions will be based on local conditions. It is possible to use $3,000 to buy one computer system with dual disk drives, 48K of memory, several hundred dollars worth of programs, and a good quality printer. On the other hand, the same $3,000 might be used to buy three computers with 16K of memory, cassette storage instead of disks, and one inexpensive printer. If you are planning to offer a computer literacy class for fifteen high school juniors it would probably be better to spend the money on three limited systems than on one expensive system.

If there is some assurance of additional funds in the future it may be possible to start with a minimal system and upgrade by adding disk drives, better printers, and more software later. On the other hand, if your application will not permit you to begin with a minimal system and upgrade later there may be another alternative—leasing. Several companies, including a division of Tandy (parent company of Radio Shack) have leasing arrangements that allow you to lease the equipment you need, pay the lease costs once a year when your budget is approved, and buy the equipment for a small amount at the end of the lease. Should you decide to investigate the possibility of leasing be sure to check carefully the terms of the lease. Recently we talked with two educational districts about their leases. One had leased around

$10,000 of computer equipment for $350 a month on a thirty-six-month lease. At the end of the lease they will be able to buy the equipment for $1. That means they will pay under $13,000 in lease payments for equipment that would cost $10,000 in today's dollars. That seemed to be a fair lease. At the end of thirty-six months the school system will own the equipment for far less than it would have cost to finance the purchase over thirty-six months at current interest rates.

The other lease carried by an educational institution was not so fair. It involved less than $8,000 of computer equipment and less than $700 of computer software. It was also a thirty-six-month lease with an option to buy at the end of the lease. The price to buy at the end was $800 rather than $1, and the monthly rental was $680 per month. This educational institution will pay almost $25,000 for less than $9,000 of computer equipment. This lease also had a number of sticky clauses in it as well. For example, if the leasee decided not to pay the $800 for the equipment at the end of the lease the company would take the equipment back, charge whatever they felt was appropriate for refurbishing it, and sell it themselves. If the sale price did not equal the $800 plus whatever the company charged for refurbishing, the leasee had to pay the difference. Check a lease very carefully before signing.

STEP SIX. TRY IT OUT

Now that you know how you want to use a computer and have a fairly good idea of what is affordable, you can begin the tire-kicking phase. Read reviews of computers in journals and magazines, arrange for local stores and computer suppliers to demonstrate their systems at your school, visit local computer club meetings, browse at retail computer outlets, and attend educational conventions that have computer displays.

We would suggest that you limit yourself to computers already on the market rather than those announced as being available *in the near future*. In this industry the near future can be as long as three years. In some cases, new models which are announced (and for which orders are accepted) never appear.

The same sort of problem can happen with computer accessories. If you want a computer with a compatible printer from the same company, look only at systems with acceptable printers already available and working rather than systems for which a fantastic printer is in the works.

One final point—no amount of reading reviews will take the place of an actual demonstration. The computer you finally select should be one you have tried out personally, one that you know is easy and comfortable for you and your students to use. Be sure to try it before you buy it.

STEP SEVEN. SURVEY SOURCES

Steps 6 and 7 should probably be completed at the same time. As you check out different types of computers for suitability, also evaluate the potential sources of supply. Most computers are purchased from one of three sources: a local retail store, a mail order supplier, or the manufacturer. Few manufacturers are willing to sell directly to consumers. Most prefer instead to deal with distributors and dealers who in turn sell to consumers. This frees the factory to concentrate on production and development. They count on their dealers or service centers to provide most of the customer service.

The other two alternatives, retail stores and mail order suppliers, are a mixed bag. There are excellent examples of ethical, responsible businesses in both categories. There are also examples of crooks, inept ne'er-do-wells, and fast buck olympians in both categories. If you are considering buying a computer that is supposed to be serviced by the retailer, a good local store with a top-notch technician who provides service on time is a valuable commodity. Prices at such a store may be higher than they are from mail order discount dealers, but many people feel that the slightly higher price is worth it if the person responsible for the warranty is just down the street. If you're not sure about a store, take the time to get opinions from computer owners in your area. We once considered buying a computer from a local dealer so we could get quick service. You can imagine how we felt when we discovered the dealer had no service personnel at all for that computer. When a system went down (needed repair) it was shipped back to the factory in California. Since the dealer's price was $200 more than the mail order price, we reconsidered the purchase. Apparently many other people did the same. The store is no longer in business. In educational applications it is essential that the equipment be reliable. In areas where quick service is not available, school systems often purchase backup systems which can be used when a computer is in need of repair. In communities with several dealers, school systems often consider the availability of timely service a prime requirement before buying equipment. In general, we would recommend school systems buy from a local dealer who provides good service. However, there are instances when buying by mail is in order.

Few generalizations can be made about mail order computer companies. Some have good track records. Many mail order suppliers have a staff of service technicians and provide quality repair service. Others are slow at delivering goods in the first place and even slower at handling service requests. One way to protect yourself is to read the letters and commentaries about mail order companies in the computer magazines and talk with other computer owners in your area who purchase equipment by mail. In general, you will avoid most of these problems if you buy from a retailer.

STEP EIGHT. BUY IT.

There's not much else to say. Once you've done your homework it's time for bid requests, purchase orders, and computers.

POTENTIALLY IMPORTANT FEATURES

Video Display

All the popular small computers use a video display for normal operation. All video displays are not created equal, however. Some computers display as few as 12 lines on the screen at one time and have 32 or fewer characters on each line. That is a little on the skimpy side. The standard displays for small computers can put either 24 lines of 40 characters or 16 lines of 64 characters on the screen at once. More expensive systems use a 24 by 80 format.

For recreational computing, many educational applications, and some business applications, two other features – color and graphics – are more important than the character display capacity. Several models now offer color displays rather than the traditional black and white. Color adds zest to games and makes computer aided learning more interesting.

Most computers have at least some graphics capability. That means that in addition to letters and numbers, the computer can display figures, graphs, charts, game boards, or computer-generated pictures on the screen. On some computers the graphics features are limited but useful. Other computers can handle very sophisticated graphics. In addition to educational and game applications, businesses can use color graphics to create sales displays as well as charts and figures.

Two other points should be made about video display. First, while most computers have video display capacity, many do not come with video monitors. Some are designed to be connected to a standard television, and some require you to buy a video monitor. Monitors cost from $125 to $700 depending on their quality and whether the monitor is color or black and white. Second, while all systems will display letters and numbers some display only uppercase or capital letters. We prefer a display with both upper and lowercase letters, but your pattern of usage will determine whether that feature is important.

Keyboard

Perhaps we're fanatics about keyboards, but they can determine whether working with the computer is a joy or a pain. Some manufacturers have produced computers with midget-sized keyboards resembling those on calculators. The keys are small and closely spaced. They are hard to use without making errors, and there is no way to touch type on these tiny keyboards.

A full-sized typewriter style keyboard is not the only thing to look for. A good keyboard should offer smooth resistance to the touch without catching and the whole assembly should be firmly mounted with no flexing or give in the keyboard when you press a key. Finally, the keyboard should be free of *key-*

bounce. You have keybounce when you type an A on the keyboard and AA or AAA appears on the screen. Keyboards with contact points exposed to dust are particularly susceptible to keybounce.

Computers such as the TRS-80 Model III, the Apple II, and the ATARI 800 use a very good standard size keyboard while the ATARI 400 uses a touch sensitive *membrane* keyboard. The keyboard on the ATARI 400 is functional and less expensive than a typewriter style keyboard. The membrane keyboards are fine for some applications (e.g., providing CAI which does not require extensive use of the keyboard). Since membrane keyboards are impervious to spills and also dustproof they may be the preferred type if you plan to use the computer in some environments (e.g., in a chemistry lab, in an elementary school, or with young children who like to use the computer while drinking their milk).

Membrane keyboards are not very good for word processing or for projects that require you to spend many hours typing in programs on the computer. Before selecting a computer, we suggest you sit down at the keyboard and work with it for awhile. Consider your probable uses for the system and decide whether the keyboard will be acceptable to you.

Storage Medium Options

Virtually all small computers come with cassette storage systems. Programs or data you want to save and use again later can be recorded on regular (but good quality) audio cassettes. Cassette storage is cheap, generally reliable, and easy to use. Unfortunately, it is slow. A large program can take as long as three minutes or more to load. That may not sound like a long time now, but when you're trying to help students load their programs in a class that only lasts 50 minutes it can be forever, particularly if there are problems with the load and you have to do it again...and again...and again. It is also easy to end up with a hundred or more tapes. Finding the one you need can take a considerable amount of time. Actually, we should not be so negative about cassette storage. Good systems can be very pleasant and easy to use. A poorly designed one is very trying.

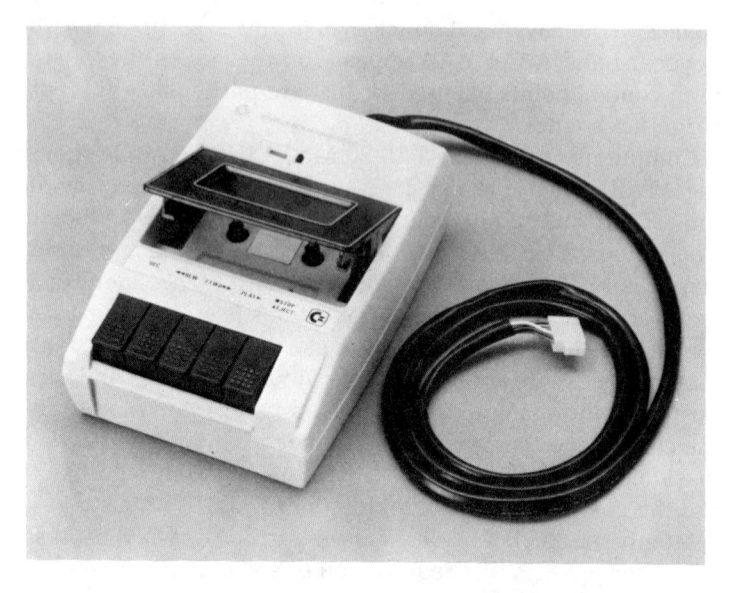

Figure 3.20 Commodore computers use this special cassette for data and program storage. *Photo courtesy Commodore.*

A popular alternative to cassette storage is the *floppy diskette*. Users with a floppy disk system use small diskettes that look like 45 RPM records for program or data storage rather than cassette tapes. A diskette slides in a slot on a disk drive. The disk drive then spins the diskette and reads or writes information on the diskette.

Floppy disk systems are very fast, very reliable, and as you might expect, expensive. Count on paying at least $400, perhaps as much as $900, for a small single drive system. Dual drive systems cost even more. For the money you get a high speed, reliable storage system that can put many programs on each of the little 5¼-inch disks. Many business computers have built-in disk drives in lieu of cassette systems. They are generally in the $3,000+ price range, but give businesses the speed and storage capacity required for large scale applications. Disk drives can also be added to most of the small computers as well.

Selecting Educational Computers • 79

Figure 3.21 The Apple II computer with two disk drives, a printer, and a monitor. *Photo courtesy Apple Computer, Inc.*

Figure 3.22 Several companies offer disk drive kits for popular computers at prices considerably less than buying from the manufacturer. This Percom kit fits a TRS-80 Model III. *Photo courtesy Percom Data Corporation.*

80 • Computers, Teaching and Learning

Figure 3.23 The 8050 dual disk drive from Commodore stores half a million characters on each diskette! That is three times the capacity of some drives. *Photo courtesy Commodore.*

Figure 3.24 A dual 8-inch system from Morrow Designs. *Photo courtesy Morrow Designs.*

Figure 3.25 A hard disk system is capable of storing millions of characters. *Photo courtesy Morrow Designs.*

Actually disk drives come in two sizes: 5¼-inch and 8-inch. The capacity of the diskettes vary according to size and type, but a great deal of data can be stored with even the smallest, least sophisticated disk drive. While there have been some quality control problems with a few of the drive manufacturers, many of these have been corrected. The overall quality in floppy disk systems is reasonably high.

In addition to the flexible or floppy disk systems there are also *hard disk* drives. These drives store data on rigid disks which spin at high speed. Hard disk drives were once very expensive, but it is now possible to buy a hard disk system for a small computer for as little as $2,000. Millions of characters can be stored on each hard disk; where large amounts of data must be stored they are more economical than floppy disk drives since it would be necessary to buy many floppy disk drives to equal the capacity of only one or two hard disk drives.

Base Cost and Expansion Costs

It is probably natural to compare computer prices by looking at the price tag on the basic computer. But that may not tell the whole story. Consider a familiar example. When you shop for a new car the sticker prices on two cars can vary by as much as $5,000 even when both cars are being sold by the same dealer and are the same make and model. The difference in sticker prices can be accounted for by options. One may have air conditioning, power steering and brakes, a moon roof, special accent and protective molding, a custom engine and transmission, special paint job, and an optional AM/FM stereo cassette player. The same thing can happen with computers. One dealer may quote you a very low price for a computer while another dealer may offer to sell you a system for hundreds of dollars more. The higher bid may mean the dealer has listened to you describe what you want to do with your computer and is offering a system that includes all the accessories needed to do that job. There is the base price of the computer and there is the cost of expanding the computer to do a particular job. The base price may not include the cost of a cassette recorder, disk drive, extra memory, or a printer. Many first time buyers of computers are shocked to find that the cost of accessories can easily add up to several times the cost of the computer itself. People are used to buying a $7,000 car and looking at options and accessories that cost only a fraction of the cost of the car. With a computer it is possible to buy disk drives or printers that cost much more than the computer itself. That means the base price of the computer is not of major importance to many people. The important number is the cost of expanding the system to do the work you want it to do. It would be easy for a company to put a very competitive price on their computer to attract buyers and then make the cost of expanding the system very high. This has been done by several companies. The TRS-80 Model III computer includes the circuits needed to add a printer to the computer in the base price of the least expensive model. The Apple II, on the other hand, does not. When adding a printer to your Apple II you must buy the printer and buy a printer card that can cost over $100.

The point is, always consider the cost of expanding a basic system to meet your specific needs, not just the price of a bare bones computer.

Section Two

COMPUTER LANGUAGES

4

BASIC

One question you may have at this point is, "How do I get the computer to do something?" You may already have discovered that just having the machine in front of you doesn't accomplish much. You probably are also aware that in order to get it to do anything, you must have a program.

A program is simply a detailed set of instructions that tells the computer what to do step-by-step. It's like writing down a set of instructions for another person when you want to make sure that a precise task is accomplished. As you read, think of the term program as direction giving.

There are two ways to get a program. You can buy a ready-made program, or you can develop your own. Does the first option sound best? Sometimes commercial software is the obvious way to go, and you will probably want to use many store-bought programs. However, there are times when you may want to write your own program. There may also be times when you will want to modify a commercial program to fit a special need. In order to program the computer yourself, or to modify a commercial program, you will have to communicate with the computer. Basically, you want to let it know what you want it to do. "But," you say, "I don't speak its language!" That brings us to the purpose of this chapter—to provide you with enough information about one language (BASIC) to allow you to begin communicating with the computer. An overview of the nature of computer languages will be provided as well.

COMPUTER LANGUAGES

Just as people use many different languages to communicate with one another, there are a number of different languages for computers. Computer languages can be categorized into three levels: machine, assembly, and higher-level languages.

Machine Language

In actual fact computers speak only one language—machine language. There are many machine languages. Different computers use different central processing units (CPUs). The machine language varies with the CPU used.

The CPU, the heart of most small computers, consists of a maze of electronic components. In order to program the computer, instructions must be sent through this CPU electronically. When you program in machine language, you are in direct contact with the CPU. The instructions you use are understood and acted upon without any translation.

Before you rush into learning machine language be aware that few people actually use this language to write programs. Why? Because program development at this level is a complicated process from the programmer's point of view. Even something as simple as adding two numbers takes several instructions. Machine language programs are also difficult to correct and generally can be used only in computers very similar to the one for which they were developed. Another disadvantage is that the instructions are written in numbers rather than in letters. This would be like writing down a set of directions for your students in a code instead of in English. In this case, the code is difficult to learn because the numbers have no relationship to the real world. Unless the programmer is able to memorize which number belongs to which instruction, programming is slow and laborious.

Rest assured that people who know little or nothing about machine language are able to do marvelous things with computers. As a computer user, you simply need to know that such a language does exist and what it does.

Assembly Language

To facilitate ease and efficiency in programming, assembly languages were developed. Most computers can be programmed in an assembly language. Because the vocabulary is made up of wordlike codes rather than numbers, assembly languages are easier to use than machine languages. These wordlike codes are often referred to as *mnemonics*. A mnemonic is something that assists memory (like a string tied around your finger that reminds you to pick up bread at the market). In assembly language the instruction to load data can be represented by the letters LD, while in machine language this instruction might be represented by the number 36. LD is certainly more likely to remind you of the message "load" than the number 36. The closer you get to a vocabulary that resembles the English language, the easier that vocabulary is to understand and use.

A disadvantage of assembly language is that it requires an assembler which is itself a program that takes up memory (storage space within the computer). Considering the steady trend toward memory being offered at a lower cost, this is not a serious disadvantage for most people. A greater disadvantage is that, while easier to work with than machine language, programming in assembly language is still rather cumbersome and tedious. Consequently, few people do much programming in assembly language.

Higher-Level Languages

Suppose you are suddenly transported to a foreign country where you don't know a single word of the native language. If you are to communicate with the people there, one of three things must happen: you must learn to speak their language, they must learn to speak your language, or you must work through an interpreter. Given these three alternatives, an obvious choice would be the interpreter – someone who could take your words and convert them to words that the natives could understand. Although an oversimplification, this is basically what happens when you use a higher-level computer language.

Simply put, a higher-level language is a language whose instructions are easy for the programmer to understand since they use English or English-like words. The problem is that the computer can't understand them. This problem, as you may have guessed, is solved by an interpreter – a program that translates the vocabulary you understand into vocabulary the machine can understand (i.e., machine language).

A higher-level language is a language that closely resembles English and is easy to learn, yet precise enough for the computer to follow without confusion. English itself is not precise enough for the computer. Higher-level languages are the next best thing to simply talking to the computer in your everyday language.

BASIC

The most popular higher-level language used with personal computers today is BASIC (Beginners All-Purpose Symbolic Instruction Code). BASIC, developed in 1963 at Dartmouth College, has since been revised and expanded many times.

Advantages

BASIC originally was developed as a conversational language; the programmer is in an *interactive* mode with the computer. The programmer and the computer are in direct contact with each other, as opposed to a *batch* mode, where the programmer takes a program to someone who puts it into the computer, waits for the computer to get around to running it, then gives the results (printout) back to the programmer. In the interactive or conversational mode, the programmer types a message to the computer, and the computer can respond immediately. It is rather like talking to another person face to face as opposed to communicating by an exchange of letters.

In the interactive mode a program can be entered simply by typing each line in on the keyboard. When the program is all typed in, the programmer can instruct the computer to process or execute the program (i.e., go ahead and follow the instructions). The programmer tells the computer to process the program by typing RUN. When RUN is typed the computer processes the program and when it comes to a line which contains an error, it stops and notifies the programmer of the location and nature of the error.

One advantage of the interactive mode is that small segments of a program can be run separately to see if they do what they are supposed to do. This is invaluable in getting a program debugged (getting the flaws out).

As a general purpose language, BASIC is not restricted to a specific or narrow purpose as are some computer languages. Consequently, with this one language you can use the computer to do many different tasks.

Perhaps its greatest advantage is the fact that it is so easy to learn. In one afternoon it is possible to learn enough BASIC to write your own simple programs.

Disadvantages

Since it was first introduced BASIC has been changed and expanded to keep up with dramatic hardware changes. True, it is now possible to do more with BASIC, but with the language still in a state of evolution, different computer designers have incorporated modifications which are peculiar to their own machines. Consequently, BASIC is not a highly standardized language. For example a program written in TRS-80 Level II BASIC (a BASIC used by Radio Shack's Model 1 computer) may not run in the Apple or PET computer. Although attempts are now being made by the American National Standards Institute to standardize BASIC, there is at present no such standardization between different popular versions.

This lack of standardization will not affect you as long as you are programming on your computer or using ready-made programs written for that computer. However, it will affect you when you find a program written for another computer in a book or magazine and decide you want to use it. You may find that after you have typed it in and eliminated all of your typing errors, the program still will not run. As you gain more experience, you might be able to make the necessary modifications so that the program will run on your machine. In the beginning, however, you may need to consult an experienced programmer for help.

Two other disadvantages are associated with BASIC: it is slow (relatively speaking) and requires more memory than other languages. To say that BASIC is slow simply means that the computer may take more time to perform a given task when the program is written in BASIC as opposed to machine or assembly language. To some computer users, this fact is critical—but usually not for the educator who is using a small computer. The speed at which a small computer, programmed in BASIC, can perform complicated tasks is still phenomenal. You may very well wonder whether performing tasks any faster would be an advantage. The need for more memory is also becoming less and less of a disadvantage with BASIC since memory is now very inexpensive.

GETTING STARTED

Now that you have an idea of what computer languages are and what they do let's get started. Keep in mind that various makes and models of computers have some of their own idiosyncrasies with respect to BASIC. You may need to consult a user's manual on your particular machine. The programs used in this chapter will run for the TRS-80 computer and are consistent with TRS-80 Level II BASIC.

The first requirement for using BASIC is that the computer must be ready to accept BASIC. Either an interpreter or compiler (a program by itself) must be in place to translate BASIC instructions into machine language instructions. Some computers have such a program already in the computer's memory. They are ready to accept BASIC right away. Other computers require you to get this program into the machine yourself. The interpreter or compiler, if not in memory already, is usually recorded on either a cassette tape or a magnetic disk. If the computer you are using requires that such a program be put into the computer before you begin using BASIC, consult your user's manual.

Once the machine is turned on and prepared to be programmed in BASIC, it will flash the word READY on the screen. This means exactly what it says—the machine is ready for you to talk to it. Now let's learn how.

STRUCTURE

BASIC, as do all languages, has a structure. A sentence always begins with a capital letter and ends with a period or some other appropriate punctuation mark. Each sentence has a subject and a predicate. Computer languages also have a structure governed by various rules. These rules must be adhered to rigidly or your program will not work. If you thought your high school English teacher was intolerant of rule violations, "you ain't seen nothin' yet!" Don't be discouraged, however. The rules are quite simple, and you can start with only a few of them and then add new ones as you gain experience.

Line Numbers

When you write in English you combine words and punctuation marks according to certain rules and thus form sentences. Sentences are then combined to form paragraphs. In BASIC, you combine words and punctuation marks according to certain rules to form *statements*. One or more statements form a program line. Each line is assigned a number. These numbers must be positive whole numbers (i.e., 1, 2, 3, ... 10; not −5 or 2.6). It is a common convention to assign line numbers in increments of 10 (i.e., 10, 20, 30 ... 100). The purpose of doing so is to allow you to insert additional lines into the program later. For example, you might decide that you need a line between lines 10 and 20; you could assign this line the number 15. You do not have to type in the line numbers in order; the computer will order them from low to high for you. In other words, if you type lines in the following order:

  10
  20
  40
  30

The computer will order them:

  10
  20
  30
  40

BASIC Characters

BASIC uses the twenty-six upper-case letters of the English alphabet (ABCDEFGHIJKLMNOPQRSTUVWXYZ) and the ten basic Arabic numerals (0 1 2 3 4 5 6 7 8 9). In addition to these characters, BASIC uses a variety of arithmetic symbols and punctuation marks. The most commonly used arithmetic symbols are:

$$+ \quad - \quad * \quad / \quad = \quad < \quad > \quad <>$$

The most commonly used punctuation marks are:

. , ; : " $

The way in which these symbols and marks are used will be explained in example programs throughout the remainder of this chapter.

A PROGRAM

You already know that a program is a set of instructions that tells the computer what you want it to do. Now let's take a look at a very simple program:

PROGRAM 4.1

```
10 LET X = 3
20 LET Y = 2
30 LET Z = X + Y
40 PRINT Z
```

This program tells the computer to add 3 plus 2 and print the answer on the screen. It consists of four program lines, each containing a statement.

Statements

You will recall that a program is made up of program lines, each containing one or more statements. To keep things simple for now, assume that each program line consists of only one statement.

A statement is somewhat similar to a sentence in written English. It is composed of words, numbers, and symbols arranged according to certain rules. A statement that is properly constructed can be decoded by the computer and acted upon appropriately.

Syntax

The term *syntax* is used to denote the way in which words are put together to form phrases and sentences in a human language. Syntax is also used to denote specific rules for putting elements of a computer language together. Although an analogy can be made between English sentences and BASIC statements, there are some important differences.

In English the meaning will usually be clear even if a word or two is mispronounced or misspelled. BASIC and other computer languages are not so forgiving. You must say precisely what you intend and say it exactly as the computer expects. For example, words must be spelled correctly. The computer does not grant the least degree of allowance for spelling errors. In English, if you wrote lode when you meant load, the reader would understand what you meant from contextual clues. In BASIC, the computer understands the command LOAD, but LODE would not mean the same thing.

Another difference is the way punctuation is handled. Commas, semicolons, and periods clarify the meaning of written English, but the rules for their use vary. You could still understand a letter from Uncle Harry even if he managed to write a whole page without a comma or period. In BASIC these punctuation marks are often as important as the letters and numbers. Leaving out one comma can prevent an entire program from running properly.

Finally, English is a very rich language. There are usually several words that have similar meanings. A 1956 Chevrolet could appropriately be called a car, auto, automobile, or vehicle. BASIC is not so well endowed. There are often only a few ways of saying something.

Key Words

The words BASIC understands are called *key words*. Each statement begins with a key word (exceptions to this will be explained later). In many statements a beginning key word is a cue to what the statement will instruct the computer to do.

Commands

A statement is only one type of instruction that the computer can understand. It can also understand a type of instruction called a *command*. It is important to understand the difference. A command is an instruction which is acted upon immediately by the computer. For example, you could solve the 3+2 problem with a simple command:

PRINT 3+2

After typing in this command and pressing the ENTER key on the keyboard, the computer would respond with 5 (displayed on the monitor screen).

Some instructions can be used as either a statement or a command. PRINT is one of these instructions. We have just seen how it can be used as a command to tell us the sum of 3 + 2. Look at Program 4.1. Note that line 40 uses PRINT as a statement. Since PRINT is assigned a line number, the computer will not act upon this instruction until it has acted on lines 10, 20, and 30.

PRINT, RUN, LIST, and ENTER are commands which you will need to be familiar with from the start.

PRINT. This command has to be followed by some additional information (such as 3 + 2). It tells the computer to print something out on the screen.

RUN. When you have typed in a program and you want the computer to execute, or run it, you instruct the computer to do so by typing the command RUN and pressing the ENTER key. The computer will then act on each program line.

LIST. This command tells the computer to display your program on the screen as it is presently registered, or entered in the computer. It does not do anything with it; it simply shows you what you have. By typing LIST and pressing ENTER, the program lines, with their numbers, will appear on the screen in numerical order, even if you have entered a program line out of sequence.

We have considered these three commands – PRINT, RUN, LIST – in terms of writing your own program. RUN and LIST also are essential when you are using a program that has already been written for you. To get the computer to execute your program, you give the command RUN. If you want to see what the program looks like, you give the command LIST.

ENTER. The ENTER command is a special command given by simply pressing the key labeled ENTER on the keyboard (this is the case on the TRS-80; on other computers this key may be labeled something else). ENTER is essential to getting information into the computer. Look again at program 4.1. To get a program line into the computer, you first type the line number, then the statement:

10 LET X = 3

Then press the ENTER key. Until the time you actually press the ENTER key, all that has transpired is the characters

    10 LET X = 3

have appeared on the screen. At this point you can change any or all of these characters by using some editing keys on the keyboard. Once you press the ENTER key, however, you have entered the statement into the computer and it has been registered as a line in your program.

Immediate and Delayed Modes

We have seen that there are two different ways of telling the computer to solve a simple arithmetic problem. One is to use a command, which is acted upon immediately by the computer. The other is to use a series of statements, contained in program lines, which the computer acts on individually in numeric order. When commands are used, the programmer is working in the *immediate mode*, and when statements are used, the programmer is working in the *delayed mode*.

ANALYSIS OF PROGRAM 4.1

Now that you understand a few concepts, let's look at Program 4.1 again to see exactly what it does and how it does it. Each program line begins with a line number and is followed by a statement; each statement begins with a key word.

LET. The key word in lines 10, 20, and 30 is LET. LET tells the computer that you want to assign a value to a variable. A variable is something that is capable of changing (varying) in value. Instead of using a constant (e.g., 6) you may want to use a variable. Let's say you call the variable X. Now you can assign different values to X. As we progress you will see the advantages of using variables. A variable can be represented by one letter, two letters, or one letter followed by a number. For example, X, Y, XY, X1, and X2 are all legal variables.

In Program 4.1 you want the computer to add two numbers and give the answer. Instead of simply telling it to add the constants 3 and 2, variables were chosen and then assigned desired values. The first variable was arbitrarily called X. In line 10 we tell the computer that we want to use a variable X and to assign the value 3 to that variable. The format for using LET is:

LET variable = expression

In this case, the variable is X and the expression is 3. So we have:

LET X = 3

The statement in line 20 is exactly the same, with Y as the variable and 2 as the expression.

In line 30 observe that an expression can be more than a number; it can also be a mathematical operation (X + Y). Other examples of valid mathematical operations could be (X/Y), (A + B*5) and (23 – T). The / symbol indicates division while * indicates multiplication.

SUMMARY OF PROGRAM 4.1

Thus far, the program has assigned the value of 3 to the variable X and the value of 2 to the variable Y. It has stored these values in memory. It then adds them and assigns the sum to variable Z. Now you are ready for the answer. In line 40, PRINT tells the computer to display on the screen the value of Z.

INPUT AND OUTPUT

If you have not already done so, type in and run Program 4.1. Notice the small blinking block on your screen. This is the cursor. It lets you know where the next character you type will be displayed. Remember, after typing each program line, to press ENTER. Your program will appear on the screen just as it has been registered in the computer. If you have made any typing errors, correct them at this time. Most computers have an edit mode that allows you to change, delete, and insert characters in a program line. The edit mode will allow you to do rather complex editing on the lines. Your user's manual will explain the editing mode. For now, if you have made an error, simply type that line (including the line number) over again. When you enter the corrected line, the computer will register the new version and delete the old version. It will also place the new version in its proper sequence in the program.

Now type the command RUN, press ENTER and the number 5 should appear on the screen. Congratulations! You have just had your first conversation with the computer.

That was some effort just to get the computer to tell you that 3+2 equals 5, wasn't it? But you are beginning to learn the rudiments of programming in BASIC. To illustrate what the program can do, however, try Program 4.2.

PROGRAM 4.2

```
10 LET X= 25049.2
20 LET Y= 501003.2
30 LET Z= X/Y
40 PRINT Z
```

Notice the new character in line 30: / (slash). In BASIC, this slash is the division symbol. Placing it between any two values tells the computer to divide the first value by the second. Again, as in Program 4.1, you could accomplish the same thing by telling the computer:

PRINT 25049.2/501003.2

Keep in mind that the task at hand is not to divide numbers, but to learn some programming skills.

YOU AS A PROGRAMMER

Suppose again that you are in a foreign country. You decide to learn the language of that country. On the first day of your visit, you don't speak or understand a single word of the new language. Six months later you can communicate quite well in it. At what point did you learn the language? Perhaps after the first day you could speak a few phrases. Gradually, with practice, you added more words to your vocabulary and were able to build these words into more elegant sentences. The same is true in learning BASIC. Now you can say, "Hello," "How are you," and a few more things. With a few more words and a few more rules, you will be able to get the computer to do some more complex things. It simply takes practice.

REMARKS STATEMENTS (REM)

A very important aspect of computer programming is *style*. Documentation is an important part of style. Documentation means labeling and explaining things so that other people can easily understand what a program does and how it does it. In BASIC the REM statement is a very convenient way to document a program. When the computer encounters REM, it ignores whatever follows on that line. This allows the programmer to type in whatever remarks are needed, and these remarks will be listed in the program but will not affect its execution. Examples of REM statements will be found in Program 4.3.

SOME ESSENTIAL STATEMENTS

The following program can be used for an individualized addition facts drill:

PROGRAM 4.3

```
10 REM CLEAR THE SCREEN
20 CLS
30 REM GENERATE RANDOM NUMBERS
40 X=RND(9): Y=RND(9)
50 REM FIND CORRECT ANSWER AND PRESENT
   PROBLEM
60 LET Z=X+Y
70 PRINT X;" + ";Y;"="
80 REM GET STUDENT'S ANSWER, MATCH WITH
   CORRECT ANSWER AND GIVE FEEDBACK
90 INPUT A
100 IF A=Z THEN PRINT "GOOD THAT'S RIGHT!"
    ELSE PRINT "OOPS"
110 REM DELAY
120 PRINT "PRESS 'ENTER' TO CONTINUE"
130 INPUT S
140 GOTO 20
```

When Program 4.3 is run, it may put the following on the screen:

5+7=

BASIC • 99

The student taking the drill types in an answer. If the answer is 12, a message appears on the screen:

GOOD THAT'S RIGHT!

When the student presses ENTER again, the screen is cleared, and a new combination of numbers appears. The student then responds with an answer. When a wrong answer is given, the message OOPS appears on the screen. This process will continue indefinitely. The computer will continue to provide additional problems using randomly selected numbers ranging from 0 through 9 and will continue to inform the student whether the answer is right or wrong, as long as he or she keeps pressing the ENTER key.

ANALYSIS OF PROGRAM 4.3

Several new instructions will be introduced in this section. In addition to these new instructions, some programming conventions will be introduced. These instructions and conventions will be explained as they are used in program lines.

Now take a look at each individual line of Program 4.3 in order to understand what is happening. Notice that REM statements have been inserted in this program to document what various segments of the program do.

Line 20. CLS. This is a new instruction. CLS, like PRINT, can be used as both a statement and a command. In this particular case, CLS is a statement; it tells the computer to clear the screen. It erases anything that is on the screen and moves the cursor to the upper left corner.

Line 40. Line 40 is a multiple statement line. Rather than having each statement take up a separate program line, you can add additional statements to the same line by placing a colon (:) after each statement, thus telling the computer that one statement is complete and another will follow.

RND. This statement tells the computer that instead of assigning a value to X as in Programs 4.1 and 4.2, you want the computer to randomly select some numbers for you. The RND instruction is one of a group of instructions called arithmetic functions. The format for RND is:

RND(x)

The x can be any positive integer (whole number) up to a certain limit depending on your computer. The number you place in parentheses following RND tells the computer to randomly select numbers up to this number. In line 40 of Program 4.3 (9) was used. If you wanted to use larger numbers in the math drill, you could increase the number. RND(100), for example, would give you random numbers ranging from 0 to 100.

The second statement in line 40, Y = RND(9), again assigns a randomly selected number to the variable Y.

Line 60. This line is exactly like line 30 in Programs 4.1 and 4.2 and requires no further explanation.

Line 70. PRINT. The PRINT statement will tell the computer to print out the addition problem:

X + Y =

Alphanumeric Strings

The term *alphanumeric string* is usually shortened to *string*. It refers to a sequence of characters you want the computer to print out exactly as they appear in the statement. The same process is also used to get the computer to print out words. Whenever you want to print a string, you must enclose the string in quotation marks. This tells the computer to print the actual character rather than dealing with it as a variable name or a mathematical function. To illustrate, the commands PRINT X and PRINT "X" would do two different things. PRINT X would print out the value of X. PRINT "X", on the other hand, would print the character X.

In line 70, the computer is instructed first to print the number it has selected and assigned to X; then print a + sign; then, the value of Y; and finally, an = sign. In this statement, after you ask for a variable value to be printed, you ask for a string to be printed. It is necessary to separate these statements in some way. You can do this with either a comma (,) or a semicolon (;).

In a single line across the monitor screen, there are four predetermined print locations. An element in a PRINT statement which is separated from other elements by a comma (,) will be placed in the next available tab location. Therefore, the comma in BASIC works a little like the tab function on a typewriter. When you use the semicolon (;) to separate the elements of a PRINT statement, each element is printed without any spaces. You have to build the desired spacing into the statement.

In summary, in line 70, you first tell the computer print the value of X. X is the first element of your statement and you want to maintain control over where the elements are printed so you follow X with a semicolon. Second, you want the computer to print the plus sign, and you tell it to do so by using quotation marks on both sides of the plus sign. Notice the blank space before and after the + sign. The computer will print a blank space and move over to the next position, print +, and then print another blank space. Next the value of Y is printed, and finally the = sign. So the student is asked the question:

X + Y =

Line 90. INPUT. One way of getting information into the computer is by using the INPUT instruction. When the computer comes to the key word INPUT, it prompts the user with a question mark (?). In essence it is saying, "Okay, it's your turn to talk." Some kind of information must be entered for the program to continue. The computer recognizes information as having been entered when the ENTER key is pressed. In this instance, you have told the computer that you will input the value of variable A, which in this program will be the answer. You have just been asked a question; you now provide an answer.

In line 90, when the computer comes to INPUT it has displayed an addition problem followed by a question mark. It then stops and waits until the ENTER key is pressed before it continues. It doesn't really care whether you provide an answer to the question. It moves on to the next step in the program when you press ENTER. If you press ENTER without giving an answer, the computer assumes that the answer is 0. What generally happens in this program is that a number will be typed in (e.g., 9), ENTER is pressed, and the computer moves on to the next step in the program.

String and Numeric Information

The computer is concerned with two types of information: string and numeric. When you use INPUT, you must specify which type of information you want to "input;" the computer then will accept only that type of information. Numeric information is specified simply by a variable name (A, X, BC). "String" information (e.g., BILL, HELLO, XYZ) is specified by attaching a dollar sign ($) to the variable name (A$, X$, BC$). The computer deals with the two types of information differently. Numeric information is treated as a value, while string information is treated as one or more characters. For example, the numeric variable A can have a value assigned to it, let's say 9. The computer will then treat A as a 9. You can now add, subtract, and multiply with this 9. If, however, A$ were the string "XYZ", the computer would treat A$ as the characters "XYZ." You can print this A out and do other things with it, but you can't add it to 5 or multiply it by 3.

Line 100. IF THEN. In line 100 of program 4.3 you encounter the IF THEN statement. IF THEN, part of a family of statements, is used in conjunction with other key words to form more complex statements. It is one way of telling the computer that you want it to make a decision. The format for a simple IF THEN statement is: IF (followed by a true or false expression), THEN (an action clause). For example:

IF S = 5 THEN PRINT S

tells the computer that if the expression S = 5 is true, then you want it to print the value of S. There are many possible true or false expressions that could be used in place of S = 5 and a number of action clauses that could be used in place of PRINT S. At this point, however, let's simply consider the difference between a true expression and a false expression. In the above example, S = 5 can either be a true statement or a false statement depending on the value of S. If S has the value of 5 assigned to it, you are simply saying 5 = 5, and that is true. If, however, another value has been assigned to S, let's say 2, then you are saying 2 = 5, and that is not true. What is important here is what the computer does with a true expression as opposed to a false expression. When the expression is true, the computer carries out the action clause (in this example, PRINT S). When the expression is false, the computer moves on to the next line number (unless it is told differently) and ignores the action clause.

In line 100 the expression is A = Z and the action-clause is PRINT "GOOD THAT'S RIGHT!". When the conditions of the expression are met (when A does in fact equal Z), the computer will print:

GOOD THAT'S RIGHT!

When the conditions are not met (the expression is not true because A and Z are assigned two different values), the computer does not execute the action clause.

In line 100 a third element is also added to the IF THEN statement. It is ELSE. ELSE allows you to tell the computer to do something "else" when the conditions of the expression are not met. Rather than proceeding to the next program line, in this case it will print "OOPS!"

Look again at line 100 and see exactly what happens. The number typed in by the student has been assigned to the variable A. The sum of X + Y (which is the correct answer) has been assigned to the variable Z. When the student's answer (A) is the same as the correct answer (Z), the student is told "GOOD THAT'S RIGHT!" When it is not correct the student is told "OOPS!"

Lines 120 and 130. Delaying the PRINT Instruction. One peculiarity of the computer is that it just keeps on going until you tell it to stop. This presents a problem whenever a print statement is used. The information may be printed out on the screen, but it may be pushed off the top of the screen as the computer moves on to the next statements. The INPUT statement stops the computer until it is signaled to move on again. INPUT S is used to stop action so that you can see

GOOD THAT'S RIGHT!

When line 120 is encountered, "PRESS 'ENTER' TO CONTINUE" appears on the screen. When line 130 is encountered everything stops and a ? appears. The student has to press ENTER to continue the program. Since you aren't using the variable S in the program for any real purpose, it doesn't matter what value you assign to it. And if you don't assign any value to it, the computer will assign the value 0. The computer is perfectly happy with this value and is willing to continue. All that is really happening, is that the ENTER key is being used to signal the computer to move on.

Using Loops

The purpose of line 140 is to create a *loop*. A loop means that the computer is to go back to some previous point in the program and sequence down through the program again. You may want this looping action to occur one or more times. In the case of Program 4.3, without the loop, it would present only one addition problem. GOTO, simply tells the computer to shift control back to line 20. Once this is done the computer will continue sequencing—20, 30, 40, 50, 60, 70, 80, 90, 100, 110, 120, 130, 140—then return to 20, and on and on.

There are several different ways to create a loop within a program, as well as several ways to limit the number of times the loop is to occur. In Program 4.3, you have no set limits. The student can keep on answering math facts as long as he or she wants or until someone pulls the plug on the machine, or presses the BREAK key.

A LITTLE MORE SOPHISTICATION

Add a few more tricks, and the addition drill will do a few more things.

PROGRAM 4.4

5 REM CLEARS SCREEN AND FINDS OUT HOW MANY PROBLEMS THE STUDENT WANTS TO DO
10 CLS: INPUT "HOW MANY PROBLEMS WILL WE DO TODAY"; PR
15 REM CLEARS SCREEN, COUNTS LOOPS, GENERATES RANDOM NUMBERS, PRESENTS PROBLEM AND ACCEPTS STUDENT'S ANSWER
20 CLS: N = N + 1: X = RND(9): Y = RND(9): PRINT X;" + ";Y;" = ":INPUT A:Z = X + Y
25 REM COMPARES STUDENT'S ANSWER WITH CORRECT ANSWER AND COUNTS CORRECT AND INCORRECT RESPONSES
30 IF A = Z THEN C = C + 1 ELSE IC = IC + 1
35 REM GIVES FEEDBACK, TELLING THE STUDENT WHAT THE CORRECT ANSWER IS WHEN STUDENT ANSWER IS INCORRECT
40 IF A = Z PRINT "CORRECT!" ELSE PRINT "OOPS! THE CORRECT ANSWER IS";Z
45 REM DELAY AND DECISION ON WHETHER TO CONTINUE

```
50 INPUT "PRESS ENTER TO CONTINUE";S: IF N<PR
   GOTO 20
55 REM TELLS STUDENT RATIO OF CORRECT AND
   INCORRECT ANSWERS
60 PRINT:PRINT:PRINT:PRINT "YOU MISSED ";IC;
   " OUT OF ";PR;" AND YOU GOT ";C;
   " OUT OF ";PR;" CORRECT"
70 END
```

Program 4.4 has three additional features. It allows the teacher or the student to designate how many problems will be presented. The program not only tells the student whether the answer is right or wrong, it tells what the right answer is when an incorrect answer is given. It also scores the drill and puts the score (number correct and number incorrect) on the screen at the end of the drill.

ANALYSIS OF PROGRAM 4.4

With several new instructions in this program, let's again look at it line by line. Only the new key words and procedures will be explained.

Line 10. String Variables. The INPUT statement this time has one additional feature: a string which acts as a prompt to the user. The format is:

INPUT "string"; variable.

Instead of just a ? as a prompt, the user will see "HOW MANY PROBLEMS WILL WE DO TODAY?" The user responds with a number (which is represented by the variable PR). Using mnemonics—or variable names that remind you of the actual thing you are dealing with—will be helpful (e.g., PR for PROBLEM). Note that each program line includes several statements which are separated by colons.

Line 20. Counters. In programming you often need to count each time something happens. In this case you want to count how many times a problem is presented (in actuality, how many times the program loops). N, our variable for number, will act as a counter. Until you assign a value to N, it is equal to 0. The first time through the program N=N (or 0)+1. In other words, after one problem has been presented the counter (N) will equal 1. The second time, N will equal 1 + 1 (or 2), and so on. You are simply increasing N by 1 each time you go to line 20.

Line 30. In line 30 the student's answer (A) is compared with the correct answer (Z). If they are the same, the variable C (correct) is increased by 1; if not, the variable IC (incorrect) is increased by 1. C and IC are counters just like N, and simply count the number of correct and incorrect responses.

Line 40. Line 40 is just like line 50 in Program 4.3 with one exception. The computer knows what the correct answer to each problem is — it is Z. So you tell the computer that, if the student's answer (A) is incorrect, it should print "OOPS! THE CORRECT ANSWER IS 6" or whatever Z happens to equal at the time, since it will always be the correct answer.

Line 50. The Dummy Input Statement. In line 50 the dummy INPUT stops the sequence and causes the computer to make a decision whether to stop or present more problems. As long as N (number of problems) is less than PR (number of problems wanted), the computer will go back to line 20 and loop through again. Once N is equal to PR, however, the conditions of the IF THEN statement will be met and the computer will proceed to line 60.

Line 60. Using PRINT as a Spacer. Each time the computer encounters the PRINT statement it drops down a line. When PRINT is by itself, with nothing to print, the computer simply spaces for you — it's like hitting the return key on the typewriter if you want to leave a blank line.

In line 60 the computer spaces down four lines to spread the information out and make it easier to read. Next, the computer prints "YOU MISSED (number incorrect) OUT OF (number given) AND YOU GOT (number correct) OUT OF (number given). Now out of the loop, there is no place for the computer to go since it is at the end of the program. It then encounters line 70 END and says READY, indicating it is awaiting further instructions.

WORKING WITH STRINGS AND ARRAYS

You have now been exposed to some of the fundamentals of programming in BASIC. If you have tried these programs in the computer, you should begin to get a feel for the language.

PROGRAM 4.5

```
5 REM SETS ASIDE MEMORY SPACE FOR AN ARRAY
10 DIM L$ (5,5) : CLS
15 REM STARTS OUTER LOOP
20 FOR I = 1 TO 5
25 REM STARTS A NESTED LOOP
30 FOR J = 1 TO 5
35 REM READS VALUES OF THE ARRAY
   SEQUENTIALLY
40 READ L$ (I,J)
45 REM SENDS LOOPING ACTION BACK TO START
   OF NESTED LOOP
50 NEXT J
55 REM SENDS LOOPING ACTION BACK TO START
   OF OUTER LOOP
60 NEXT I
65 REM DATA STATEMENTS
70 DATA "WHIN", "WENN", "WEN", "WIN", "WIN"
80 DATA "TIHM", "TIME", "TEIM", "TIEM", "TIME"
90 DATA "GIRLZ", "GRILS", "GIRLS", "GURLS", "GIRLS"
100 DATA "DULLER", "DOLLER", "DOLLAR", "DOLAR",
    "DOLLAR"
110 DATA "SIENCE", "SCEINCE", "SEINCE", "SCIENCE",
    "SCIENCE"
115 REM STARTS OUTER LOOP
120 FOR I = 1 TO 5
125 REM STARTS NESTED LOOP
130 FOR J = 1 TO 4
135 REM PRINTS FOUR SPELLINGS OF ONE WORD
    ON SCREEN
140 PRINT L$ (I,J),
150 NEXT J
155 REM ASKS FOR AND ACCEPTS STUDENT'S
    SELECTION
160 INPUT "WHICH ONE IS CORRECT"; A$
165 REM COMPARES STUDENT'S WORD WITH
    CORRECT WORD AND GIVES FEEDBACK
170 C = C + 1 : IF L$ (I,5) = A$ PRINT "THAT IS RIGHT"
    ELSE PRINT "OOPS, THE CORRECT SPELLING
    IS";L$ (I,5)
```

```
175 REM TIME DELAY WITH FOR NEXT LOOP
180 FOR K=1 TO 900
190 NEXT K
200 CLS
210 NEXT I
212 REM PRINTS RATIO OF CORRECT AND
    INCORRECT
220 PRINT "YOU ANSWERED"; C; "OUT OF 5 RIGHT"
```

Program 4.5, a spelling drill, is more complicated than the earlier programs used as examples. Unfortunately, you can't program the computer to randomly select words internally, so you must put the words you want to use into the program. The program will display four words across the screen, only one of which is spelled correctly (e.g., TIHM TIME TEIM TIEM). The student will be asked which word is spelled correctly. The student types in the answer and the computer indicates whether the response is right or wrong and shows the correct answer. As in Program 4.4, the student's performance will be scored and the results printed out at the end of the program.

SOME NEW SKILLS

Four major new programming skills are introduced in Program 4.5 that will be very useful to you in writing your own programs. First, it uses an *array*. Next, it works with string variables whereas previously we have only manipulated numeric variables. Third it makes use of the FOR NEXT statement to create a loop. And finally it uses a delay mechanism so that we can read what is printed on the screen rather than the dummy INPUT statement used previously.

Arrays

An array is a group of elements such as a list or a table. The arrays you will work with are either "one-dimensional" or "two-dimensional". A one-dimensional array consists of one row of elements (e.g., E1 E2 E3 E4). A two-dimensional array consists of more than one row of elements as well as more than one column of elements as shown below:

```
E11  E12  E13  E14
E21  E22  E23  E24
E31  E32  E33  E34
```

Subscripted Variables. Using a variable name to denote the array, you have a twelve element array arranged in three rows and four columns. BASIC provides a quick way to work with this type of information. It involves using *subscripted variables*. A subscripted variable is a method of referring to one single element in an array. This allows you to identify each element of the array so that it can be singled out for some purpose in a program. It is like looking out over a classroom where a group of students are seated in several rows of desks. As the teacher you want to address one of these students so you call that student by name. Subscripted variables allow you to give a name to each element in the array.

As with any other variable, a subscripted variable must have a name. Let's assign the variable name E to the above array. The format for a subscripted variable is:

variable name (row number, column number).

In this case, E(1,1) would refer to E11 in the upper left hand corner of the array. The second element in the first row (E12), would be referred to as E(1,2).

Using subscripted variables to work with arrays is a great convenience in programming. It allows the programmer to manipulate large amounts of information very quickly and with only a fraction of the program lines it would take to deal with each element of a list or table as a completely separate entity.

In Program 4.5 the array consists of five rows and five columns and is made up of words. Line 70 contains five spellings of the word WIN, two of which are spelled correctly and three of which are spelled incorrectly. Lines 70 through 110 simply list the array. Each of these lines has the key word, "DATA", immediately following the line number. These "data statements" from 70 to 110 are a way of listing information (words or numbers) in the program so that it can be accessed by the computer. In this case our array looks like this:

WHIN	WENN	WEN	WIN	WIN
TIHM	TIME	TEIM	TIEM	TIME
GIRLZ	GRILS	GIRLS	GURLS	GIRLS
DULLER	DOLLER	DOLLAR	DOLAR	DOLLAR
SIENCE	SCEINCE	SEINCE	SCIENCE	SCIENCE

In Program 4.5 the variable name L$ refers to the elements in this array. We could refer to the word WHIN with L$ (1,1), and the word DULLER with L$ (4,1).

Dimensioning an Array. Whenever you use an array in a program, the computer must at some point while executing the program set aside memory space to store the elements of the array. There are two ways to tell the computer to set aside this memory. The first is by default and the second is by using the DIM instruction.

1. Default. The first time you use the variable name of an array, space is set aside for that array. If the subscripted variable KN (3) were encountered, the computer would interpret this to mean the third element of a one-dimensional array — only one row of elements. It would then, by default, set aside storage space for 11 elements of information (11 is the default number).

E0 E1 E2 E3 E4 E5 E6 E7 E8 E9 E10

As actual pieces of information with the variable name KN were fed into the computer, they would be stored in the space which was set aside. If you were using a two-dimensional array (more than one row and more than one column) and you referred to an element in this array, such as KN(3,3), the computer would set aside eleven rows and eleven columns of storage space.

One problem with using the default method is that you may set aside storage space and only use a small portion of it. This is inefficient, of course, and you may use up all of your available memory needlessly. The other problem, of course, is that an 11 by 11 array may not be large enough.

2. DIM. You can designate exactly how much storage space to set aside by using a DIM (dimension) statement. The format for the DIM statement is: DIM variable name (number of rows, number of columns). For example, if you wanted to use an array with six rows and four columns and use the variable name PR, you would dimension the array this way:

DIM PR(6,4).

Some BASICs designate the first element of an array 0 rather than 1. When this is the case, a three by three array could be dimensioned E(2,2). The elements of this array would be designated as follows:

E00 E01 E02
E10 E11 E12
E20 E21 E22

ANALYSIS OF PROGRAM 4.5

In Program 4.5, the first thing you do in line 10 is dimension the array. Whenever a DIM statement is used, it must come before any use of the array in the program. Since you will be working with an array consisting of five rows and five columns, you dimension the array like this:

DIM L$(5,5).

String Variables

Since elements of the array in Program 4.5 are words rather than numbers, they are string variables. When you use a string variable, you designate it as such by using the $. The following are all legal string variable names: A$, AB$, B1$, L4$. In some versions of BASIC, whatever string of characters you want to assign to a string variable must be enclosed in quotation marks (" ").

FOR NEXT With Arrays. One common way to manipulate elements of an array in a program is to use the FOR NEXT sequence.

The format for the FOR NEXT sequence is:

FOR *counter = expression* TO *expression*.

Body of sequence consisting of one or more program lines.

NEXT counter.

Line 20 in Program 4.5 illustrates the FOR NEXT statement: I is set up as a counter. It is increased by 1 each time the FOR statement is encountered. The first expression (in this case, 1) tells the computer where to start the counter, and the second expression (in this case, 5) tells the computer how high to count.

In line 20 you tell the computer to start at 1 and count to 5. Again you are setting up a loop, starting with the key word FOR and ending with the key word NEXT. Consequently, you have set up a loop going from line 20 to line 60. Each time the computer encounters line 60 (NEXT I), it will loop back to line 20, increase I by 1, and proceed again toward line 60. Each time the computer passes through the loop, lines 25-55 are executed. It will do this only five times and then it will proceed through the program.

In Program 4.5 note the introduction of a *nested loop* – a loop within a loop. Line 30 to line 50 sets up a loop with the counter J and the limits 1 to 5.

```
 ┌─20 FOR I = 1 to 5
 │ ┌─30 FOR J = 1 to 5
 │ │  40 READ L$ (I,J)
 │ └─50 NEXT J
 └──60 NEXT I
```

Figure 4.1

Figure 4.1 helps to visualize the sequencing of program lines with nested loops. Starting with line 20, the computer sets I equal to 1. It then encounters line 30 and sets J equal to 1. It then executes line 40, then encounters line 50, which tells it that it is at the end of the inner loop (30 to 50); so it goes back to 30, increases J by 1 (J now equals 2). This continues until J equals 5. Then the sequencing drops past 50 to line 60, which tells the computer to loop back to line 20. Now I is increased by 1 and the sequencing continues. Next, line 30 is encountered again and the sequencing goes from 30 to 50 and back again five more times. The inner loop is executed five times for every time the outer loop is executed. When I finally equals five, the program goes on to the next program line.

Look at line 40 and you will see what is happening from line 10 through 110. This program segment loads into the memory an array which consists of the words for the spelling drill – lines 70 through 110. This is done with the READ statement in line 40 – it tells the computer to READ information contained in the DATA statements. The first time through the program, I equals 1 and J equals 1; so the READ statement as far as the computer is concerned, says READ L$(1,1). In other words, read the word for the first column of the first row—WHIN. Now the value of J will change to 2. The second time line 40 is encountered, it will be saying READ L$ (1,2)—first row, second column; or WENN. Through the looping action, then, first the entire first row will be read, then the second row, and so on until I and J both equal 5 which will be when the word in the fifth column of the fifth row (SCIENCE) is read. Now all of the elements in the array are stored in the computer's memory in an order which will allow you to call up any word you choose at any time.

The key word READ tells the computer to look for information stored in a DATA line. Each time a READ instruction is encountered the computer uses the next unused value in the DATA statement.

Lines 120 through 170. This segment of the program tells the computer to print on the screen the first four words in a row of the array. Notice again the nested loop. Once the first four words of a line are printed across the screen, the student is asked, "WHICH ONE IS CORRECT?" The student's best guess is then typed (A$). The computer can make decisions about the equality of two string variables just as with numeric variables. In line 170 the last element of each row designates the correct spelling of each word. When the words are printed out for the student to see, only the first four words (one is correct and three are incorrect) appear. The fifth word of each row is the correct word. You use this fifth word to compare with the student's word (IF L$ (I,5) = A$). When the words are the same, the student has chosen the correct word; when they are not, an incorrect word has been chosen.

Lines 180-190. Delay Factor. Lines 180 and 190 contain a delay factor. You will recall that in the math drill programs a dummy INPUT statement was used to stop program execution so that you could hold what was printed on the screen for as long as you liked. In this program, you tell the computer to pause after telling the student whether the correct word was selected so that the message can be read and the student can continue. This is done by using a FOR NEXT statement. This time, however, you don't actually have the computer do anything in the loop. You tell it to go from line 180 to line 190 and back to 180 and continue looping between these two lines 900 times. The effect of this is to simply cause a delay of about 15 seconds. You could make the delay longer or shorter by changing the second number in line 180. Some BASICs have more efficient ways of creating a pause than the one used here.

WHERE TO GO FROM HERE

Now that you have been exposed to BASIC and have acquired some skills, you need to consult your computer's user's guide for BASIC. This will provide you with details on the peculiarities of the BASIC your computer uses. It will also provide you with many more statements and special functions that are a part of BASIC.

HOW TO USE WHAT YOU HAVE LEARNED

You have been exposed to some of the standard BASIC terminology and practices. You have also been exposed to what a computer language is like and how it is used to communicate with the computer. This background should allow you to:

1. Write some programs yourself. You will probably start simply; but with some time and the help of your user's manual, your programs will become more and more powerful.

2. Read other people's programs. This is important, since you may want to use them with some of your own modifications. You will not be able to immediately understand complex programs—remember, you are still quite new to the language. Again, as you use the knowledge you have now, your understanding will grow.

3. Get some practice. Like learning a foreign language or learning to play a musical instrument, there is no substitute for practice. You can't learn much by just reading about BASIC. You need to get access to a computer, turn it on, and start programming, or at least begin using some programs. If you haven't done so already, try the programs in this chapter. Once you put the programs in and run them, you will begin to get a feel for the language. Next you should try changing the programs. These programs could easily be converted into sub-

traction, multiplication, or division drills. The complexity of the drills could also be increased. The messages which the computer prints out on the screen could be modified and personalized. Try taking one of the programs presented here and modifying it to do bigger and better things. Once you have done this, start from scratch and write a program that will solve a problem for you. Keep it simple at first.

SAVING YOUR PROGRAM

We haven't talked about ways to save your program in this chapter. So far, when you turn the computer off, the program is gone and you have to retype it the next time you want to use it. This, of course, is extremely inefficient. Your computer is probably equipped with either a tape recorder or a disk drive unit. By using commands like CLOAD and CSAVE, you can record your program on a cassette when you are finished and then load it back into the computer when you want to use it again. Consult your user's manual for details on how to do this. You may also have a printer available. With a little searching in your manual and a little practice, you can have information printed out on paper rather than on the monitor screen. Usually this is done simply by changing any PRINT statements or commands to LPRNT.

Look at Other Programs. When you are learning a new language, it is helpful to hear other people speak the language. The same is true with BASIC. Study other programs, observing the way the programmer got the computer to perform a specific task.

Go to Other Sources. Many books have been written on BASIC. *Instant BASIC*, by Gerald Brown (dilithium Press, 1978) is a good example of such a book. You also may want to consult some specialized books. The possibility of drawing pictures with computer graphics has not even been considered here. You may want to consult a book on graphics, such as *Atari Graphics and Sound* by Jerry Willis and Merl Miller (dilithium Press, 1983).

A careful study of this chapter and some practice on the computer, along with the use of some reference materials, will get you started as a programmer in BASIC. You will be surprised at how quickly you and the computer will begin communicating. It will do some amazing things for you once you know how to talk to it. One advantage of being able to program the computer yourself is that you can tailor programs to fit your specific situations. Happy computing!

5

PILOT

Five children in Mr. Smith's fourth grade class have just gathered around a small computer in a corner of the room. It is 8:15 A.M. and class is just about to begin. Mr. Smith turns on the computer and the following conversation takes place:

Computer: Hi kids, how are you this morning?

First Student: We are fine, how are you?

Computer: Not so good! I didn't sleep well last night.

Second Student: What was the problem?

Computer: Well its like this, you see I ate too much candy before going to bed, and I had bad dreams all night.

Third Student: What did you dream about?

Computer: MATH, I dreamed about math. I was trying to solve a problem. Say, what is your name?

First Student: Jim.

Computer: Jim, maybe you and your friends could help me with this problem. A friend of mine wants to buy a used bicycle. The price of the bicycle is $27.00. The owner says that this is only ⅓ of what the bicycle cost new. I want to know how much the bicycle cost new. Can you tell me the answer, Jim?

First Student: Yes I can figure it out.

Computer: Good, when you have the answer please tell me.

Computer programs which create this type of conversational interaction between the student and the computer are possible using a programming language called PILOT.

In addition to general purpose higher-level languages such as BASIC, there are also some specialized languages. A specialized language is one which is designed to be very efficient for a particular type of application. Such a language may do a specific job more efficiently than other languages, but what it gains in efficiency for a specific use, it may lose for general use.

PILOT is one specialized langage which is becoming more and more popular with educators. It is, in fact, a specialized language developed for efficiency in computer assisted instruction (CAI). Those who use PILOT are discovering that it is a good language for many uses. Gregory Yob in an article in *Creative Computing* ("PILOT," May/June 1977, p. 57-63) discussed four ways in which computers are used in education, 1) to teach students about computers; 2) to pass the curricula to the student; 3) to solve problems within a course of study; 4) to allow the student self expression and personal growth. PILOT is proving to be an effective language in all four of these areas.

An important reason for PILOT's popularity is that it is a conversational language. It uses English-like words almost exclusively, as opposed to the algebraic-like statements used by many other languages. It is also very flexible and has very few rules of syntax. (Syntax is the equivalent of grammar in a spoken language.) PILOT is a little like being with down-home folks where you don't have to worry too much about your grammar.

That doesn't mean PILOT lacks refinements. Very ingenious programs can be written with this language. Some things can be done with it that would be extremely awkward, if not impossible, in other languages.

Some computer experts feel that PILOT is likely to become the preferred language for small computers in education. "Elegant, but not simple-minded" characterizes PILOT. It can do the things that it was designed to do very effectively and at the same time it is not cluttered by unnecessary elements.

ADVANTAGES

Three distinct advantages of PILOT over competitive languages like BASIC recommend it to educators, 1) it is very easy to learn and to use; 2) it is conversational in nature; 3) it lends itself to sound pedagogical principles.

The simplicity of PILOT is perhaps best illustrated by the fact that children learn it quickly and efficiently. Bob Albrecht has described how five-year-old children have been learning PILOT in the Golden Gate Montessori School in San Francisco for several years (*Interface Age*, Sept., 1978, p. 68-70).

The simplicity factor is very important. If computers are going to be effective teaching and learning tools they have to be accessible in more than just a physical sense to the majority of teachers and students. The computer may be in the classroom, but if it is viewed as something beyond comprehension it will contribute little. Even BASIC, as easy as it is to learn, is often dismissed at first glance by some educators because it looks like algebra. Some educators, and many students, never develop a feel for mathematics. They never really learn the language of mathematics and sometimes develop a type of mental block toward it. These same people tend to deal with concepts in general language much more effectively than in mathematical language.

PILOT looks like something that is familiar to the nonmath oriented person. Educators may experience success very quickly and are less likely to dismiss the computer as a tool that can only be mastered by those gifted in mathematics.

Good computer programming requires a great deal of organizational skill and creativity. These skills are not the sole province of math-oriented people. Word-oriented people may also be blessed with these skills. PILOT allows the word-oriented person to interact with the computer comfortably.

PILOT is not popular with teachers and students just because it is easy for them to master. The teaching and learning process is heavily laden with language. Good teaching involves flexibility of expression. When a question is asked, for example, there may be many acceptable answers. Languages like BASIC and FORTRAN are not as flexible as PILOT in the range of answers they can accept.

A well designed PILOT program may come close to giving the student a feeling that the computer is actually speaking on a personal basis. This, incidentally, helps to dispel the myth that the use of computers in education is part of a cold, impersonal educational philosophy.

Perhaps the most exciting advantage of PILOT is that it lends itself to student programming. When the children begin to build programs in their own words and on their own level the computer begins to fulfill its promise in education. The version of PILOT for the Atari computers is particularly suited to student programming.

The general constructs of computer programming are similar regardless of the computer language used. Many skills gained from learning to write short programs in a language that is easy to manage will transfer to more complex programming in that language and in other languages.

WHAT IT'S LIKE

It is easy to see that PILOT relates closely to education by looking at its name – Programmed Inquiry Learning or Teaching. PILOT was originally developed by John Starkweather at the University of California Medical Center. It can be described as a programming system for controlling interactive conversation. In a PILOT program just five simple program lines can produce the following dialogue with the student:

Computer: Hi, how are you today?

Student: I'm feeling fine (or any other similarly positive response).

Computer: Good, I'm glad to hear you are feeling well. (Or if a negative response was given by the student, such as not very well, lousy, or I'm sick), the computer could respond: I'm sorry you're not feeling well, is there anything I can do?

To program this same type of dialogue in most other languages would take many more statements and would require much more sophistication from the programmer.

PILOT was developed in 1969. After its original development, Stanford University used it in an experimental educational research project. During the course of this project revisions were made in the language. At the same time other institutions such as Western Washington University began to develop their own dialects of PILOT. An organization called MICROPI (2445 N. Nugent, Lummi Island, WA 98262) pulled together features from several dialects into what they called COMMON PILOT.

One of the major problems with PILOT is the lack of standardization. Just as with other computer languages, everyone wants to add their pet ideas. This is particularly a problem with PILOT. Programmers who are experienced in other languages, but new to PILOT, often propose extensions which they believe would make the language more sophisticated. These extensions, however, are often not necessary and may detract from one of the most eloquent aspects of the language, its simplicity.

There are many different versions of PILOT on the market today and more are being introduced all the time. Some of the early versions are quite weak. Some, though adequate for demonstrating the basic features of PILOT, have some problems which limit their usefulness. Radio Shack has made available their own version called "TRS-80 Micropilot" which has promise. Atari also has a very good version of PILOT for the ATARI 800 and 400 computers. Color graphics and sound are features of the Atari PILOT.

One of the most highly touted versions of PILOT is Southwest Technical Products Corporation's (SWTPC) PILOT 1.0 (219 West Rhapsody, San Antonio TX 78216). This version, a direct descendant of COMMON PILOT, claims to be a sophisticated microcomputer language which may soon outdate textbooks and correspondence schools. It sounds like a line from a snake oil salesman doesn't it?

PILOT, of course, will not be a panacea. There are some basic differences between the versions; some are much more flexible than others. Some versions have more sophisticated mathematical capability than others. The SWTPC PILOT v 1.0 has a full range of math functions, while other versions have none. In order for PILOT to have real power, mathematical functions must be available.

Some versions of PILOT have the capability to tap into the host language and use its mathematical capabilities. For example, suppose the PILOT version you are using has no built-in capability for instructing the computer to generate random numbers. If you were working in one of the versions that allowed you to use elements in the host language (by host language we mean the language used to write the PILOT language program) you could use the host language to generate random numbers. If the host language is BASIC, you could use BASIC's RND function and the computer would generate a random number within your specified limits each time RND was encountered.

A version of PILOT written in BASIC is available. This version is one which you can gain access to by typing in a BASIC program. The BASIC program creates a PILOT Interpreter (Hawkins, R. "PILOT – The language of computer-aided instruction," *Microcomputing*, July, 1981, p. 122-142). In this do-it-yourself version, all the standard BASIC instructions can be used. This seems to have some real potential for power and it is certainly a bargain. For the price of one issue of the magazine and about an hour of typing you can have PILOT up and running. The article also includes programs which teach you how to write programs and use PILOT.

The above discussion really highlights the greatest limitation of PILOT. Being a specialized language, it is very good for some things and not as good for others. It was not designed for data processing and it is inferior to many other languages whenever number manipulation is involved to any great extent.

GETTING STARTED

You won't be ready to program in PILOT simply by turning on your computer. PILOT must be loaded in either from cassette tape or disk (or a PILOT cartridge must be inserted). Each computer configuration is going to require a different method of getting the language into the computer, so we'll leave that to you and your instruction manual. When you have PILOT up and ready to go, however, we can get started. There are three basic things that the computer can do, 1) it can accept or take in information; 2) it can manipulate this information; 3) it can output information. PILOT uses eight simple commands and two *conditioners* to accomplish these three things.

We will begin by learning how to use three of the eight commands:

> **T** tells the computer to type something onto the screen. The computer will type whatever we want it to.

A tells the computer to accept information — usually an answer to a question.

M tells the computer to match the answer with a criterion set by the programmer.

The two conditioners used in PILOT are:

Y for yes. This can be combined with one of the other instructions. It tells the computer to execute the instruction only if the answer matched the criteria.

N for no. This tells the computer to execute an instruction only if there was not a match.

Each of the commands T, A, or M by themselves or combined with Y or N tells the computer to do something. Each command must be followed by a colon (:). Sometimes the command by itself (A:) accomplishes our purpose. At other times it will be followed by an expression (T:PILOT). The command and the expression combined with a command are called statements. A program is made up of a series of statements which the computer follows in a sequential order to accomplish the task the programmer has set for it.

Let's look at a short program which incorporates T, A, M, Y AND N. This program should look familiar.

PROGRAM 5.1

T: HI HOW ARE YOU TODAY?
A:
M: FINE, ALRIGHT, OK, GOOD, WONDERFUL, TERRIFIC.
TN: I'M SORRY YOU'RE NOT FEELING WELL. IS THERE ANYTHING I CAN DO?
TY: GOOD, I'M GLAD TO HEAR YOU ARE FEELING WELL.

Now let's see what happens. When the computer is told to execute the program, (this is done in different ways, but often by typing RUN and pressing the ENTER key on the keyboard) it will first encounter T: HOW ARE YOU TODAY? The command T tells the computer to Type whatever is on the right side of the :.

In this case the computer flashed HI HOW ARE YOU TODAY? The next program line which begins with "A:" tells the computer to expect an answer. It waits until one is supplied via the keyboard. A typical answer might be FINE. Now the computer moves on to the 3rd line which is a "Match" statement. It contains six words separated by commas which establish the criteria for the match. Any word or combination of words could be put in this line. We simply included some typical responses a person might give if he or she were feeling well. The situation could also have been reversed by matching for negative expressions like: Bad, terrible, not so good, etc.

In the next statement we have used the conditioner "N". The command TN tells the computer that on the condition that the answer given does not match anything in the Match Statement, it is to type the expression following the :. Let's assume that the user responds to the initial question HI HOW ARE YOU TODAY? with TERRIBLE, I'M FEELING LOUSY. This, of course, doesn't match anything in our match statement, so the No condition would be fulfilled and the computer would type I'M SORRY YOU'RE NOT FEELING WELL. IS THERE ANYTHING I CAN DO? If the No condition had not been met — let's say the user responded with I'M FEELING TERRIFIC (TERRIFIC makes the match) — then the computer would move on to the next program statement which instructs it to type GOOD, I'M GLAD TO HEAR YOU ARE FEELING WELL.

At this point the computer would be at the end of the program, and some versions would flash an error message on the screen saying something to the effect that the end of the program was not indicated. With some versions the command E for END must be the last line in the program.

In this simple program, you have seen the one attribute of PILOT which gives it much of its power as a conversational language, the matching statement. This statement is really the heart of the language. It is almost unrestricted by syntax, and there is no restriction on length since the expression can be carried over to additional program lines. The programmer's imagination is really the only major limiting factor involved. Using matching combined with the conditioners N and Y, the computer can seem almost human.

In addition to T, A, and M there are five other commands which need to be explained before we consider another program:

- **J** tells the computer to jump to a different place in the program. This allows the programmer to gain control of the sequencing of the program. Since PILOT does not use program line numbers a line must be labeled (usually with a word) if a program is to be sent to it. In that case, J will be followed by a label (e.g., J: START). An example of this will be provided later.

- **U** tells the computer to go to a subroutine, a short segment of the program which may be used over and over again. Rather than writing it in the program each time we want to use it, we simply send the computer to it each time we want it executed. U works much like J, but with one important difference. J does only one thing, U does several things. J sends the program sequence from point A to point B. The program is then sequenced in order starting at point B. U on the other hand, sends the program sequence from point A to point B and after the subroutine at point B has been executed U sends the program back to the next program line following point A. The program then continues from that point. For example, U:CALK will send the computer to a set of instructions where the first statement is preceded by the label CALK. The program lines making up the subroutine CALK will be executed. Then the program will go back to the program line just after U:CALK and continue from there.

- **E** We have already seen one use of this command. It tells the computer that the end of the program has been encountered. It has a second function, however, and that is to signal the end of a subroutine. When U is used the program starts with the labeled line indicated by the U command and continues until it encounters an E command. Then it returns to the line just following the U command.

- **R** This instruction, remarks, tells the computer to ignore whatever follows it on that line. It is exactly like the

REM statement in BASIC. It is used to place remarks in the program which will cue a person looking at the program as to what a particular segment of the program is designed to do.

C In some versions C is used strictly as a counter. A counter can be set to increase each time an event occurs. Counters are used in a variety of ways. In this case, the counter works like this: C tells the computer to increase a variable by one each time it encounters this program line. C:X, for example, would add 1 to the value of X. In other versions C can also represent compute. Its function in this case is to tell the computer to perform a mathematical operation such as C: 2+4.

All of the basic commands have now been explained. Depending on the version you are working with you may encounter additional commands or expressions such as:

Z can be used in conjunction with C to reset a counter back to zero. C:ZX, for example, would change the value of X to zero.

D Some versions allow the use of one or two dimensional arrays. D then is a dimension command which tells the computer to set aside array space. See the chapter on BASIC for an explanation of arrays.

There are also some other instructions, but they are peculiar to certain versions of PILOT and are not necessary for an understanding of how the language works.

One other convention does need to be explained. It has already been mentioned that a program line can be labeled for reference by J or U. The process of labeling and using labeled statements in a program requires three syntax rules: First, the label (any label or name you want to assign) must be preceded by an asterisk (*). (*CALL) for example, would label a program line CALL, and the program could be sent to that program line with the statement J:CALL. Second, the label which is assigned to a program line can also be used as a variable. In order to use the label as a variable, the label is followed by a space and then a command. (*CALL A:) tells the computer to assign whatever answer is provided by the student to the variable CALL. Third, the answer which has been assigned to CALL can now be referenced or called up by the program. In order to do this the label must be preceded by a slash(/). (T: /CALL would then print out whatever was assigned to CALL.

We will next consider a program which when executed becomes a simple addition drill. A similar program written in BASIC is presented in Chapter 4.

PROGRAM 5.2

```
T: WHAT IS YOUR NAME?
*NAME A:
*START C:X = RND(9)
C:Y = RND(9)
C:Z = X + Y
*START T: WHAT IS X + Y
A:
M: Z
TY: VERY GOOD /NAME THAT WAS CORRECT!
JY: QUEST
T: OOPS SORRY /NAME THAT IS NOT CORRECT, TRY
   IT AGAIN.
A:
M: Z
JN: ERROR
TY: THERE YOU GOT IT.
JY: QUEST
*ERROR T: /NAME X + Y = Z.
*QUEST T: DO YOU WANT ANOTHER PROBLEM?
A:
M: Y, YES, OK, I GUESS SO, ALRIGHT
JY: START
T: OK /NAME SEE YOU LATER!
E:
```

Because the method for generating random numbers differs widely among versions of PILOT you will need to determine how this is done in the version you are using. To be practical as an addition drill, random numbers must be generated. The numbers must be handled as integer variables and their sums computed. The third and fourth lines in the program assign random numbers to X and Y.

Now let's look at Program 5.2 in detail. First the program asks, WHAT IS YOUR NAME? The student then types in a name—BOB, for example. Notice that BOB is now stored or saved in memory under the variable name "NAME". Now two random numbers are generated. Different versions of PILOT will do this in different ways. TRS-80 MicroPILOT uses C:variable name=RND(value). If the value is 0, a random number ranging between 0 and 1 will be assigned to the variable. If the value is a number greater than 1, a random number ranging between 1 and the value will be assigned to the variable. In program 5.2, C:X=RND(9) and C:Y=RND(9) will result in a number ranging from 1 to 9 being assigned to both X and Y. Next the first problem is presented (we will assume that the first two numbers generated are 3 and 5) WHAT IS 3+5? We have labeled this line as START so that we can send the sequencing of the program back to it.

The computer is now waiting for an answer. When the answer is supplied by the student the computer matches it with 8. If the answer is 8 then the yes condition has been met. On the next line TY will, when the yes condition has been met, type VERY GOOD BOB THAT IS CORRECT! Based on the yes condition again, the next line, with JY, will jump to the line labeled QUEST. The QUEST line asks if the student wants another problem. His answer is then matched with various potential positive answers. If he has given a positive response such as I GUESS SO the yes condition has been met and the program will jump to the line labeled START.

Now another problem will be presented. This time let's assume that the first response is something other than the correct answer so that the no condition is met. Picking up the program at the T: OOPS ... line, the message OOPS SORRY BOB THAT IS NOT CORRECT, TRY IT AGAIN is typed. An answer is then given by the student and accepted by the computer. This answer is then matched and if correct the yes condition has been met. In that case the computer would then type THERE YOU GOT IT. The QUEST Line is then jumped to and another problem is presented if the student responds that he wants one.

If, however, the second answer was also incorrect (did not match) the no condition would have been met. If we pick up the program at the JN:ERROR line, the computer is told that if the no condition is met, it should jump to the line labeled ERROR. Now the computer types BOB, 5 + 3 IS 8 (or whatever set of numbers is being used at this point).

QUEST is now encountered and the student is asked if he wants another problem.

If the student responds positively to the request for another problem, the program goes again to START. If the student responds negatively, however, the message OK BOB SEE YOU LATER! is typed. The end statement is then encountered and the computer waits for further instructions.

Let's look at one more program. Program 5.3 is a spelling drill. Again, it is similar to the spelling drill program written in BASIC and discussed in Chapter 4. You may want to compare the two.

In Program 3 all eight of the most common PILOT commands are used at least once. This program not only gives you a good look at how the language is used, but if you are able to run it, will also give you a flavor of its conversational nature.

PROGRAM 5.3

Segment 1
R: PROGRAM SENT TO SUBROUTINE CLS WHICH
   CLEARS THE SCREEN
U:CLS

Segment 2
R: NAME IS OBTAINED AND A GREETING IS MADE
  T: WHAT IS YOUR NAME?
*NAME A:
  T: HI /NAME HOW ARE YOU TODAY?
  A:
  M: FINE, GOOD, OK, ALRIGHT, EXCELLENT, NOT
      BAD, WONDERFUL
  T:
  T:
  T:
  TY: GOOD I'M GLAD YOU'RE FEELING WELL
      TODAY /NAME
  TN: I'M SORRY YOU'RE NOT DOING SO WELL
      TODAY /NAME

Segment 3

R: STOPS SEQUENCING FOR TYPED MESSAGES TO BE READ
   T: WHEN YOU ARE READY JUST PRESS THE E N T E R KEY
   A:

Segment 4

R: DIRECTIONS ARE GIVEN AND THE COUNTER "J" IS ACTIVATED
C:ZL
U:CLS
   T: /NAME WE ARE GOING TO DO SOME SPELLING
   T:
   T:
   T: I'M GOING TO SHOW YOU SOME WORDS AND THEN I WANT YOU TO TYPE THE WORD THAT YOU THINK IS SPELLED CORRECTLY
*COUNT C:J
J(J>4):STOP
U:CLS

Segment 5

R: FOUR ALTERNATIVES ARE PRESENTED AND CHOICE CALLED FOR
   T: WHICH OF THESE WORDS IS SPELLED CORRECTLY /NAME?
   T:
   T:
T(J=1):WHIN   WENN   WEN   WIN
J(J=1):ANSR
T(J=2):GIRLS   GRILS   GURLS   GIRLS
J(J=2):ANSR
T(J=3):DULLER   DOLLAR   DOLLER   DOLAR
J(J=3):ANSR
T(J=4):SCIENCE   SIENCE   SEINCE   SCEINCE
J(J=4):ANSR

Segment 6

R: RESPONSE MATCHED, DECISION TO CONTINUE MADE, BRANCHES TO EITHER STOP OR COUNT

*ANSR A:
M: WIN, TIME, GIRLS, DOLLAR, SCIENCE
T:
T:
TY: GOOD /NAME YOU GOT IT ON THE FIRST TRY!
JN: CONT

Segment 7

T: READY FOR ANOTHER ONE?
   A:
   M: Y, OK, ALL RIGHT
   JN: STOP
   *CONT C:ZL
   UY:CLS
   JY:COUNT

Segment 8

R: SECOND TRY, CONTINUE REQUESTED,
   BRANCHING OCCURS
   T: SORRY /NAME THAT WAS THE WRONG WORD.
      LOOK CAREFULLY AND TRY AGAIN.
   A:
   M: WIN, TIME, GIRLS, DOLLAR, SCIENCE
   JN: ERROR
   TY: OK, THAT TIME YOU GOT IT. WANT ANOTHER
      ONE?
   A:
   M: Y, OK, ALL RIGHT
   JY: COUNT
   JN: STOP

Segment 9

R: THIRD TRY, BRANCHING
   *ERROR T: OH, I'M SORRY THAT ISN'T RIGHT
      EITHER /NAME
   T: HAVING TROUBLE WITH THIS ONE AREN'T
      YOU? TRY AGAIN!
   A:
   M: WIN, TIME, GIRLS, DOLLAR, SCIENCE
   JN: ERROR2
   TY: CONGRATULATIONS YOU GOT IT RIGHT!
   T: PRESS E N T E R AND LET'S TRY ANOTHER
      WORD.

A:
J: COUNT

Segment 10

R: FOURTH TRY, BRANCHING
   *ERROR2 T: WELL THERE IS ONLY ONE CHOICE LEFT. TRY IT!
   A:
   M: WIN, GIRLS, DOLLAR, SCIENCE
   JN: ERROR3
   U: CLS
   TY: OK /NAME YOU GOT IT THROUGH THE PROCESS OF ELIMINATION
   T: PLEASE PRESS E N T E R WE WILL CONTINUE
   A:
   J: COUNT
   *ERROR3 T: OH WELL BETTER LUCK NEXT TIME
   T: PRESS E N T E R
   A:
   J: COUNT

Segment 11

R: SUBROUTINE TO CLEAR SCREEN
   *CLS
   *COUNT C:L
   T:
   J(L< 15):CLS
   E:

Segment 12

R: SIGN OFF AND END
   *STOP T:
   T:
   T:
   T: OK, THAT'S ALL FOR NOW SEE YOU AGAIN SOON.
   E:

This program has been divided into segments by using remarks statements (R). Rather than discuss each program line separately, each segment will be discussed as a unit.

Segment 1. U:CLS sends the program to a subroutine labeled CLS in segment 11. Subroutine CLS clears the screen. In the version of PILOT used here there is no single command for clearing the screen, so for aesthetic purposes the subroutine CLS is incorporated into the program. How this works will be explained in the discussion of segment 11.

Segment 2. This segment looks almost exactly like part of program 5.2 and needs no further discussion except to point out that the type statement is used as a dummy spacer for aesthetic purposes. Now we get:

WHAT IS YOUR NAME?

HI BOB HOW ARE YOU TODAY?

Rather than:

WHAT IS YOUR NAME?
HI BOB HOW ARE YOU TODAY?

Segment 3. As was the case in BASIC it is sometimes necessary to have the computer pause in its sequencing of the program so that the type statements will remain on the screen long enough to be read. This is accomplished in PILOT by putting in a dummy A statement. That is a statement which tells the computer to stop and wait for an answer. It is called a "dummy" statement because no answer is really wanted – since no question was asked – and it is used only to stop the sequencing. This trick fools the computer into stopping for awhile. Once the sequencing is stopped, the student has to know (if he doesn't already) how to get the thing going again. So he is told to press the ENTER key. When the ENTER key is pressed the computer thinks it has been given an answer; our charade is complete – the sequencing continues.

Segment 4. In this segment the counter command is used for the first time. C:ZL set the counter L back to zero. L is used as a counter in subroutine CLS (Segment 11). Each time the program is sent to CLS, L needs to be set at zero, or CLS will not accomplish its purpose. So just prior to U:CLS, L needs to be set to zero as it is here.

*COUNT C:J activates the counter J and each time the program returns to *COUNT C:J, J is increased by one.

J(J>4):STOP is brand new to you. It says jump to the line labeled STOP if the value of J is greater than 4. Since only 4 spelling words are included in this program (you may include as many as you like) once each of the words has been presented and responded to, the program ends. J keeps track of how many words have been presented.

Segment 5. Here the four spellings of the word WIN will be presented to the student first, GIRLS second, and so on through SCIENCE. This is accomplished by making use of our counter J again. The computer is told that when J is equal to 1 it should type GIRLS and so on with SCIENCE being typed only when J=4.

Segment 6. In this segment the computer simply accepts the student's answer, matches it, and responds according to whether the answer was right or wrong. If the correct answer was chosen the student is asked if another word is desired. If one is, the program goes to COUNT and a new word is presented. If the student does not want another word the program goes to STOP and ends.

Segments 7, 8, and 9. These segments do the same thing. The student is asked to make another try and match the response. If correct we give the student a chance to try another word. If the response was wrong the program goes to the next segment for another try.

Segment 10. The only difference between this segment and segments seven and eight is that when the student chooses the wrong word this time he is all out of alternatives. The computer now says "OH WELL BETTER LUCK NEXT TIME" and goes back for another word.

Segment 11. This, of course, is the screen clearing subroutine. What occurs here is a looping action. As the program passes to C:L (L always equals 0 when the program gets here because of our C:ZL statements) L is increased by one. There is now a dummy T – the computer prints a blank. Then as long as the value of L is less than 15 the program jumps back to *CLS and the process is repeated. When this has happened fifteen times the entire screen has been cleared and the program returns to the line following the U:CLS statement that sent the computer here in the first place.

Segment 12. This segment needs no explanation. It is just a way of telling both the student and the computer that the program is finished.

At this point you may not be a proficient PILOT programmer, but you should have a fair idea of what PILOT is like. The next step is to sit down at the computer and do some programming. If you have access to PILOT you need to do three things to get started: First, consult your user's manual and figure out how to get PILOT into your machine. Second, check to see if there are any obvious differences between your version and the one we used here. Most of the differences will be subtle and shouldn't get in your way in getting started. Many versions of PILOT, however, have keywords for creating sophisticated color graphics, music, and sound. These keywords are generally specific to a particular computer. Third, you will need to learn how to use the editing mode if your version has one. This allows you to correct errors and make changes in your program.

More information about PILOT is needed and should be forthcoming. The PILOT Information Exchange has a newsletter with information on implementations, users, seed programs, manuals, technical specifications, applications articles, and a library of unpublished PILOT materials. PILOT materials are available for the cost of copying. (The PILOT Information Exchange, c/o LoopCenter, 8099 La Plaza, Cotati, California 45628.)

There are several versions of PILOT available for the Apple II, PET, ATARI, Commodore 64 and TRS-80 computers. If you have a TRS-80 computer you could quickly get your own PILOT by using Randy Hawkins' do-it-yourself version referenced earlier in this chapter.

We believe that PILOT will become a widely used language among educators.

6
Logo

This chapter will depart somewhat from the pattern of the other two chapters on BASIC and PILOT. Logo, along with its developer, Seymour Papert, represents a departure from the typical. BASIC is a very good general-purpose programming language and PILOT is a language designed to help educators do their job more effectively. Both are, more or less, traditional languages which represent efforts to help people do existing jobs better. Logo is different. It is an effort to develop a language that does new jobs.

Logo was developed by Seymour Papert, a professor at the Massachusetts Institute of Technology. It is very much a product of Papert and his background. Papert's father was an entomologist who, with his family, lived and worked in the South African bush for several years. Later, when Papert was eight, the family moved to Johannesburg where he attended secondary school. After a brief stay at Cambridge University, he settled down to serious work at the University of Paris. Afterward Papert studied and worked for five years with the Swiss psychologist Jean Piaget in Geneva. The influence of the theories of Piaget are obvious in Papert's writing. It is the foundation upon which Papert builds a theory of educational computing and a language—Logo. We will discuss Piagetian developmental theory in more detail in the next section.

While Papert is a Piagetian psychologist, he is also a mathematician—one who is intrigued with mathematical relationships and their relevance to both the real world and to thinking. Finally, Papert firmly believes in the potential of the computer for education. His vision of the future is not of hundreds of computers teaching children everything from math facts to graduate level physics. For Papert, the traditional approach of computer-assisted instruction is just a way of having the computer program the child. According to Papert, the future of educational computing lies in allowing the child to teach or program the computer. Dr. Sylvia Weir, a physician who uses Logo in her work with exceptional children, put it this way:

> We reverse the usual relationship between computer and student that is found in a conventional computer-assisted instruction situation. There, the clever program teaches a "dumb" student. In contrast, in the Logo system, the student is required—gets a chance to—teach this dumb computer how to carry out the task in question.
>
> The first step is to set up a miniature communications system linking up various devices to a computer so that the student can instruct (program) the computer to perform actions. Next we need a world interesting enough to inspire young students to want to teach the computer.... The development of the Logo language has included the invention of such domains. The best known of these is Turtle Geometry. (Sylvia Weir, "Logo and the Exceptional Child," *Microcomputing*, September, 1981, p. 76-84).

The purpose of having the student teach the computer is cognitive development. Piagetian psychologists believe children learn best by doing, and they learn best when they decide what, when, and how they will learn. Since the Piagetian perspective is one of the foundations upon which Logo is built, we will consider the theory in more detail in the next section.

PIAGET AND CHILD DEVELOPMENT

Jean Piaget is probably the most influential developmental psychologist in this century. By the time he died in 1980, he had published hundreds of papers and books and had changed the direction of developmental psychology in both

Europe and North America. In the early part of this century, Piaget was not well accepted, not even well known, in the United States. For most of his professional career he held the post of Director at the Jean Jacques Rousseau Institute in Geneva, Switzerland. Several of his early books were not even translated into English until long after their original publication.

While American psychologists were trying to find "truth" in aseptic laboratories by conducting research under tightly controlled experimental conditions, Piaget was studying children in their natural environment. He wrote several books describing work he had done with his own children as subjects. Instead of concentrating on how many correct answers children gave, Piaget would focus on what the children were thinking—how they arrived at their answers even if they were wrong. During a period when rewards were considered by many to be important, perhaps essential for learning, Piaget said that learning was its own reward—children naturally seek knowledge about the world in which they live. Perhaps more than any other theorist, Piaget concentrated on the cognitive aspects of development—how children think, the quality and structure of their reasoning, and the changes which occur as children grow.

While acceptance was slow in coming for Piaget, especially in the United States, his theories gradually gained a wide following in several fields. During the past twenty years hundreds of books and thousands of articles have been written about Piaget's theory. In the space available here we can only present a few aspects of the theory. The discussion will concentrate on those features which are most relevant to the development of Logo and Papert's view of educational computing.

Nature versus Nurture

Does the environment in which a child develops determine the type of person he or she becomes? Or is the essential nature of the person a product of nature? This is a point which has been debated for centuries. The massive social programs of the Kennedy and Johnson era were based on the assumption that nurture (or environment) plays a major role in development. Head Start is probably the best known federal program in this tradition.

Another way to look at this issue is to ask whether development is a process of *unfolding* or a process of *molding*. Theorists who take the unfolding view say the way a child develops and grows is set by nature. Parents watch the child develop or unfold in much the same way they watch a flower develop and bloom. On the other hand, theorists who consider development a molding process feel parents and teachers must take a more active role in the child's life. The molding theory treats the child as a lump of clay which can be shaped into many different things. What the clay or the child becomes depends on the treatment or experiences it has.

Piagetian theory supports the unfolding view. Piaget felt that nature sets a timetable or sequence for cognitive development which should not, even could not, be influenced by eager parents and teachers who want to speed up the cognitive growth of children. Attempts to teach young children concepts for which they were not ready would only produce pseudolearning in which children might memorize the correct answers but would not readily understand what they were saying. Papert diverges considerably from Piaget on this point. Papert believes providing a rich computer environment for children can enhance and speed up their cognitive development.

Role of Environment

If environment determines what a child becomes, we must be sure to provide the child with the right experiences. Many molding theorists argue that parents and teachers should plan the experiences of children in such a way that they learn and develop quickly. A book by Siegfried Englemann, entitled *Give Your Child a Superior Mind*, is a good example of this approach. Englemann outlines an entire curriculum for young children which, he feels, will enable them to learn such academic subjects as reading and math at a much younger age than they would under normal circumstances. The head start this approach provides is supposed to enable children to get ahead and stay ahead of children who do not receive such training.

For Piaget and his followers such an approach is not possible. Since nature, not nurture, sets the pace and timing of development, providing an enriched environment will not speed up development. It may even cause problems. However, Piaget did not believe children will develop normally in a totally barren environment. When the child is ready to take another step in cognitive development, that step is made through interaction with the environment. Infants do not realize that those tiny hands and feet are part of them while the blanket, crib, and toys are not. Babies gradually acquire an awareness of themselves as separate beings through experience and interaction with the environment. If the environment is barren or inadequate, the child's thinking skills may not develop and grow even though he or she is ready.

Thus, even Piaget believed that the environment was important. A flower planted in poor soil and watered infrequently may never bloom even though it has the natural ability to do so. Likewise, a child's natural curiosity and willingness to learn may never express itself if the environment is unsuitable. On the other hand, even with rich soil and abundant moisture you cannot force a flower to bloom just a few days after it sprouts. There is a natural sequence of development for the flower and there is a natural sequence of development for a child. A good environment allows that sequence to occur but does not change it. So says Piaget.

Is Cognitive Development Quantitative or Qualitative?

Does a child think like an adult? For Piaget the answer is a definite no. Children are different from adults, not because they have fewer thoughts, but because the way they think is different. According to Piagetian theory, children use experiences to build mental models of the world around them. At first the models they build are crude and often inaccurate. They are also limited by the concrete quality of their thinking. As children develop, two things happen. First, additional experiences enable children to adapt, modify, and refine their mental models (*schemas* in Piagetian terms) of the world. Second, as children go about the process of interacting with their world, their abilities to reason change. In the area of language, for example, young children are limited because they can classify objects and events along only one continuum at a time. They can put all the red balls in one box and all the blue ones in another, but they cannot put the big red balls in one box and the small blue ones in another. They cannot categorize objects by size and color at the same time. In addition, young children's language or communication is *egocentric*. That means they can only see things from their own perspective. They do not realize that other people may use words in different ways than they do, or that a situation seen from someone else's perspective may look different. It is difficult for young children to understand how it is correct for them to call one person daddy while it is appropriate for one of their friends to use that label for a different person. As the child develops, thinking and reasoning become more sophisticated and allow for more sophisticated language usage.

Pathways to Learning

Piaget argued that young children do not have the same sort of thinking skills as adults. Young children are unable to deal with abstract concepts. They deal with the concrete—what can be seen, felt, touched, manipulated. Children learn by doing. Young children learn more from actually experiencing something than they do from having the experience explained to them with words. It is not until they approach adolescence that children begin to be able to deal effectively with abstract concepts and symbols. That means children will learn best when they have an opportunity to manipulate and deal with things directly. Teaching subtraction by placing three pieces of fruit on the table, asking the child to eat one, and then asking how many are left is preferable to trying to explain the concept of subtraction to a child. Learning by doing is an important aspect of Piaget's approach to education.

PIAGET APPLIED TO EDUCATION

There are several educational approaches which claim the philosophical and theoretical heritage of Piaget. Though they differ in some ways, virtually all emphasize these points:

1. Learning environments should allow children to learn on their own and to discover things for themselves.

2. Since preadolescent children think in concrete terms, their educational experiences should involve direct contact and manipulation of materials. Lecturing about a concept, even demonstrating a concept, is not as good as letting the children try things out for themselves.

3. Children should be provided with opportunities to interact with other children at the same stage of cognitive development. Since their thinking will differ considerably from that of adults it is sometimes more effective to have children "teach" each other.

4. Teacher/pupil interaction should take place on an individual basis. Children in a typical class will not be at the same stage of cognitive development and may need different experiences. If a teacher is to be aware of where a particular child is, he or she must have individual contact with that child. This contact should involve more than just determining whether the child can give the correct answer. Children must be encouraged to explain how they arrived at their conclusions. The process is more important than the actual answer given.

5. Children must be given opportunities to develop their own mental models of the world. Trying to force your own models on them will not work. They must create their own models or schemas through their own experiences. Provide experiences which encourage children to grow and develop cognitively.

Most applications of Logo follow these basic points. Logo allows children to pursue their own course, to discover things on their own with only a small amount of teacher guidance. Logo also allows the child to experience directly the consequences of his or her actions. The computer is given instructions, the child observes the consequences of those instructions, and may then modify them to better accomplish a goal. This process of trying something out, modifying it, and trying it again nicely fits the model of cognitive development espoused by Piaget.

In addition, most schools that use Logo encourage children to work together, to share information and skills. Teachers also generally participate and work with the children, though not as directors or shapers of behavior.

THE LOGO LANGUAGE

The original versions of Logo were written for large computers. The versions for bigger computers contain a set of instructions children can use to guide the movement of a small mechanical "turtle." The turtle is a motorized device with a pen which can be told to move in different directions, and to put its pen on the paper it is moving over to draw different figures.

Figure 6.1 The Logo turtle. *Photo courtesy Terrapin, Inc.*

Today most applications of Logo use a microcomputer version of the language. A company appropriately named Terrapin, Inc. in Cambridge, Massachusetts markets a version of Logo for small computers such as the Apple II. The Terrapin version of Logo uses a mechanical turtle just like the versions for larger computers. The most popular variations of Logo for small computers use a video turtle. Instead of a mechanical turtle which moves around on the floor, there is a video turtle

Logo • 145

Figure 6.2 The mechanical turtle can be used with a version of Logo for the Apple II computer. *Photo courtesy Terrapin, Inc.*

which allows students to draw figures on a color monitor. The first microcomputer to have a commercial version of Logo with a video turtle was the Texas Instruments 99/4. TI has been a generous corporate supporter of the computer projects at MIT. The TI version of Logo comes in a separate cartridge which is plugged into the computer. At least two Apple versions of Logo are also available. There is also an excellent Logo for the Commodore 64 and a version for computers that use a disk operating system called CP/M. A Logo cartridge is available for the TRS-80 Color Computer. In addition, the Atari version of PILOT incorporates several aspects of the Logo language (e.g., turtle graphics commands). If Logo becomes popular there should be versions available for most of the small computers used in schools.

In this chapter, we will use the TI version of Logo as the basis for our discussion since it was the only one available when the chapter was written. The Apple version is similar to the TI version but at least one Apple Logo version lacks the "sprites" that are an important aspect of TI Logo. Sprites will be discussed later in this chapter.

Before beginning our discussion of TI Logo, we should note that our focus is on the use of Logo with young children. Proponents of Logo can correctly point out the fact that Logo is used in many other settings as well, including university level math courses.

Turtle Graphics

The best known and most powerful aspect of Logo is turtle graphics. Instead of a mechanical robot which would draw designs on paper, TI Logo has a small triangle which appears on the video display. Logo contains a whole set of instructions which control what the turtle does. Here is a summary of the most important turtle instructions:

TELL TURTLE – Causes the computer to enter the turtle graphics mode and put the turtle (small triangle) in the center of the screen. The center location is called HOME.

FORWARD – The point of the triangle indicates the current direction of the turtle. FORWARD 20 will cause the turtle to draw a line which is 20 "steps" long. If the point of the triangle is aimed toward the top of the screen and the turtle is in the middle of the screen the line drawn will start in the middle of the screen and extend straight up for 20 steps. (A "step" is a unit of measurement which is a fraction of an inch long.) In TI Logo some space is reserved at the bottom of the screen for the program you are writing. The bottom quarter of the screen will display the instructions you type in while the top three quarters are used for turtle graphics displays.

BACK – Works the same as FORWARD except movement is in the opposite direction of the triangle's point.

RIGHT and LEFT – These two instructions direct the triangle (the turtle) to rotate a certain number of degrees. If the triangle is pointing straight up (i.e., north), then the instruction RIGHT 90 would cause it to turn and point to the right (i.e., EAST) while LEFT 90 would cause it to point to the left (i.e., WEST).

With just these five commands you can create a variety of simple shapes. To draw a small square the following instructions are required:

TELL TURTLE
FORWARD 10

RIGHT 90
FORWARD 10
RIGHT 90
FORWARD 10
RIGHT 90
FORWARD 10

If you forget to give the computer all the instruction (e.g., FORWARD instead of FORWARD 10) the computer will say TELL ME MORE. If you make an error in one of your instructions, e.g., FOORWARD 10 instead of FORWARD 10) the computer will say TELL ME HOW TO FOORWARD. You can then correct your error. TI Logo has very good editing features which allow you to change, edit, and correct the programs you write.

CLEARSCREEN – Once you draw a few figures, the screen may get very cluttered. CLEARSCREEN will erase all your work (and the program you've written at the bottom of the screen) and put the turtle in the center of the screen pointing straight up. If a printer, cassette, or disk drive is attached to the computer you can save or print a copy of your programs before erasing them.

HOME – If you want to put the turtle in the middle of the screen but don't want to erase everything use the HOME instruction.

HIDETURTLE – This instuction makes the turtle invisible. It will still respond to your instructions, but it will not be visible on the screen.

SHOWTURTLE – As you might expect this makes the turtle visible again.

PENUP – The form of this instruction was set when the turtle was actually a mechanical device with a pen attached. PENUP causes the mechanical turtle to lift its pen from the paper. An instruction such as FORWARD 20 would then cause the turtle to move, but it would not draw a line. In the micro versions the instruction works the same way. After PENUP the turtle moves when instructed to do so but does not draw a line as it moves.

PENDOWN – After a PENUP instruction this one tells it to start drawing lines again.

PENERASE – If you create a line with FORWARD 20 you can erase it by typing:

PENERASE
BACKWARD 20

The turtle will move back over the line just drawn and erase it.

Figure 6.3 A number of schools provide Logo experiences to most of their students. *Photo courtesy Terrapin, Inc.*

PENREVERSE – This instruction is a bit difficult to understand. After PENREVERSE, any movement of the turtle will cause two things to happen. If the turtle moves over or along a line that has already been drawn, it will erase that line. If the turtle moves across parts of the screen where no line is drawn, it will create a line there.

NOTURTLE – When you are through with turtle graphics this instruction will remove the turtle from the screen and all your creations will disappear.

Sprites and Shapes

Another fascinating aspect of TI Logo is the ability to create and use several different graphic symbols or shapes. TI Logo has five shapes which are built in. These shapes are a plane, truck, rocket, ball, and box. TI Logo also has an imaginary entity called a "sprite" which can take on or "carry" any of these five shapes. Here is an example which might help:

TELL SPRITE 1
CARRY :TRUCK
SETCOLOR :ORANGE
HOME

The four instructions above tell the computer to assign the truck shape to Sprite 1, to color the truck orange, and to put it in the middle of the screen. In Logo when you are assigning a name or label to something, you put a space after the instruction (e.g., CARRY); then you type a ":" and the name (e.g., CARRY :TRUCK).

Sprites can be assigned any of thirty-two different shapes (you must create most of them yourself) and any of sixteen different colors. The colors available are quite varied and range from white, gray, rust, and cyan to yellow, lemon, olive, purple, black, and lime. Below are additional instructions which can be used with sprites:

COLORBACKGROUND – This instruction lets you change the background color of the screen to any of sixteen different colors.

SETSPEED – We can make our truck move at varying speeds. SETSPEED 127 calls for the maximum speed while SETSPEED 1 is the slowest speed available (very slow). You can also use negative numbers (SETSPEED −127) in which case the sprite will move in the opposite direction. In this version of Logo, a sprite that reaches the edge of the screen will wrap around the screen. That is, if it moves off the left side of the screen it will reappear on the right side and continue across the screen again.

SETHEADING – It would be boring if the sprites could only move in one direction. If you want a sprite to travel straight up you can use the instruction SETHEADING 0 or SETHEADING :NORTH. To travel to the right SETHEADING 90 or SETHEADING :EAST is used. This instruction will accept either degrees from 0 to 359 or compass directions (North, South, East, West).

HOME – Tells the sprite to move to the home position (center of the screen). If it was moving it will go to the home position and then continue moving in the direction and at the speed specified by earlier instructions.

FREEZE and THAW – FREEZE will cause the sprite to stop moving until you give it the THAW command.

Here is an example of a program that will cause one sprite to assume the shape of a yellow ball and move diagonally across the screen at a fairly rapid rate:

TELL SPRITE 1
CARRY :BALL
COLOR :YELLOW
SETHEADING 45
SETSPEED 115

Now suppose you want to put a blue ball on the screen which will travel diagonally from right to left at the same speed as the yellow ball. Here is how it would be done:

TELL SPRITE 2
CARRY :BALL
COLOR :BLUE
SETHEADING 315
SETSPEED 115

With more than one sprite on the screen you may want to give instructions to a single sprite or to all the sprites at once. To give an instruction to all sprites use the following instruction:

TELL :ALL

Any instructions given after TELL: ALL will be applied to all sprites. When you want to instruct only one sprite, issue the following instruction:

TELL SPRITE #

where # indicates the number of the sprite you want to direct. If you forget which sprite you are working with, the instruction WHO will cause the computer to reply with:

TELL ME WHAT TO DO WITH SPRITE #

where # indicates the sprite which will follow your instructions.

You can also write the TELL command like this:

TELL [1 3 6]

The numbers inside the brackets tell the computer that instructions which follow are to be applied to sprites 1, 3, and 6.

Finally, you can give a set of sprites a name and then use that name rather than their numbers thereafter. Suppose that you want to write a program that will use sprites 2, 7, and 11 as a group in several places. If you type in the instruction:

CALL [2 7 11] "ART"

you will be able to use the name ART in place of the numbers for each sprite in that group. Instead of saying TELL [2 7 11] you can say TELL :ART.

Creating New Shapes

In addition to the five standard shapes, a Logo user can create shapes that fit a particular need. The process of creating a shape begins with the instruction MAKESHAPE #. When you issue this command the screen changes color and a grid appears on the screen which is 16 squares wide by 16 squares high. This grid is actually an enlarged pattern for the shape you will create. If you type MAKESHAPE 4, the grid will contain the pattern of the ball since it is the shape number 4. MAKESHAPE 11 will cause a blank grid to be displayed since there is no standard shape with that number. In TI Logo you can change or create a shape by using special keys on the keyboard. Each of the squares in the grid represents one element in the shape. You can fill in any of the squares using the special keys on the keyboard. When you have the shape the way you want it, pressing the BACK key puts that shape into the computer's memory under the number you used in the MAKESHAPE instruction. If you used the number 11 you could put that shape on the screen in a light blue color with the following instructions:

TELL SPRITE 11
CARRY 15
SETCOLOR :SKY
HOME

Now sprite 11 will carry the shape. It would appear in the center of the screen in a light blue color (SKY).

Sprite number 11 was used in this example, but you could use any number from 0 to 31. If you use the numbers 1, 2, 3, 4 or 5 your shape will replace one of the standard shapes. As with the turtle graphics program you can save your shapes on cassette or diskette, or get a copy of them on your printer.

TI Logo also has an instruction, MAKECHAR, which permits the user to create new characters that are the size of the regular letters and numbers. Thus you could create Greek or Russian letters, scientific symbols, or a secret code. The steps in creating new characters are similar to those required to create new shapes. A special instruction, PUTTILE, enables a user to put a standard character or a specially created character at any location on the screen. The screen is divided into a large, invisible grid which has 32 positions across (0 to 31) and 23 positions down the side (0 to 22). That means there are 32 × 23 different locations or squares on the screen where a character can be placed. The instruction PUTTILE 36, 16, 12 would place a $ in the center of the screen. The first number, 36, is the code number assigned to $ while 16 specifies the column location and 12 indicates the row location.

Teaching the Computer

A powerful feature of Logo is its ability to let the user teach the computer new skills. There are two terms in Logo which relate to this feature—*primitive* and *procedure*. A primitive is something the computer speaking Logo already understands. For example, the computer knows instructions such as FORWARD and BACK; it knows five shapes for sprites, and it knows the letters and characters on the keyboard. A procedure is something you teach the computer. It doesn't know it in the beginning but it can learn. Suppose that you would like to teach the computer to draw a triangle. You might start by typing this:

TRIANGLE

The computer would then respond:

TELL ME HOW TO TRIANGLE

You would then type the following:

TO TRIANGLE
FORWARD 40
RIGHT 120
FORWARD 40
RIGHT 120
FORWARD 40
END

After typing this you press the BACK key. The computer now understands another instruction, TRIANGLE. To make the triangle appear on the screen give the following instructions:
TELL TURTLE
TRIANGLE

Now the computer will put a triangle on the screen. Whenever you want to draw a triangle on the screen you will not have to do it using primitives, the instructions that are built into the computer. You have taught it a procedure, TRIANGLE, which will create a triangle for you. Procedures can be very complex, involving the creation of several shapes with movement, color, and changing conditions all specified in the procedure you teach the computer. Several procedures can be combined on the screen to create different effects. Procedures can be written for sprites or for characters.

Although turtle graphics get most of the attention in many articles about Logo, the provisions for teaching the computer may well prove to be one of its most innovative and useful features because it permits children to explore the consequences of their own ideas and concepts. A student using Logo can think through an idea, try it out by teaching the computer to do something, and then modify and improve the idea after seeing the results of the instructions given the computer.

Other Logo Instructions

Logo also understands many other instructions which make it easier to use the computer or give it more power. Some of these instructions are explained below:
Math Operations – Logo understands the standard math operations of addition (+), subtraction (–), multiplication (*), and division (/). The instruction FORWARD 20/4 would cause the turtle to move forward 5 steps since 20 divided by 4 is 5.
These math operations enable the computer to function as a calculator although it is far more limited than the typical $5 pocket calculator. The limitations are primarily due to the fact that TI Logo uses only integers (i.e. whole numbers). That is, this Logo will add 5+6 but not 5.6+7.05. In addition, if an operation such as 12/7 produces an answer that includes a decimal, only the integer portion of the answer is printed. To

Figure 6.4 Children working with the TI version of Logo. *Photo courtesy Texas Instruments.*

TI Logo 12/7 equals 1. TI Logo is also limited to numbers between $-32,767$ and $+32,767$.

RANDOM – This instruction will create a number between 0 and 9. It is handy in writing procedures that produce changing effects on the screen.

WAIT – causes the computer to pause or halt operations for a specified time. WAIT 60 tells the computer to pause for 1 second. The number following WAIT indicates the time in sixtieths of a second.

SET X and SET Y – These two instructions allow you to put a sprite, turtle, or group of sprites or turtles at any particular location on the screen. In Logo each location on the screen is identified by two numbers, one for the horizontal (X) location and one for the vertical (Y). With these two instructions the exact center of the screen is 0 on both coordinates. The top right position on the screen is X127 and Y96. Top left is X – 127 and Y96. Bottom right is X127 and Y – 96. The following instructions would put sprite 8 at the bottom left of the screen:

TELL 8
SET Y -96
SET X -127

Another way to do the same thing is

TELL 8
SXY -127 (-96)

The SXY command is really a combination of SET Y and SET X.

DOT – This instruction tells the computer to put a dot at a particular location on the screen. DOT is followed by two numbers (e.g., DOT 50 80) which specify the location. The first number is the X coordinate and the second is the Y coordinate. DOT uses the same numbering system as SX and SY.

BEEP and NOBEEP – The instruction BEEP turns on a tone and NOBEEP turns it off. The instructions:

BEEP
WAIT 120
NOBEEP

would cause the computer to emit a tone for two seconds.

REPEAT – When you want to tell the computer to execute a primitive or a procedure several times, REPEAT will do it easily. REPEAT requires you to tell the computer how many times you want something done, and exactly what you want done. Here is an example:

REPEAT 20 [TRIANGLE]

The word TRIANGLE in the line above stands for the name of a procedure you have created. The REPEAT 20 instruction will cause that procedure to be executed twenty times. You can replace the word TRIANGLE with any other word that designates a procedure the computer can perform.

TEST, IFT, and IFF – These instructions allow the Logo user to give conditional instructions. That is, you can tell the computer to do something if and only if certain conditions are met. IFT stands for IF TRUE and IFF stands for IF FALSE. Suppose you are moving a turtle across the screen and you want it to go up if it is past a certain point on the screen and down if it is not. Here is how that might be done:

```
TEST YCOR⌐85
IFT TURN 90
IFF FORWARD 10
```

The TEST instruction checks to see if the turtle is more than half the distance between the center of the screen and the right margin (YCOR⌐85). If it is, the test is true and the instruction after IFT is executed. If the turtle is not that far to the right, the TEST is false and the instruction after IFF is executed instead. Logo also has another way of giving conditional instructions – IF... THEN... ELSE. This instruction is virtually identical to the IF THEN ELSE instruction in BASIC.

Before ending our discussion of Logo instructions we should point out that each instruction has a short form which can be used in place of the full terms. BACKGROUND, for example, can be shortened to BG. MAKESHAPE can be written as MS. The short forms make it easy to write Logo programs quickly.

Using Logo in Schools

Just what can be done with a language like Logo? Clearly it is not set up for drill and practice and exercises. It is also not particularly suited to teacher directed activities which require one teacher to stand at the front of the class and feed information to the students. Logo is particularly suited to a learning environment designed along Piagetian lines because:

1. Children learn on their own.
2. Children are able to manipulate the environment directly.
3. They can share and communicate their learning with other children.
4. The teacher can observe the reasoning children use and adjust the learning environment accordingly.
5. Children can create their own mental models of their world.

In an ideal classroom of fifteen to twenty children there may be five to ten computers which children use regularly. There is some group instruction, particularly in the early stages of use, so that children understand how to turn systems on, load and save programs, and how to use some of the primitives available in Logo. There may even be some procedures available which have been written by teachers. Such procedures would take into consideration the cognitive stages of the children. They might simplify the use of Logo for children who are not ready to deal with several concepts at once (e.g., speed, direction, and color of a sprite) or provide practice on concepts they are just beginning to acquire (e.g., use of degree designations to indicate direction of movement).

In our ideal classroom, children would work at the computer either individually or in small groups, often dyads, on a regular basis. As they discover ways of creating interesting things, their programs or procedures would be eagerly shared with other students who might take them and modify, enhance, or adapt them to their own uses. As all this happens the teacher is in the background, observing progress, guiding children when needed, and planning experiences for the future. If students seem to have mastered the use of sprites and turtle graphics using straight lines only, the teacher may then introduce students to the idea of creating curved shapes and movement patterns. Given a start by the teacher, students do their own experimenting with the idea until it becomes their own.

Much of the focus in a Logo session is on the child teaching the computer to do something. If a child is trying to create a square or a triangle on the screen, the steps required to create the shape put the child in direct contact with the elements of that shape. Through Logo primitives the child manipulates the external world, sees the result of his or her manipulation, and gradually develops a clearer, more sophisticated mental concept of what a triangle or square really is. A child's initial efforts to create shapes are likely to be faulty. In computer terms, there is a "bug" in the program. That, however, is not a terrible thing. The child sees there is a problem, troubleshoots (rethinks) the program, tries another way of doing it, and checks to see if the bug is fixed. Papert, Piaget, and many other psychologists argue that this is the natural road to understanding. Answers do not spring fully developed from our thoughts. They evolve slowly and through a process of creating, testing, and reformulating, and retesting. Especially in the areas of mathematical and spatial concepts, Logo seems likely to facilitate the cognitive development of children.

That brings us to some of the criticisms of Logo. Perhaps the most common criticism is that it purports to develop thinking and reasoning in children in a general way while, in reality, it concentrates on mathematical and spatial concepts, the cognitive areas which were of most interest to its developer, Seymour Papert. To some extent, we agree with this criticism. On the other hand, if that is to be a major point against this computer language it seems to us that critics are obligated to provide an alternative computing language that provides experiences in other areas of cognitive development. To our knowledge, Logo stands alone among computer languages. Today it is Logo or nothing. Perhaps the future will bring other languages which will compete with Logo, but there are none available today.

A final criticism relates to the developers and proponents of Logo rather than the language itself. Logo is often presented as a replacement for other languages and for traditional teaching approaches. The impression left is often that Logo is THE answer to the problems of education today, that Logo is a competitor to CAI, CMI, and traditional learning methods. It is unfortunate that many Logo enthusiasts view the world in that fashion, particularly at a time when many of the basic tenets of Piaget's theory are being challenged by researchers conducting careful tests of the theory. From our perspective, Logo is an excellent educational tool, one that hopefully will be used intelligently in many classrooms in coming years. However, it does not replace other forms of learning. Even the greatest mathematician must once have learned some basic math facts and the gifted concert pianist must have practiced scales. There is a place for drill and practice, for tutorials, for lectures, demonstrations, and much more in the schools of today and tomorrow. There is probably no one best method of teaching children; each approach is probably more suited to some learning goals than others. An educator who uses only one method of teaching is likely to accomplish some goals well and others poorly or not at all. Logo appears to be an excellent means of accomplishing some very important educational goals.

Section Three

TYPES OF EDUCATIONAL APPLICATIONS

7

Computer-Assisted Instruction

In Chapter 1 we briefly discussed the various types of computer-aided learning using Taylor's tutor, tool, and tutee models. In this section of the book the focus will be on the different ways a computer can serve as a tutor.

There are a number of categorical schemes which could provide a framework from which to discuss the tutorial or teaching role of computers. In this book we will use a relatively simple one which labels the tutorial function as Computer-Assisted Learning or CAL. Under the broad term CAL there are several more specific terms which refer to the major types of CAL:

Computer-Assisted Instruction (CAI) – the computer takes some of the responsibility for actually teaching the student.

Computer-Managed Instruction (CMI) – as part of a particular course or program of study, the computer may keep records, make lesson assignments, administer tests, and compute grade or progress reports, but it does not actually do any of the teaching.

Diagnostic/Prescriptive Applications – the computer is used to administer and score tests, to evaluate diagnostic tests and evaluations and may generate a report or prescription for future learning experiences. Diagnostic/Prescriptive applications are often considered one type of CMI. We have separated the two in this book because we feel they will follow different patterns of development in the future.

In this chapter we will deal with Computer-Assisted Instruction or CAI. The following chapter is concerned with

CMI, and chapter 9 covers the use of a computer in the diagnostic/prescriptive process.

COMPUTER-ASSISTED INSTRUCTION

CAI is actually a general category that includes three forms of instruction, each with unique features and formats. Drill and Practice is the simplest form of CAI and involves providing computer practice of skills already learned. For example, an elementary school teacher may teach students a new math skill such as long division and then use a computer to provide students with an opportunity to practice the new skill. There is a drill and practice program in basic math facts for virtually every computer in existence today.

A more sophisticated form of CAI is tutorial CAI. Tutorial CAI programs actually take some or all of the responsibility for teaching the student (note that Taylor in his tool, tutor, tutee model uses the term tutor in a broader sense than we do here). In its simplest form Tutorial CAI presents information in relatively small segments, gives the student an opportunity to deal with or manipulate the information, and then tests the student's mastery of the information being taught. If the student demonstrates mastery the computer moves on to the next segment. If the student has difficulty the computer may reteach the information, give the student remedial instruction, or suggest additional study.

Perhaps the most interesting and attractive form of CAI is the simulation. Simulations attempt to teach by allowing the student to play a role in the simulation of a situation or circumstance. Many business majors in college today spend some of their computer time in business or industrial simulation games. A simple business simulation might create an imaginary market in which two competing companies try to capture a large share of the market by adept managment and by deployment of their capital resources, their personnel, and their equipment. Other simulations deal with city government politics, operation of nuclear power plants, special education classrooms, and much more.

In the following sections of this chapter we will consider each type of CAI, discuss the advantages and disadvantages of each approach, and provide a few examples of CAI software currently available.

Drill and Practice

Drill and Practice (D&P) is perhaps the easiest form of CAI to develop and use. In D&P it is assumed that the student will arrive at the computer with some prior training. Thus it is not necessary to write a very complicated program that actually does the teaching. D&P just provides practice. Students may practice diagramming sentences, computing square roots, or solving algebraic equations, but they learn to do those things in some other way, often through traditional teacher-centered classroom instruction.

Drill and Practice programs get mixed reviews from both computer educators and others. Many see D&P as a throwback to the concept of mental exercises so prevalent a century ago in Western education. Millions of students learned by rote everything from morality poems to Latin grammar on the assumption that such mental activity would strengthen the brain in much the same way that physical exercise strengthens the muscles. That view is virtually dead today, but many educators tend to equate drill and practice exercises, whether they be on a computer or not, with the mental exercise theory. Many argue that drill and practice, rote memorization, and similar pedagogical practices are useless. Children must develop cognitive understanding, and discover things for themselves if true learning is to take place.

In our view neither extreme is correct. There is a place for drill and practice, but it is not the most important technique in education. It should neither be abandoned nor elevated to a primary position. Even great pianists spend hours practicing their scales, great novelists had to learn their ABC's, and theoretical physicists had to master the routine, sometimes boring fundamentals of basic integer math.

On the other hand, traditional drill and practice methods such as mimeographed sheets of exercises, flashcards, and memorization rituals are somewhat inefficient since it is difficult to individualize them and to tailor the amount of practice to the needs of the child. Computer-based drill and practice has the potential to identify through pretesting areas in which the student needs practice and to keep a running record of performance, which can be used to determine whether the student needs more practice on the current lesson or work at a different level.

Admittedly many drill and practice programs available today do not come close to the ideal. Many are no more than electronic versions of mimeographed practice sheets or flash cards. The Texas Instruments Little Professor, for example, is an electronic version of an old method rather than a new method of teaching math skills. That is not necessarily all bad, however. Parents and teacher who buy such hand held learning aids find their mode of operation familiar and not at all anxiety provoking. The fact that they are electronic makes them attractive and interesting. The same children who voluntarily play for hours with The Little Professor or Speak and Spell might groan loudly when presented with another set of dittoed practice sheets.

Drill and practice programs, whether they be in the form of hand held learning aids or programs which can be run on general purpose computers, are likely to be much more sophisticated in the future. Robert Vojack, a New Jersey educator, described four criteria for drill and practice programs in an article entitled "Drill and the Microcomputer" which appeared in *The Computing Teacher* (1980, 8, 1, 60-62). Drill and practice programs should be:

1. Easy to use.
2. Adaptable to a variety of user levels.
3. Interesting to the learner.
4. Educationally valid.

A majority of the currently available drill and practice programs probably do not meet at least one of these criteria. The ability to adapt to a variety of user levels is the feature most often lacking. If every child must go through the same number of practice exercises in the same sequence there are cheaper ways to provide such practice than CAI.

In terms of use in the classroom, drill and practice programs are probably best used in areas where mastery requires a significant amount of practice and different students require widely varying amounts of practice. Examples of such areas include letter and shape recognition for preschoolers, basic computational skills in the elementary school, algebra in high school, and note recognition in music. There are, of course, many more topics which are quite suitable for drill and practice programs.

Computer-Assisted Instruction • 163

Figure 7.1 Students can do drill and practice exercises while the teacher works with others. *Photo courtesy Milton Bradley.*

Figure 7.2 Screen display from a Milton Bradley program on mixed numbers. *Photo courtesy Milton Bradley.*

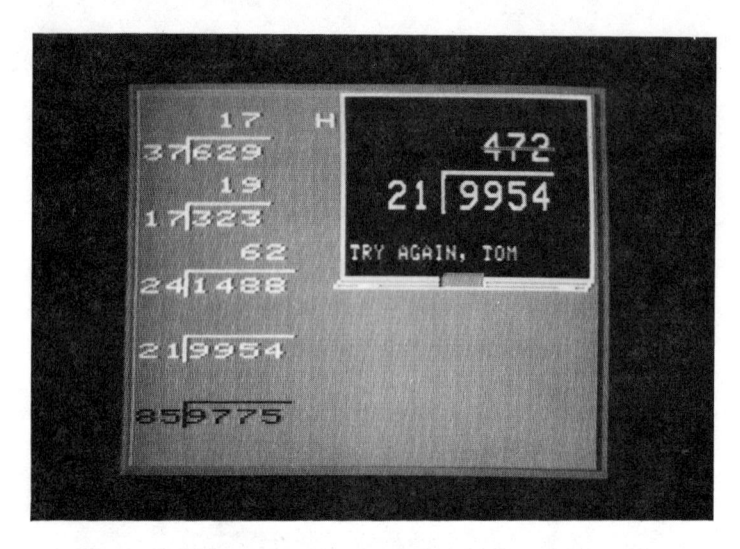

Figure 7.3 When errors occur, a gentle indication can be provided. *Photo courtesy Milton Bradley.*

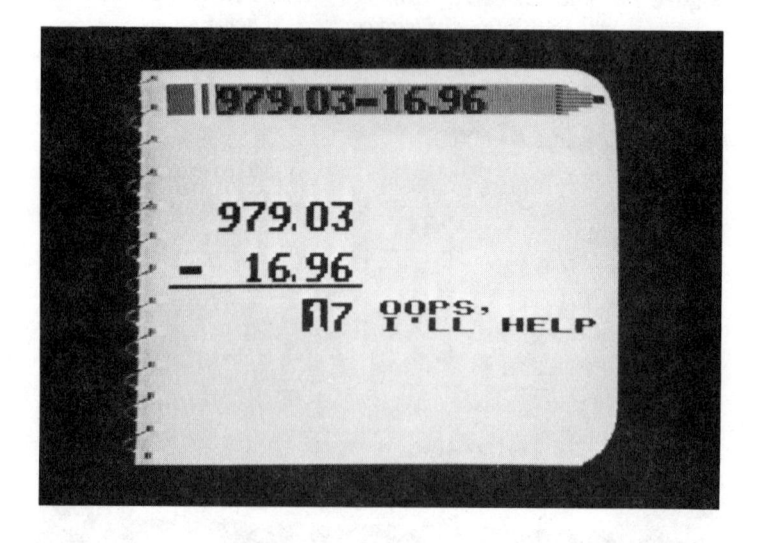

Figure 7.4 Good graphics and guidance when errors occur are desirable features in D&P programs. *Photo courtesy Milton Bradley.*

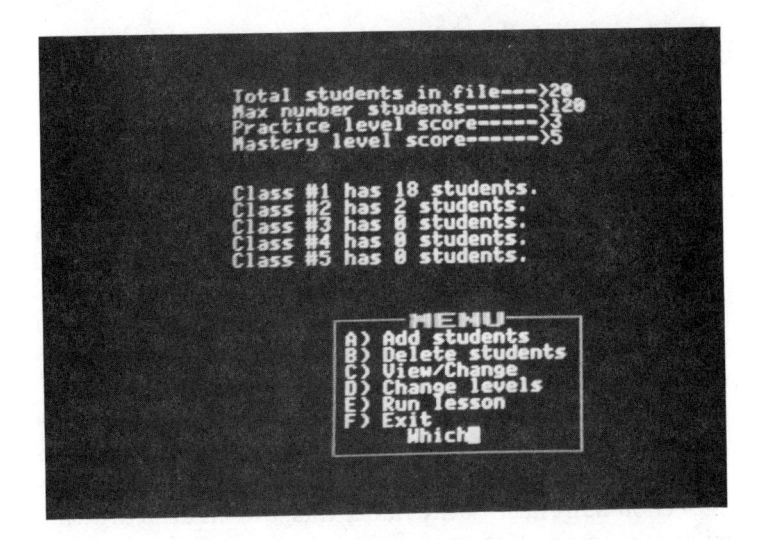

Figure 7.5 Many D&P programs allow the teacher to keep track of students in several classes. *Photo courtesy Milton Bradley.*

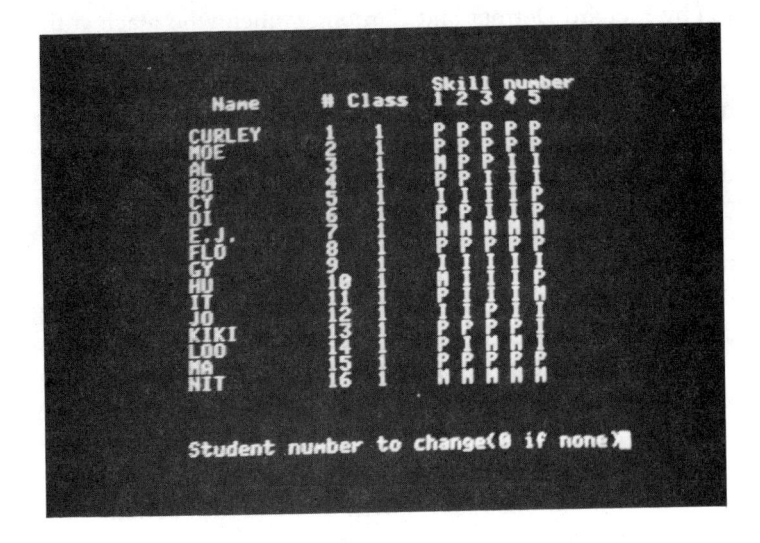

Figure 7.6 Some programs permit the teacher to keep track of each student's progress. *Photo courtesy Milton Bradley.*

An ideal drill and practice program for any of these areas should be capable of providing practice over a range of skills, should use the student's performance to determine how much and what type of practice to provide, and should provide some form of feedback to the teacher on the performance of individual students as well as class patterns. Our ideal program would also be enjoyable for students, provide feedback on the correctness of their answers, and when errors occurred provide information that helps the student identify errors and correct them. In addition, many applications are enhanced if the computer remembers areas in which the student is having particular difficulty and provides extra training in those areas.

Not many drill and practice programs today meet all the requirements outlined thus far, and those that do tend to be expensive. In fact, the examples we will describe in the following section don't necessarily fit our image of an ideal drill and practice program. The examples, however, will give you an idea of what is available.

Algebra Drill and Practice I. This program is available from Conduit (Box 388, Iowa City, Iowa 52244). It was written by Richard Detmer and Clinton Smullen who teach at the University of Tennessee at Chattanooga. The cost of the program is $110. An Apple II version, available on diskette, requires an Apple II computer with 48K of memory and at least one disk drive. The program can also be purchased in a standard BASIC version which can be used on many small computers.

Algebra Drill and Practice I is designed to give students taking a high school or college level course in algebra an opportunity for guided practice on problems similar to those being dealt with in class. There is no diagnostic component in this program, and the program provides only limited assistance when the student makes an error. The student can select any of several different programs for practice:

Alcomy – Provides practice with addition, subtraction, multiplication, division, and reduction of algebraic fractions.
Fracts – provides practice with numeric fractions.
Simple – provides practice with simplifying algebraic expressions including use of the distributive property.

Lines — provides practice finding slopes and equations of lines.
Signs — provides practice with signed numbers and with order of arithmetic operations.
Percent — provides practice with percents.

All the drill programs mentioned above use the same format. First, the computer presents a sample problem and works out the correct solution to it. Then the student is given a series of problems similar to the example and asked to solve them. In some cases the computer will provide hints if asked. If the student misses a problem twice he or she can ask to see the solution or can proceed to another problem. A student who misses several problems will be presented with another example problem with a solution before the computer gives any more problems.

In addition to the six types of drill and practice programs noted above there are three programs which require the student to solve word problems of a particular sort. Students can select any of three levels of difficulty for the word problems. At the lowest level the solution can be obtained using only arithmetic skills; no algebra is required. A second level requires the student to understand expressions and variables, while the third level calls for the use of linear equations as well. The fourth and most difficult level is similar to the third level but gives no hints or help as the student tries to solve the problem.

Touch Typing. This program is available from Atari dealers. It runs on an ATARI 800 computer and is supplied on a cassette. The program has several levels of practice and a number of sophisticated features. The beginning typing level gives the student practice on individual letters which are presented in groups of five. A novice begins with drills on the A, S, D, F, and G keys, the home keys for the left hand. The student progresses through all the letters, numbers, and punctuation symbols on the keyboard and then begins to type words or letter groups followed by sentences and paragraphs. The program keeps track of errors and identifies characters the student has difficulty with; it also times the student and prints out a speed in words per minute after each exercise. *Typing Tutor* puts a color coded display of the keyboard on the screen in the beginning lessons. If the student omits a word during an exercise, the computer changes the color of the word missed. The computer also remembers troublesome words or letters and gives more practice on them than on words and letters that are usually typed correctly.

There are typing programs for virtually all the popular small computers. One of the first such programs was *Microtype*. It was written by Dr. Bill Engel at the University of South Florida for the TRS-80 computer and is available from Hayden Book Company.

Bilingual Math. This program was written by Marvin Mallon and published in *Interface Age* (September, 1978, 130-133). Thus it is free to anyone who can get that issue of the magazine. Bilingual math is a general purpose math program which provides drill for students in addition, subtraction, multiplication, or division. It does print out a summary of each student's performance at the end of each session, but it does not adjust the types of problems being presented during the session. Instead it allows students (or the teacher) to specify what types of problems will be provided. It will also present the problems in either English or Spanish, a feature which makes this program popular in the Southwest and California. It is not a sophisticated program but the price is certainly right!

Milliken Math Sequence, Grades 1-8+. Milliken (1100 Research Boulevard, St. Louis, Missouri 63123) is a small educational publishing house that moved into educational computing early. Their math software package is designed to provide several types of drill and practice for students in grades one through eight. The version for the Apple II costs $450 and comes on 12 diskettes. Less extensive versions are available for the TRS-80 and the PET computers.

As with other drill and practice software the Milliken series does not attempt to teach anything. Instead it serves as an automated practice system for students who are in regular math classes. The Apple II version includes practice on twelve different skills (e.g., number readiness, addition, integers, fractions, percents, measurement formulas). Each skill is divided into many different levels of difficulty. There are sixty different levels of addition, sixty-two for multiplication, and thirty-six for fractions. While not keyed to a particular basal math series the difficulty levels are in the approximate order and sequence found in most basal series. The teacher's manual provides a complete overview of the programs and offers a number of suggestions about how to integrate the programs into a regular math program. Teachers with little or no computing background find it easy to use this package. There are, however, substantial requirements made of the teacher. He or she must be quite familiar with the system since it is the teacher who selects the particular drills a student will take. The teacher even has a password which must be given before the computer will print out student performance records or allow changes to be made in the sequence of exercises. Each student in the class has a file which contains plans for future lessons, a record of lessons already done, and a performance summary. For each student the teacher can specify which exercises are to be provided, the number of problems per exercise, the mastery level (e.g., 90% correct on 10 or more problems allows a student to proceed to the exit lesson), the failure level (e.g., 45% errors and student is routed to a different exercise), and the minimum number of problems to be provided in each exercise. (The teacher can also specify a class sequence which all students will follow unless there is an individual plan for a particular student). The program is capable of keeping individual and class records on as many as one hundred students for an entire year.

Students who use the program must first type in their password as well as their name and other information. The sign on procedure may be difficult for many children in the primary grades. In addition, the instructions given during the lesson are well within the reading level of an average student in the upper elementary grades but may be a problem for younger students. The computer then looks at their record and selects the appropriate exercises. The exercises are presented in large, easy to read type with animated displays used for reinforcement (e.g., a colorful jack-in-the-box pops up on the screen when the student answers several items correctly.) A feature which is criticized by some educators is the use of large red Xs, which are printed across the screen after the student makes two mistakes in solving a problem. After the red Xs appear the screen begins to flash on and off. Such theatrics are not generally considered educationally useful and may even be detrimental to learning.

Actual problems are presented in a relatively traditional format that appears to be generally well thought out. Some problems would probably be easier to understand and master if greater use was made of the graphics capabilities inherent in the Apple II, but that would increase the size of the programs drastically. In general, the *Milliken Math Sequence* is a good example of the type of software packages we are likely to see more often in the future. Recently, SRA began marketing a similar software package which can be used on the Apple II or ATARI 800 computers. SRA, Milliken, and McGraw Hill also have drill and practice packages for elementary grades in reading, phonics, and other standard school subjects.

Shape/Letter Discrimination For Preschoolers. This program was developed at the Educational Computing Center of Texas Tech University (Lubbock, Texas 79409). It is available in versions for the TRS-80 Model I and Model III computers and costs $19. The program has two sections. The first deals with shapes such as circles, squares, rectangles, and triangles. Children press a key when they think the two shapes on the screen are the same. They press a different key if they think the two shapes are different.

The goal of the program is to help children master the skills of shape discrimination, first with standard geometric shapes and then with large primary style letters. These prereading skills can be taught to preschool children as well as to older children with some types of learning difficulties. The sequence of shapes presented is determined by research on shape recognition (i.e., circles and squares before triangles and rectangles). Correct answers cause the computer to display a large happy face on the screen. Errors cause a small, unhappy face to appear briefly at the bottom of the screen. Then, one of the two shapes moves across the screen until it is on top of the other shape. The child can then see where the shapes differ or that they are identical. Children progress through several levels of difficulty when they reach a criterion score (e.g., 8 out of 10 correct). Students who do not do well at a particular level are given easier problems.

The letter discrimination segment works much like the shape discrimination section except that the letters are grouped according to difficulty and differences. Easily identified letters appear with other letters that are very dissimilar in the beginning levels. Later, the child is required to differentiate between letter pairs such as "b" and "d". In addition, several types of training are provided. One letter may be displayed at the top of the screen with a row of four or five letters at the bottom. The student must select the letter at the bottom that matches the letter at the top.

Shape discrimination is only one small part of the skill we call reading, but it is one that many children find difficult. This program can be used for individual students who are having problems, or in preschool centers with readiness programs.

Tutorial CAI

Tutorial Computer-Assisted Instruction is the form of computer aided learning perhaps most familiar to most educators. That is somewhat surprising because there are fewer good tutorial programs than either drill and practice or simulation programs. Tutorial, however, is what many people expect when CAI is discussed.

Tutorial programs teach as well as monitor the progress of learning. To many, the tutorial program represents technology's way of providing each student with an individual tutor that is patient, responsive to student needs, and tireless. Tutorial CAI is sometimes seen as a total substitute for tutors and teachers. The term dialogue is often used rather than tutorial to describe this type of CAI. That is because good programs resemble a dialogue between an experienced teacher and a student. Learning is not passive. The program accomplishes the learning goals not so much by teaching as by guiding the student through questions, from one concept to another until the student grasps the whole meaning of the lesson. There is no predetermined sequence. The student's response determines the next step.

Will such programs really replace teachers? We have a difficult time accepting that vision of the present or the future. Perhaps perfectly written tutorial programs with elegant graphs, illustrations, animated displays, and an almost unlimited ability to predict what a student will misunderstand would be competitive with a human teacher or tutor. We have never seen even one perfect tutorial program and have serious doubts that we will see many, if any, in our lifetime. Tutorial programs are best considered aids rather than replacements for human educators. A good tutorial program requires a good educator if it is to be used effectively and properly. (Good tutorial programs, however, can easily replace poor or mediocre teachers, and save money in the process!)

Still, tutorial programs do have a great deal to offer. In a typical classroom the teacher must teach new information or skills to groups of students. There are severe limits on just how much a teacher can adapt his or her instruction to the needs of individual students. The typical classroom is not populated by identical students who are at the same level and learn at the same rate. Teaching that is at the right level for some students will be too advanced for some and boring for others. In addition, it is very difficult for a teacher to provide for significant amounts of student interaction and participation when making group presentations. A few students usually make most of the responses and the teacher is often in the dark as to whether most of the students are following the instructions or not. There are many differences between one educator educating one student, and one teacher trying to educate thirty-five fifth graders. It is a credit to teachers that they do the job as well as they do.

All of the problems mentioned above are potentially solved by good tutorial programs. A student learning about the geography of the Pacific Northwest, for example, can sit down at a computer and work through a series of programs which deal with many aspects of the topic. Through graphs, video maps, figures, and written instructional material presented on the screen, the tutorial program may proceed to teach the student about the topic. At regular intervals the computer will stop and ask the student a series of questions about the material just covered. If the student answers the questions correctly, the next segment is presented. If the student answers some questions incorrectly, the program may branch to remedial material that concentrates on the concepts the student does not understand. (In simple tutorial CAI the program may simply return to the material presented earlier and instruct the student to work through it again.) In any case tutorial CAI usually breaks the material down into small, digestible bits, requires the student to make regular responses, checks those responses to be sure the student understands, and tailors the next phase of instruction to the needs of the student. It all sounds very nice. It also sounds a lot like programmed instruction hiding in a computer.

Many tutorial programs are, indeed, no more than programmed instruction books presented electronically rather than in printed form. That is fine for some subjects—those that are easily divided into small segments and those that have a logical, cumulative structure. Some subjects, however, do not easily lend themselves to the programmed instruction format, and the result can be rather boring software that is seen as either busywork or drudgery for the students who must endure it.

Many tutorial programs closely resemble programmed instruction with its frame by frame approach. It is easy to write programs in that mode. Like a minister's sermon guidelines of "three main points and a prayer" many authors of tutorial CAI seem to follow the dictum of "ten lines of instruction, three multiple choice questions, do it again if incorrect, go ahead if correct." That need not be the case and each month the quality of the tutorial software available for small computers improves. Below are descriptions of some examples which represent relatively good tutorial CAI:

Milton Bradley Language Skills Programs. Milton Bradley, known primarily as a toy and educational game manufacturer, now offers a line of moderately priced educational programs for the Apple II computer. There are four programs in their language skills series.

All the programs take advantage of the color graphics features of the Apple Computer. The language skills series includes:

Vocabulary Skills
  Prefixes, Suffixes, Root Words
  Context Clues
Punctuation Skills
  End Marks, Semicolon and Colon
  Commas

Each of the programs costs $45 and is intended for use in grades six through eight. They come on a diskette and have relatively good teacher's guides.

These programs are not drill and practice programs since they actually teach the student skills. Practice is an important component of all the programs. We have reproduced several illustrations of screen displays from this Milton Bradley series to show you how they work. Although the photos are black and white, the actual programs use color graphics.

```
┌─── CONTEXT ───┐
      CLUES
    YOU CAN FIND SOME WORD
    MEANINGS DEFINED RIGHT
    IN THE SENTENCE YOU
    ARE READING.
    SIGNAL CLUES FOR
    THESE MEANINGS ARE:
    IS, THAT IS,
    OR THE USE OF
    COMMAS.
    ─PRESS SPACE BAR─
```

Figure 7.7 Display from the Language Skills series. *Photo courtesy Milton Bradley.*

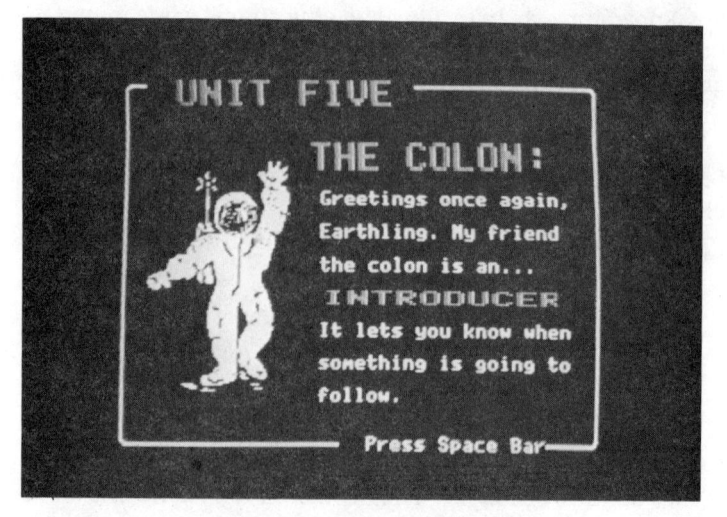

```
┌─── UNIT FIVE ───┐
    THE COLON:
    Greetings once again,
    Earthling. My friend
    the colon is an...
    INTRODUCER
    It lets you know when
    something is going to
    follow.
    ─Press Space Bar─
```

Figure 7.8 Display from the Language Skills series. *Photo courtesy Milton Bradley.*

Computer-Assisted Instruction • 175

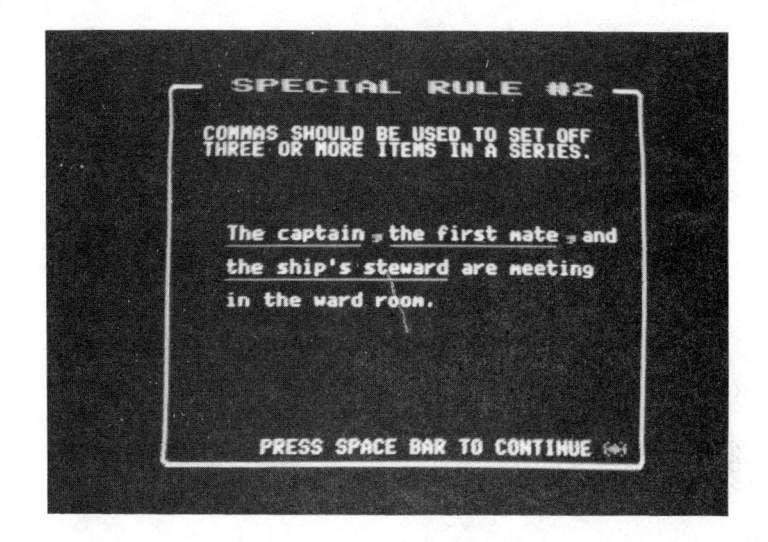

```
┌─── SPECIAL RULE #2 ───┐
│                        │
│ COMMAS SHOULD BE USED TO SET OFF │
│ THREE OR MORE ITEMS IN A SERIES. │
│                        │
│                        │
│  The captain , the first mate , and │
│  the ship's steward are meeting │
│  in the ward room.     │
│                        │
│                        │
│                        │
│   PRESS SPACE BAR TO CONTINUE  │
└────────────────────────┘
```

Figure 7.9 Display from the Language Skills series. *Photo courtesy Milton Bradley.*

```
          LATIN ROOTS

            Cred=Believe
               As in
            That's inCREDible.

            Press Space bar

   CORP=BODY              VOC=VOICE
            MORT=DEATH
   CRED=BELIEVE           VIV=LIVE
```

Figure 7.10 Display from the Language Skills series. *Photo courtesy Milton Bradley.*

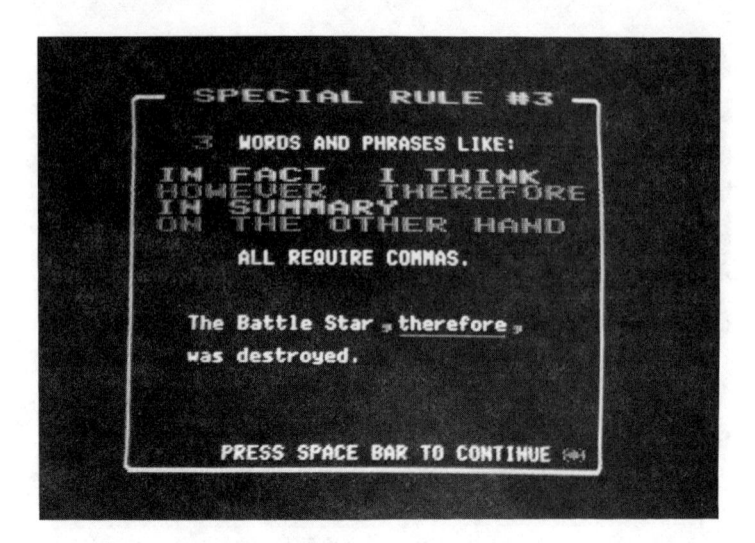

[Figure display showing:]

```
┌─ SPECIAL RULE #3 ─┐
  3 WORDS AND PHRASES LIKE:
  IN FACT      I THINK
  HOWEVER      THEREFORE
  IN SUMMARY
  ON THE OTHER HAND
  ALL REQUIRE COMMAS.

  The Battle Star , therefore ,
  was destroyed.


  PRESS SPACE BAR TO CONTINUE
```

Figure 7.11 Display from the Language Skills series. *Photo courtesy Milton Bradley.*

Nold/Cannom Programs in Pylon. The July/August issue of *People's Computers* (6, 1, 1977) contained several programs written by Ellen Nold and Sallie Cannom of Stanford University. These programs are written in Pylon (a language very similar to PILOT) for use in freshman English composition classes. One program titled *Cumin* is designed to provide a conversation between the computer and the student on the topic of classification and prejudice. The listing below shows what might happen in a typical session. Note that the interaction in this program is much like a real conversation. The computer's responses are in uppercase letters, the student's responses are in lowercase letters.

LISTING OF A TYPICAL DIALOGUE IN CUMIN

HI. WHAT'S YOUR NAME?
Jane
THIS PROGRAM IS ABOUT CLASSIFICATION AND
  STEREOTYPING. PLEASE GIVE ME SOME INFOR-
  MATION. WHAT SEX ARE YOU?
Female

THANKS. WHAT RACE ARE YOU?
Caucasian
WHAT'S YOUR CULTURAL BACKGROUND? (ITALIAN? WEST INDIAN?)
French
O.K. I KNOW YOU'RE A STUDENT. WHAT'S YOUR MAJOR, OR YOUR INTENDED MAJOR?
Math
ALL RIGHT. ONE MORE QUESTION. WHAT'S YOUR RELIGIOUS BACKGROUND?
Protestant
FINE. NOW THAT I KNOW YOU'RE FEMALE, CAUCASIAN, FRENCH, AND PROTESTANT, HOW MUCH DO I KNOW ABOUT YOU?
I don't think you know much at all.
RIGHT. I KNOW VERY LITTLE.
IT SEEMS TO ME THAT I JUST HAVE A BUNCH OF STEREOTYPES IN MY HEAD.
LET'S EXPLORE THEM.
WE ALL KNOW ABOUT COLLEGE STUDENTS, RIGHT? PAMPERED, UNAPPRECIATIVE, SEX IN THE DORMS...
YOUR TURN. USE TWO LINES IF YOU NEED THEM.
EVERYONE KNOWS A FEMALE IS...
Dependent, illogical, emotional, indecisive, inept at technical things
NOW ABOUT THE CAUCASIAN RACE, THEY'RE...
Materialistic, exploitative, colonizers, racists, unconcerned about the problems of the third world.
THE THING ABOUT PROTESTANT PEOPLE IS THAT THEY...
are smug, self-righteous, think their way is the only way.
DO YOU KNOW HOW MUCH MATH MAJORS ARE STEREOTYPED HERE AT STANFORD?
No
GO ASK AN UPPERCLASSMAN.
ALL RIGHT, JANE:
DEPENDENT, ILLOGICAL, FICKLE
VAIN, GOOD AT MATH
COLONIZERS, EXPLOITERS, CONTROLLERS OF THE WORLD'S WEALTH

SMUG, SELF-RIGHTEOUS, DOMINATING
DOES THAT SOUND LIKE YOU?

Not really.

YOU'RE MUCH MORE COMPLEX THAN THOSE STEREOTYPES. YET, AS YOU KNOW, DECISIONS ARE OFTEN BASED ON SUCH LABELING. SOME LANDLORDS WON'T RENT TO STUDENTS BECAUSE, "THEY ALWAYS WRECK THE PLACE." MANY JOBS ARE CLOSED TO BLACKS AND CHICANOS BECAUSE, "THEY AREN'T DEPENDABLE."
HAS ANYONE EVER SAID TO YOU,
JANE, YOU REALLY SHOULDN'T DO THAT BECAUSE YOU'RE A FEMALE?

Yes, my uncle is always saying that.

YOU WERE PROBABLY PUSHING AT YOUR SEX STEREOTYPE AND MAKING SOMEONE UNCOMFORTABLE.

CLASSIFICATION OR CATEGORIZATION OF PEOPLE HAS FUNCTIONAL VALUE SOMETIMES. HOWEVER, WE NEED TO STAY AWARE OF THE DIFFERENCE BETWEEN FACT AND INFERENCE, TO BE SUSPICIOUS OF OUR STEREOTYPICAL ASSUMPTIONS, AND TO REALIZE THAT A PERSON IS DESCRIBED ONLY IN PART, AND PERHAPS IN-ACCURATELY, BY A LABEL OF ANY KIND.

BYE FOR NOW, JANE. IF YOU WANT TO DO A PRO-GRAM ON NONSTEREOTYPICAL THINKING, TRY MUSTARD. IF YOU'D LIKE TO STUDY FACT AND INFERENCE, DO MARJORAM.

THANKS

Simulations

When you drop a quarter into an arcade game and take control of an interstellar fighter with laser guns and force field shields, you are spending your money on a computer simulation. Many of the more successful arcade games are, in fact, simulations which allow you to take a role in an imaginary or simulated situation.

Simulations are models or descriptions of often complex events or conditions. There are three major functions of simulations today: recreation, decision making/problem solving, and instruction. Individuals of all ages are spending their quarters on arcade games that simulate everything from galactic warfare to the LA freeway, while giant corporations, intelligence agencies, and the military are simulating different world or national conditions in an effort to make better decisions. The Pentagon may simulate on its computers a revolution in a Middle Eastern country that threatens our oil supply. The simulation can be run with many different decision patterns (e.g., invade country, use naval forces only, remain totally neutral, support third party intervention), and the computer can offer best guesses of what might happen. On a less grandiose level, a university can use a computer to evaluate the effects of shifts in enrollment patterns and undergraduate majors and use the data to make decisions about allocation of university resources for the future.

While both recreational and problem solving simulations are fascinating, we will concentrate on instructional simulations here (which can be fun as well as educational). There are several advantages to simulations:

1. Fun. Simulations are probably easier to make attractive and interesting to students than any other form of CAI or CMI. Sometimes students have to be pried away from the keyboard.

2. Economical. Simulations are almost always far cheaper than allowing the students to learn in the real world.

3. Safe. Simulations can give students training in areas where it would be dangerous to allow students to freely experiment.

4. Realistic. Simulations bring the real world to the classroom. The cost of taking students out of the classroom and into the real world has increased dramatically in recent years. Simulations are one way of duplicating aspects of the real world in the classroom.

5. Better Transfer. Students who learn a skill in a simulation find it easier to transfer that skill to the real world than they do when training consists of the traditional lecture/demonstration.

6. Low Development Costs. Although the military may spend millions on a sophisticated simulation of landing on the deck of a carrier, it is possible for a teacher to write a credible simulation that has much educational value.

7. Less Threat and Anxiety. Simulations allow students to experiment, to try out options they might avoid in other situations. The low threat aspect of simulations makes them ideal tools for teaching divergent thinking skills whereas other forms of CAI and CMI may be better suited for teaching convergent thinking.

8. Maximum Use of Learning Time. Simulations need not duplicate the real world exactly. A simulation can concentrate on those aspects which require the most training. We have a blackjack trainer, for example, that teaches you which options to take when certain cards have been dealt to you, other players, and the dealer. The program simulates a real blackjack game, but allows the learner to eliminate patterns where the choice (e.g., hit, stand, insurance, double) is obvious. Under some circumstances simulations may be more effective than practice in a real situation.

What sorts of educational goals are best served by simulations? Some educators feel simulations are particularly valuable in teaching divergent thinking. That is, simulations provide the student with an opportunity to explore their own answers and the way those answers are obtained rather than coming up with the teacher's answers (i.e., convergent thinking). Other educators see the role of simulations as much broader than that. Simulations can also be effective in teaching simple facts. A simulation called *Civil War* recreates a number of battles in the civil war. Another program simulates space travel around our solar system. Students who play those simulations learn many facts about the civil war and the solar system.

Simulations can also teach procedures and processes. There are programs that teach technicians how to diagnose problems in radar systems, electronic ignitions, and television receivers. Other simulations teach physicians to diagnose heart problems and nuclear technicians to troubleshoot nuclear reactors.

With such potential, are there problems associated with simulations? Yes. Students who become experts in working through a simulation may not realize that there are substantial differences between the simulation and the real world. In addition, simulations may take up far more class time than their learning objectives justify because they are so captivating. These limitations are generally manageable, however, particularly when the potential of simulations is considered.

There are many different types of simulations available today for small computers. The organization Conduit markets several college and high school simulations including:

Coexist – a biology simulation that helps students understand the ecological balances in nature.

Compete – a botany simulation that helps students understand the effects of factors such as plant crowding, soil nutrients, moisture, and light availability on plant growth.

Evolut – a simulation of evolutionary development across many generations.

Tribbles – based on a famous episode from the television program "Star Trek," this simulation teaches students how to use the scientific method by making them scientists on an alien planet inhabited by cute little animals called Tribbles.

Scatter – simulates several experiments in nuclear physics which would be difficult (and expensive) for students to actually conduct.

Change Agent – allows students to take the role of a change agent in a small farm community.

Imprinting – simulates studies on imprinting with birds. Students can specify the variables they want to study, indicate the levels of those variables to be studied, and the computer will generate results.

There are hundreds of other simulations available today and many more likely to be available in the future. We will conclude this section with a description of a program we use in our courses on computer literacy for educators.

Oregon Trail. The Education section of *Newsweek* on March 19, 1981, was titled "The Classroom Computer." The article began with a description of students in a Minneapolis elementary school who were gathered around their computer playing *Oregon Trail*. That simulation is one of the most popular for both elementary and secondary students. Students playing *Oregon Trail* are part of a wagon train travelling from Independence, Missouri to the fertile valleys of Oregon. Students (settlers) must make many decisions—how much to spend on food, clothing, ammunition, and medicine; whether to shoot at riders coming toward the wagon train that look hostile, whether to push on or stop at forts for provisions. The simulation gives students in social studies and American history classes a feeling of how it might have been for settlers who headed west. Some of the versions of *Oregon Trail* use extensive color graphics.

Oregon Trail is a computer program, but it is based on historical data including diaries of settlers who actually made the trip. Thus, the odds of being attacked by bandits or suffering some other setback are based on the historically established odds. In a typical classroom application of *Oregon Trail*, the teacher might introduce students to the program and then provide them with information on that period in history (or let them go to the library to look up the information themselves). The more knowledge about the period the students have, the more likely they are to make it to Oregon alive. Playing *Oregon Trail* can thus be a powerful motivator to study harder. In addition, the simulation also helps students learn systematic problem solving skills since they must make many decisions that can have important consequences later in the simulation.

Selecting Educational Software

Regardless of the type of CAI you need, the current situation in the software marketplace dictates that you will probably have to sift through a lot of sand before you find a pearl. The median level of quality is currently quite low. That does not mean good software is not available. It is. Unfortunately the good programs constitute only a small portion of the programs currently offered for sale. Chapter 10 contains a number of suggestions on where to get more information about educational software. This chapter concludes with some general guidelines for selecting software:

1. Carefully define your learning objectives and goals before shopping for software.
2. Keep time and use patterns in mind when shopping. A program that requires two continuous hours of computer time

for each student to complete won't fit into a thirty minute time slot for computer literacy, especially if you plan to run 200 students through that program each semester.

3. Consider the program/machine match. If your computers use cassette storage and have 16K of memory, you won't be able to run programs that require disk drives and 48K of memory.

4. Consider the context in which the programs will be used. Some programs require a great deal of scheduled and/or unscheduled teacher intervention. Others can be used by students with minimal supervision. Drill and practice programs assume some initial training has been provided before the students reach the computer.

5. Look for interactive programs. Many educational programs are really no more than textbooks typed into the computer. It is easier and cheaper to use textbooks if that is all you need.

6. Programs should be *user friendly*. That is, educational software should not require a Ph.D. just to understand how to make it run properly. Mistakes should not be fatal (i.e., cause the program to stop running).

7. Programs should be interesting. That is true for any educational media, although some topics are harder to make interesting than others.

8. Programs should be well organized, use good learning principles, and provide appropriate feedback to students.

9. Programs that make extensive use of graphics displays, figures, tables, and charts are usually more interesting than programs which rely solely on printed material.

10. Summaries of a student's performance in each segment of the program are helpful to the student and the teacher. Detailed class summaries are also helpful but generally not provided today.

11. Programs should work. That is, they should teach what they say they teach. AND they should do it better, quicker, or more economically than other, less expensive methods. Many of the currently available programs do not meet this basic criterion.

12. Finally, programs should have good documentation. Many good computer programs suffer because they lack manuals that show novice users how to use the program.

8

Computer-Managed Instruction

Computer-Managed Instruction (CMI) uses the computer to provide tests, develop assignments, and keep records, but it does not involve the computer in the actual teaching of material. A logical question at this point might be, "If you have the computer, why not go to CAI, and use it for instruction too? Why just limit the computer to record keeping and testing?" Fifteen years ago the answer to this question was simple. In many schools CMI became the de facto standard for computer assisted learning because computer time was too expensive to use for direct instruction. Today, even though computing time is relatively inexpensive, CMI is still popular. There are several reasons. CMI may be useful in classes where CAI is not. Educators are in the early stages of testing the limits of computer assisted learning, but we suspect many types of important learning goals can more easily be accomplished by teaching approaches that do not use a computer for instruction as CAI does. That may sound like heresy in a time when writers are predicting the demise of traditional schools and the rise of computer centered education, but our experience suggests that computers have their limits like anything else. However, even when subject matter does not lend itself to CAI, the computer, through CMI, may be a very useful tool in the classroom.

A second reason for opting for CMI over CAI is the relative amount of time it takes to develop good programs. CAI is much more labor intensive in the beginning. It can take hundreds of hours of work to produce one good hour of CAI programming for students. CMI, while not easy, takes much less time. Most of the effort invested in CMI, in fact, is directed toward reducing the clerical overhead a teacher must manage while trying to run a classroom. Some educators estimate that classroom teachers spend well over 50% of their time preparing, administering, and grading tests, keeping records, and filling out required forms. That percentage is even higher in classes that use an individualized approach. CMI appeals to many teachers because its primary goal is to take much of that clerical and managerial load off the shoulders of the teacher and give it to the computer. CMI does not have the glamorous image of CAI, but it has its own appeal.

In a typical CMI system the student would sign on at the computer by typing in his or her name, provide any information the computer requests (e.g., take a diagnostic test or a test over an assignment), receive feedback, and get an assignment from the computer. The student would then sign off and begin work on the assignment.

CMI can perform four very important roles in reducing the administrative burden in both traditional and individualized classroom settings:

1. The computer can actually administer and score tests. (Or score tests when answers are written on machine readable forms such as answer sheets or mark sense cards.)

2. The computer can provide feedback to students as they take tests. In a typical classroom, students must wait days or weeks before receiving feedback on their performance, and even then feedback is often no more than number correct/number incorrect. The computer can evaluate answers as soon as they are given, indicate correctness where appropriate, and explain to the student why an answer is correct or incorrect. Feedback provided immediately is often far more effective than feedback provided days or weeks later.

3. The computer can also provide diagnostic information and prescriptions for remediation at each testing. Suppose that a student in an American history class has taken a test over a unit on colonial governments. If the student does not reach the criteria for passing that unit, the computer can do more than tell the student to study that unit again. It can create a prescription which identifies the areas of weakness and make suggestions on what and how to study for a retake. It is true that a teacher could do much the same thing without

a computer, but few teachers have the time when they must deal with four or five classes of American history daily, each with twenty-five to thirty students. The computer makes individualized help a practical reality for every student in the class.

4. The computer can store performance records, learning plans, test scores, and remedial suggestions for all students and provide that information to the teacher in a variety of formats. A fifth grade social science teacher, for example, could ask the computer to print out the test records indicating how many units each student has passed to date, how many retakes each student has on each unit, and the number of students who are at or above the learning goals set for the class. In addition, the computer can keep track of how students perform on individual test items. Printouts of test item statistics might help identify some items that are poorly written, confusing, or ambiguous.

CMI TODAY

CMI is used in colleges and universities more than at any other level. It is also more popular in high schools than in elementary schools. Part of the reason for this pattern is that high schools and colleges usually assign teachers by subject

Figure 8.1 Many CMI programs run on small computers such as the Apple II.

matter. A sociology teacher can invest a considerable amount of time developing a CMI system for an introductory sociology class and then use that system in several different sections. The teacher who must teach math, reading, science, social studies, and art to a group of third grade students may find it harder to justify the time invested in a CMI system for any particular subject. Since most CMI programs currently available were initially developed by educators for their own use, that means there are few CMI programs for the elementary grades.

Regardless of the subject or educational level involved, CMI requires the use of standard learning methods to carry the actual teaching/learning load. The learning may occur in a variety of ways. Students can study textbooks, work on library assignments, listen to lectures, or watch live or filmed demonstrations. They go to the computer for testing and feedback. Usually the teacher will organize the materials and assignments into units or modules. These units can be chapters in a textbook, or the teacher may decide to organize the assignments along other lines, perhaps incorporating several different learning options.

Some Examples

At this point it might be useful to provide some examples of CMI systems and software in use today.
Washington School District (Phoenix, Arizona). Aly Gundlach is Coordinator of Computer Managed Instruction for Washington School District in Phoenix, Arizona. Her article in *Educational Computer Magazine* (1981, May/June, 12-15) is titled "Managing Instruction With a Micro." It describes the use of a PET computer to provide CMI to elementary schools in Phoenix. The school district uses a system called CUES, which stands for Continuous Uniform Evaluation System. The learning objectives for kindergarten through the eighth grade have been specified in three basic areas: math, reading, and communication. CUES provides measureable objectives, ordered sequentially, in all three areas with ten to fifteen minimum competency objectives provided in each subject area at each grade level. A minimum competency objective is an objective that you want every child in that grade to

achieve. In addition there are also objectives which the school system would like students to reach at each grade level, but they are not considered reachable or required for all students. The CUES system provides a test, usually consisting of around twenty items, for each objective. There is also a diagnostic test at each grade level in each subject area which provides teachers with information on each student's performance relative to the learning objectives of that grade.

The school system uses PET computers to score tests, keep complete records on student performance, and group students for instruction. The system also provides teachers with a running record of performance since students take tests as they complete work on each learning objective. It is also possible to get categorical information from the system (e.g., how well Spanish speaking students in the third grade are reaching objectives in math).

The Phoenix approach to CMI does not involve providing explicit prescriptions for accomplishing each learning objective. Instead, it provides grouping information and leaves the development of learning assignments to the teacher. That approach may be preferred in some settings. Others may call for the development of specific prescriptions for each student by the computer.

Quick Quiz. *Quick Quiz* is a software package produced by Radio Shack for the TRS-80 Model I and Model III computers. It costs $30 and comes on a diskette (you must have a disk system to use it). *Quick Quiz* is representative of the many inexpensive CMI software packages available today for small computers.

Quick Quiz allows a teacher to develop several tests, each of which can contain up to forty multiple choice questions. It is relatively easy to revise and update tests as your needs or objectives change. With this program you can have the computer administer tests to individual students or have the computer print out a copy of the test for duplication. Test results are stored on diskette by student name. The teacher can get a record of test performance for individual students or for the whole class. Even with these features *Quick Quiz* is a limited CMI system. It does not prescribe or make assignments and it keeps only the simplest of pupil records. Yet, considering the price, it is potentially useful in many classes.

A more expensive program ($125) for the Radio Shack computers is available from Fireside Computing, Inc. (5843 Montgomery Road, Elkridge, Maryland 21227). Called CAIWARE-2D the program requires a two disk system. Teachers can create tests which use multiple choice, fill-in, true-false, or short answer formats. Graphics and simple illustrations can be used to create test items where necessary, and there are provisions for providing help when students have difficulty on a particular test. The program allows teachers to specify the type of feedback each student receives, and there are provisions for relatively sophisticated student record keeping. In addition to *Quick Quiz*, Radio Shack has another program, *Author I*, which can be used to develop CMI lessons. *Author I* costs $150 and runs on Model I and Model III computers with at least one disk drive. The higher price gives educators the ability to use graphics in their CMI programs and to keep detailed records of student performance on several different CMI modules.

Individuals considering developing their own CMI programs may want to read an article titled "Writing Your Own

Figure 8.2 The *Author I* system. *Photo courtesy Tandy/Radio Shack.*

Software: Authoring Tools Make it Easy" by Glenn Kleiman and Mary Humphrey, founders of Teaching Tools: Microcomputer Services in Palo Alto, California. It appeared in *Electronic Learning*, (May/June, 1982, pp. 36-41). The article provides an excellent overview of the software development process, outlines the features to look for in programs for CMI development, and reviews several of the popular programs on the market today (including *CAIWARE-2D, Author I*, and the *ZES Authoring System* which is also described later in this chapter.) Kleiman and Humphrey also point out that there are many versions of the PILOT language, with at least one available for the Apple, Atari, Radio Shack and Commodore PET computers. PILOT is an excellent language for developing CMI programs.

Zenith Educational System (ZES). At $250 the *ZES* package is not cheap. It is, however, a very popular system for developing educational software. Avant-Garde Creations (P.O. Box 30160, Eugene, Oregon 97403) markets *ZES* which was developed by an Australian group. It requires an Apple II computer with 48K of memory and a disk drive. *ZES* is actually a set of several programs that enable a teacher to create lessons and to keep track of student progress. The 125 page manual will require some attention before a teacher can begin using *ZES*, but it is not necessary to learn to program in a language such as BASIC or PILOT to use the package.

Figure 8.3 The ZES package. *Photo courtesy Avant-Garde Creations.*

Although ZES is included in this chapter on CMI, it can be used to create drill and practice and tutorial lessons as well. Lessons may include the provision of information to the student, including tables, figures, and illustrations in color, questions the student is to answer (up to four answers can be keyed as the correct answer), and hints or remedial work for students who need help. ZES keeps track of the answers from each student as well as the time taken on each lesson. The program can also store class performance data and can perform common statistical analyses on student data.

Figure 8.4 shows the *menu* which appears on the screen when ZES begins operating. The user selects the desired option by typing a number from one to ten. If you elect to create a new lesson, the computer prints a few instructions on the screen and then begins the creation process. You must give each lesson or module a title and indicate the type and number of questions to be used as well as the amount and type of instructional material to be used (e.g., text, graphs, diagrams). Each question will, of course, have at least one correct answer associated with it, but it can also have hints and comments (for instance praise when the student selects the correct answer). Tutorial material can be interspersed between sets of questions.

DIRECTORY MENU
1. CREATE A LESSON
2. AMEND A LESSON
3. CREATE/AMEND GRAPHS
4. INSPECT GRAPHS
5. CREATE/AMEND TEXT
6. CREATE/AMEND STUDENT RECORDS
7. OBTAIN STUDENT REPORTS
8. INITIALIZE NEW MODULE DISK
9. VERIFY A LESSON
10. EXIT
ENTER YOUR CHOICE: ( )

Figure 8.4 The initial menu display for ZES. *Photo courtesy Avant-Garde Creations.*

Once the lessons have been created the teacher enters information on each of the students who will use the program. As students complete lessons, data on their performance are added to their file. ZES is one of several currently available programs for educators who want to write their own lessons. You get quite a bit for the price.

The Instructional Systems Center. Our last example of a CMI system is the Instructional Systems Center in the Psychology Department of Texas Tech University. Information on the center was provided by Dr. Douglas Chatfield who obtained a National Science Foundation grant to develop the system at Texas Tech. The Instructional Systems Center represents a state of the art application of minicomputers in CMI. We have reprinted below excerpts from the description provided to visitors of the project:
The Psychology Department at Texas Tech University uses a PDP 11/34 computer with twenty terminals to augment the instruction in several undergraduate courses. The primary instructional uses are the administration of quizzes, tutoring, and the simulation of laboratory experiments. The major CMI application is in the undergraduate general psychology course.
Content mastery in the general psychology course is measured via weekly ten-item chapter quizzes. The student may attempt each quiz once in class, and then retake the quiz in the Instructional Systems Center as many times as necessary (with a few restrictions). The Instructional Systems Center (ISC), is a large room in the basement of the Psychology Building which houses a DEC minicomputer, disk storage system, printers, and terminals for student use. The ISC was made possible by a $225,000 grant from the National Science Foundation.
Since most students taking general psychology have not used a computer before, a program called *Quiz* explains the center to students and helps them get started taking tests on the computer. Students can then take chapter quizzes at any terminal which is free. *Quiz* will randomly select ten multiple-choice questions from a chapter pool of about one hundred questions, and present them to the student one at a time. After allowing the student to recheck answers, the computer scores the test and provides feedback. If any items were missed the

computer tells the student where to find answers in the text. *Quiz* then records the results in the student's file on disk.

This whole process takes about eight minutes and permits the accommodation of over 1,000 general psychology students per week (eighteen simultaneously) using only two teaching assistants to supervise the ISC when students are taking tests.

Students may, at any time the ISC is open and not being used by another class, ask the computer to display all of their quiz grades, plus the dates each quiz was taken. Other information is also provided, such as credit earned through participation in departmental experiments and bonus points earned.

For students having special difficulties with specific chapters, and for those who just want to reinforce their studying, a tutorial program called *SALEEP* (System Augmented Learning Environment for Elementary Psychology) has been developed. This CAI program allows students who want additional help to use the computer for instructional as well as testing purposes. As the student works in *SALEEP*, progress is checked after each section of instruction via a multiple choice test. Incorrect answers lead to repetition and rephrasing of information, or review of previous terms and concepts. Correct responses allow the student to continue further into the material.

ISC also provides students in junior and senior level courses with simulations of experiments and statistical analysis. If you would like more information on ISC write to Dr. Douglas Chatfield or Dr. Charles Halcomb, Department of Psychology, Texas Tech University, Lubbock, Texas 79409.

ISSUES IN CMI

Up to this point we have discussed generally the format and components of CMI. The educator actually considering using CMI must consider carefully a number of basic issues. We will discuss a few of those in this section.

Learning Mode

CMI is compatible with most teaching strategies. That means the decision to use CMI does not provide much guidance on which learning mode to use. Do the learning objectives call for lecture/discussion approaches, individual projects, programmed instruction, peer learning, or some other system? Will learning be accomplished through reading texts, watching audio-visual presentations, or through planned experiences? CMI is a suitable partner to any of the learning modes noted above.

Size and Form of Assignments

Many CMI systems simply make assignments which are based on the textbook chapters. For many courses, that may be appropriate. CMI, however, has the potential to manage instructional programs which provide students with many different ways of mastering the learning objectives. A course which provides several different alternatives or paths to learning may be more interesting and more effective than one which makes use of only one path.

In addition, the size of the assignment must be considered. If the learning tasks are broken into a few long assignments, the student may not have sufficient opportunities to take advantage of feedback and help available from the computer as it evaluates progress. On the other hand, many short assignments may unnecessarily break up the content and prevent students from putting all the pieces together into a meaningful whole.

In general, it would seem that complex subjects in which beginning concepts form a required foundation for later skills should be broken into smaller assignments with frequent tests. Many math and science courses are good examples of this type of subject matter. In addition, subjects which do not build but involve learning specific, detailed information also seem to call for frequent testing. Learning a foreign language vocabulary is an example of this type of work. On the other hand, some courses are less concerned with the acquisition of large amounts of detailed information than with a broad understanding of the topic. A literature class might require students to develop some understanding of the relationship of themes to topics within a novel, plus an awareness of the historical context in which the novel was written. In such a class there might be fewer tests with ample time for students to read, ponder, and discuss their assignments.

Test Characteristics

We might subtitle this section The Curse of the Multiple-Choice Test. In many ways the type of test you use determines the type of learning that will occur. We would estimate that over 80% of the tests given in schools today involve no more than recall and/or recognition of information. Some have used the unpleasant term regurgitation when speaking of this type of test item. Items like "When was the battle of Hastings?"; "Who invented the typewriter?" are good (or bad) examples.

Is all that emphasis on names and dates really justified? We think not. Most teachers who use such tests don't really think so either. The reason we see names and dates so frequently on tests is that it is easier to write that type of item than any other kind. Teachers, faced with heavy demands on their time, often develop tests hurriedly and under pressure. An unfortunate side effect of that haste is often a test that measures knowledge that is easy to test rather than knowledge that is important to test. Even when teachers have access to test item files supplied by textbook publishers, they often discover the great majority of items available measure recognition and recall of facts.

Facts are not unimportant, but simple facts are only one aspect of learning. Most courses will want to measure acquisition of some facts, yet most courses also have goals and objectives that go beyond learning facts. One of the best known formats for categorizing learning objectives is Bloom's Taxonomy of Educational Objectives. In the cognitive domain Bloom divided learning objectives into six different categories:

1. Knowledge. Ability to recognize, identify, or bring to mind specific information. Most tests concentrate on this category.

2. Comprehension. Ability to appropriately translate the information into your own words.

3. Application. Ability to take the essence of the information and apply it to a given situation. An example would be determining the cubic feet in a room given the formula for cubic feet and the dimensions of the room.

4. Analysis. Ability to separate information or knowledge into component parts. An example would be conducting a quantitative analysis of a compound in a chemistry class.

5. Synthesis. Ability to put parts or elements of information together to form a whole. An example would be the ability of a stock broker to put together discrete bits of information about the economy, world conditions, and so forth to make predictions about the performance of certain stocks.

6. Evaluation. Ability to make judgments, appraise situations, and determine values based on the student's system of beliefs and values. An example might be a critical analysis of a poem.

Students who are tested only on knowledge will tend to concentrate on that aspect of learning to the detriment of other, important learning objectives. As noted earlier, it is much easier to write test items which measure knowledge than it is to write higher level items. With more effort it is possible to write quite acceptable multiple choice items at the comprehension, application, and analysis levels. With even more effort, multiple-choice items can be written for the synthesis and evaluation levels as well. The typical student's disdain for multiple-choice items is not generally shared by specialists in psychometrics, the science of test development. The difference in viewpoint is attributable primarily to the fact that students evaluate multiple-choice tests by what they see, and psychometricians take into consideration what could be rather than what is.

If you decide to develop a large test item file for CMI, we would urge you to consider carefully the percentage of items provided at each of Bloom's levels. In addition, if you have difficulty writing multiple-choice items at some of these levels, remember that languages such as PILOT can easily accommodate many different types of test items.

Entry and Exit Criteria

Another issue related to testing and test items is the specification of *entry* and *exit* criteria. Many CMI systems provide initial tests which measure skills required of students entering the course. A CMI program for a second year algebra course could initially test students on skills and concepts which should have been acquired in the first year course. If the student does not meet the minimum entry criteria for the course, remedial work might be required.

If a substantial number of students fail to meet the entry criteria in that second year course it suggests the exit criteria used in the first year course were inappropriate. Tests administered at the end of units, modules, or courses should measure the range of objectives set for that instructional unit. If the test is faulty, it is possible for students to pass without actually achieving the learning objectives.

Comprehensive Tests Versus Sampling

Another testing issue relates to how comprehensive the test will be. If you have thirty specific objectives for a particular module you could develop a test that contains at least three items on each objective. With thirty objectives and three items per objective the student must take a relatively long test (and the teacher must develop it!). Another alternative would be to have the computer randomly select items that measure at least one third of the objectives and assume that students who master the objectives tested have also mastered the others. We prefer an exit test that samples the mastery of objectives unless there is evidence to indicate such a sample will allow many students to proceed when they actually need more work.

When the computer is used to perform diagnostic testing there is another test model that may be appropriate. Since the computer can score each item as the student provides an answer, it would be possible to divide the test into several segments. Then the computer could administer a few items from each segment. These would be key items which indicate whether the student has mastered the instructional objectives measured by that segment of the test. If the student passes all the key items for a segment the computer would move on to administer other items. If the student misses some or all the key items, the computer would administer all the other items in the segment and provide a detailed profile of skills the student has not mastered.

The computer's ability to immediately score items means it can be programmed to adjust the difficulty level and type of items used. All students need not take all the items in a test.

Dealing With Failures

A related issue is the method of handling failures. When a student takes an exit test for a unit and fails to reach the criteria, many systems simply tell the student to study the material again. Others provide detailed information on exactly what to study; still other systems assign remedial work which was not a part of the original assignment. Our experience suggests that few CMI systems will function flawlessly without some human intervention, particularly when students have difficulty with exit tests. We would suggest that students who fail to meet exit criteria get help from the teacher or a teaching assistant.

ADMINISTRATIVE ISSUES

Finally, CMI systems can create administrative difficulties which must be resolved. Suppose that a high school science department decides to develop CMI materials for a chemistry class. The teacher or teachers assigned that task will undoubtedly invest a great amount of time and effort in the project. Will they receive any compensatory credit (such as extra salary or reduced teaching load) for their effort? Now suppose the science department finally has a very effective CMI system for both introductory chemistry and physics. The program is so effective that the department can handle all the students in both courses through CMI. Before CMI, those classes required the full time attention of three teachers. Will they continue to receive credit for those courses because they manage the CMI program? Or will the school administration assign additional teaching responsibilities because it is easier to teach CMI courses than traditionally taught courses? If developing CMI programs requires a great deal of effort initially and is likely to lead to more teaching assignments in the long run, few teachers are likely to move in that direction.

WHERE IS CMI APPROPRIATE?

CMI is only one of many different approaches to computer aided learning, and computer aided learning is only one of many different teaching methods that could be used in the classroom. Are there subjects which seem particularly suited to CMI? We think good candidates for CMI are subjects for which there are effective efficient teaching methods already available which do not require computers and the overhead of assessment is relatively high. Junior high school math courses, for example, have relatively well established teaching methods. Many teachers, using traditional methods, do a very good job of teaching junior high math. The subject matter is cumulative and students who do not understand a concept last week may be lost the next week because new skills build on old ones. The teacher must test students frequently if instruction is to be appropriate and on target. CMI seems a natural alternative in such classes since the teacher can continue to use teaching methods which have demonstrated their effectiveness. The computer plays an important role in reducing the testing burden on the teacher and, in the process, can provide more detailed information on performance than was possible without it.

AN EXTENSION OF CMI: CAREER COUNSELING

We will end this chapter with a discussion of a relatively new application of small computers in schools—career counseling. In career counseling instead of developing learning assignments which lead to mastery of a particular subject, the computer helps the student explore different career options. For several years a number of companies have offered computer programs which assist students who need career counseling. These systems tend to be relatively expensive and often require schools to buy terminals, install phone lines, and rent time on a computer located miles away.

One well known program is *SIGI* from Educational Testing Service (Princeton, New Jersey 08541). *SIGI* stands for System of Interactive Guidance and Information. Until 1980, schools wishing to use *SIGI* had to pay a basic fee of $2,400 per year for a four terminal system plus an additional $600 for each remote or local terminal used for *SIGI*. A school that did not have a suitable computer would have to rent computer time or purchase a very expensive minicomputer to run *SIGI*. The minicomputer installation could easily cost well over $50,000.

With a grant from the Kellog Foundation ETS adapted *SIGI* to run on a TRS-80 Model II computer. A school can now put *SIGI* to work for an annual license fee of $1,200 a year plus the cost of buying the Model II (about $6,000 for a computer with one disk drive and a printer). Adding more computers increases the licensing fee by $600 per year per computer.

Although the price is much lower when small computers are used, *SIGI* is still not cheap. What do you get for your money? *SIGI* is designed to help college bound high school seniors and college students make intelligent, informed decisions about career options. A *SIGI* session begins with the computer asking a number of questions which help identify occupational values the student considers important. Some students value jobs that are secure, while others prefer jobs that provide prestige or recognition. Still others prefer jobs that provide a great deal of contact with people. *SIGI* helps students consider and weigh ten different occupational values in the initial sessions. Once those values have been identified, the student can begin to explore career options which fit his or her value system. Occupations that attract the interest of the student can be explored in more detail. *SIGI* has a tremendous amount of information about hundreds of occupations. In addition, *SIGI* helps the student evaluate the likelihood of successfully entering that occupation. A student who made C's and D's in high school science classes and is considering medicine would be told the probability of success is low because many science classes are required in the premed undergraduate curriculum.

Once the student has explored his or her value system, identified occupations of interest, and considered the likelihood of success, *SIGI* helps plan a strategy for achieving the desired occupational goal.

A typical student will spend three to four hours spread over two or three sessions working on *SIGI*. (*SIGI* remembers information typed in previous sessions.) It does not replace a career counselor, but it does provide students with an opportunity to intensively explore both their own feelings about a career and the options which are available. *SIGI* combines personal values with detailed information about options. In coming years, *SIGI* is likely to be only one of many computer based counselling programs which allow individuals to explore and work through major decisions.

9

Applications in Assessment and Evaluation

Mrs. Jones decides it is time to give her class of thirty students a mid-term exam. Being a conscientious teacher, she has made a practice of collecting test questions on file cards. From her collection of questions in a given area, she can sort out the appropriate questions and organize them into an exam. This allows her to create a new exam each term without starting from scratch. From a total of 200 questions, she selects fifty and arranges them in order to be typed. Mrs. Jones is concerned that her students often try to look at one another's papers during testing. To help prevent this, she wonders if she could arrange the questions in a different order for each student. She rejects this thought, however, realizing it would be too timeconsuming.

After her students have taken the exam, Mrs. Jones scores it. She looks at each answer for each student and checks it against the answer key. She then totals up the raw score points for each student. Next, she converts each raw score to a percentage score and computes some descriptive statistics — mean and standard deviation. Finally, she looks at the score distribution in order to assign letter grades. She tries several different strategies and finally decides on the one she feels is fair.

Most of this process — which certainly took a lot of Mrs. Jones' time — was spent in clerical tasks: organizing, sorting, counting, checking, calculating, and rearranging. Computers often can perform these tasks quicker and more accurately than humans! If Mrs. Jones had a computer programmed to assist her with these clerical tasks, she could spend more of her time thinking about the nature of the test and its educational implications. That point leads us to the purpose of this chapter—how the computer can help you do a better job of measuring, assessing, and diagnosing.

The preceding example only touches the surface of how computers can be used in educational assessment and diagnosis. Emphasizing their potential in this area, the president of Educational Testing Service (ETS) recently commented that computers would provide "enormous flexibility in what is available when, and where, and to whom" (Turnbull, W.W. "The President's Report: Looking Ahead." *ETS Annual Report*, 1980).

Although the example at the beginning of this chapter illustrates the use of a computer in a regular classroom, we will also look carefully at the use of computers in nonclassroom settings. Each year thousands of children and adults take achievement, personality and intelligence tests as part of counseling programs, hospital intake procedures, diagnostic workups in special education classes, and many other settings. Such tests generally do not result in a grade for a student. Instead the results are helpful in making decisions about future treatment or educational services for the person taking the test. Computers can play a number of different roles in the diagnostic/prescriptive process. We will discuss several of those roles in this chapter and consider the computer's potential for testing in the classroom as well.

STATE OF THE ART

The potential of computers in assisting with assessment and diagnosis was recognized in the early stages of computer development. An early book on computer applications in the behavioral sciences predicted that computers would allow the teacher, for the most part, to "avoid the role of drillmaster or record keeper and concern himself more with the motivational, social, and inspirational aspects of the instructional process" (Borko, H. *Computer Applications in the Behavioral Sciences*. Prentice Hall, 1962, 308-312).

This indeed was a wonderful promise. Upon reading this book, however, it becomes obvious that in 1962 the technology for fulfilling the promise was not accessible to those who would need it. A review of the field in the sixties was a review of heavily funded research projects using massive computer facilities with highly trained computer experts. The classroom teacher realized few benefits from computer technology in 1962 and for a number of years thereafter.

Today 1962 is ancient history. It was not until the computer began to shrink in size and cost that the promise began to be realized. The advent of the microprocessor and its use in relatively inexpensive small computers in 1977 has added a whole new dimension to the possibilities for educators in the areas of assessment and evaluation.

Not only have advances been made in the development of the small computer; large computer systems have also changed dramatically. Changes in these systems have been toward simplicity. Systems are more accessible through terminals. The languages required to communicate with the system also have become less technical and cumbersome. As you will note later in this chapter, there is a trend toward eliminating jargon from the programs. This means a student or teacher can sit down at the computer terminal, once it is powered up, and interact with the system without learning a new language.

Another trend in large computer systems has been toward cost effectiveness. A recent study reported a comparative cost analysis involving two university math programs, one computer-based (UC, Irvine) and the other traditional (UC, San Diego). The Irvine computer-based program saved twice as much in other expenses (faculty salaries, clerical expenses, etc.) as it cost to use the computer (Franklin, S., & Marasco, J. "Interactive Computer-Based Teaching." *Journal of College Science Teaching*, 7, #1, Sept. 1977, 15-20).

Today, because of technological advances, there is greater opportunity for educators to realize the potential of the computer in assessment and diagnosis than there was a few years ago.

DEALING WITH THE OBJECTIONS

When we speak of using the computer in educational assessment and diagnosis, we run the risk of being criticized for promoting a cold, sterile approach to the educational process. Many fear that the computer will turn us all into robots. Concerning the possible use of a computer-assisted diagnostic report writing system, a school superintendent commented: "But won't the computer tend to dehumanize the report?" The article by Franklin and Morasco, cited above, describes some common myths, expressed as objections to computer-based testing. A summary of four of these myths will help put the topic in proper perspective.

Myth 1. "Forcing a student to use a computer presents an unwarranted additional obstacle in the student's attempt to attain his educational goals." Anyone sitting down at a computer for the first time, with no prior instruction or without any guidance, would probably insist that this is no myth. It does take some time and some effort to master even the simplest computer; this is usually not without its frustrations. One argument suggests that this is not a valid reason for dismissing the use of the computer because the computer can be viewed as a tool. As with any other tool, its potential can only be realized by those who know how to use it. The point is that this objection is no more valid for the computer than for any other tool designed to help us function more efficiently.

Myth 2. "Computer-based testing is crude and inflexible." How many times have you sat through the agonizing experience of taking a long multiple-choice test and felt that you knew the material but that the test did not tap your knowledge? Had the instructor been able to sit down with you personally and ask the right questions and give the right clues, he or she may have succeeded in unlocking your store of knowledge. This could have meant a successful and rewarding educational experience for you. It is said that Socrates sat on one end of a log and asked questions of his student who sat on the opposite end. Although the computer may not become another Socrates, it may be a lot more personable than passing out 200 duplicate copies of seventy-five multiple-choice questions, accompanied by a mark sense answer sheet.

Myth 3. "Interactive computer-based testing is too expensive." Two important considerations are overlooked. First, expenses are in the nature of front-end costs—when looked at over the long haul, they are not as high as they appear at first glance. Second, the trend is for the cost of electronic equipment to decrease while the cost of labor intensive programs is on the increase.

Myth 4. "Interactive computer-based testing has significant problems with security and cheating." The problem of security simply is not valid. Tests can be stored on either tape or disk, and it is no more difficult to secure these materials than tests stored in any other way. The cheating problem, however, is real. The best student in the class may take the test for other less prepared students, or resource materials may be used on a closed book test. Similar problems exist with most examination situations, however, and will need to be handled in a similar fashion. As the degree of sophistication in this area increases, these problems will likely be of less concern.

ENHANCING THE RELATIONSHIP BETWEEN TESTING AND TEACHING

In general, assessment and evaluation are inseparably connected to good educational practices. One major weakness of the testing movement has been that it has often produced instruments and methodologies which seem only loosely tied to the real world of teaching and learning. The computer has the potential for making assessment and evaluation a complementary part of education. The most natural relationship between teaching and testing is for the two to complement each other. Ideally a person observing an educational program should have a difficult time distinguishing when teaching or testing is taking place. Without going into greater detail, this is accomplished when the teacher can provide information and check for acquisition using the same methods or techniques interchangeably.

The computer has the potential to assist in making testing complement teaching. In computerese, a program which accomplishes this is termed Interactive Computer-Based Testing (ICBT). Most advantages of ICBT can be summarized under the theme of flexibility. An excellent example of this flexibility (which allows computer testing to complement teaching) is the use of multiple inputs. In traditional testing situations, when a student is asked to answer a complex question or solve a problem involving numerous steps, missing the first step leads to incorrect responses on all succeeding steps. The student then has failed a large portion of the test and testing has taken place with little learning involved. An ICBT program can check immediately for incorrect responses and either halt the process, ask the student to go on to the next question, or call attention to the error and start over.

One unique advantage of the ICBT approach is that the computer lends itself to a type of test item that ties in closely with instruction. Consider the possibilities for problem-solving questions: a problem could be presented and the student told to request the appropriate information needed to solve the problem. In this way the instructor could base an evaluation of the student's response on the degree of insight exhibited as well as on the answer. This type of question is especially well handled by PILOT (See Chapter 5). A simple example of this process is given below:

The student is told that the task is to figure out how a system works and that some things are "in" and some are "out". The program interaction with one student sitting at a small computer might look like this.

The computer displays the following on the CRT screen:

GLASS IS IN; PLASTIC IS OUT
EGGS ARE IN; BACON IS OUT
JENNY IS IN; JOHN IS OUT
MASSACHUSETTS IS IN; CALIFORNIA IS OUT

NOW TYPE A WORD
I'LL TELL YOU IF IT'S IN OR OUT

The student responds by typing:
MAN

Computer: MAN IS OUT
DO YOU KNOW THE RULE?

Student: NO

Computer: DO YOU WANT MORE EXAMPLES?

Student: YES

Computer: RIBBON IS IN; TAPE IS OUT
TREES ARE IN; BUSHES ARE OUT
BOBBY IS IN; ROBERT IS OUT
GRASS IS IN; LAWN IS OUT

WANT TO TRY SOME MORE?

Student: YES

Computer: NOW TYPE A WORD AND I'LL TELL YOU IF IT IS IN OR OUT

Student: ROBBIN

Computer: ROBBIN IS IN
DO YOU THINK YOU KNOW THE RULE?

Student: YES

Computer: OK, NOW TELL ME IF EACH OF THESE WORDS IS IN OR OUT

RIVER

Student: OUT

Computer: RIGHT

BROOK

Student: IN

Computer: GOOD, THAT'S RIGHT

BOOK

Student: IN

Computer: MIRROR

Student: IN

Computer: CORRECT

SPOIL

Student: OUT

Computer: RIGHT

SPILL

Student: IN

Computer: YOU'RE RIGHT

DANCING

Student: OUT

Computer: GREAT—LOOKS LIKE YOU'VE GOT IT! ALL WORDS WITH DOUBLE LETTERS ARE IN.

The flexibility is obvious. The instructor could then devise a scoring system to award credit based not only on discovering a rule but also on the number of examples required and on the appropriateness of calling for questions and examples. This type of interactive program allows the student to learn and the teacher to evaluate the student at the same time.

SOME SPECIFIC APPLICATIONS

Seven different ICBT approaches can be differentiated. Although many basic principles apply to all seven approaches, the goals they are designed to accomplish and the situations in which they are used are somewhat different.

Criterion-Referenced Testing

In its simplest form a criterion-referenced test is a test where meaning is derived from an individual's raw score by comparing that score to a learning goal or criterion. This is opposed to norm-referenced testing, where meaning is derived from the raw score by comparing it to the scores of other people. A norm-referenced test emphasizes relative standing, while a criterion-referenced test emphasizes task mastery. With a norm-referenced test, you may learn how Mary compares with other students her own age in reading ability. A criterion-referenced test does not take into consideration how other people scored, it measures the individual against the criterion. Can Mary divide fractions with 90% accuracy?

The criterion-referenced model is beginning to gain wide acceptance, especially in the area of special education. It is, however, fraught with some serious problems. A major one is the fact that a criterion-referenced model dictates that a good criterion-referenced test will contain many items and go into much depth and detail in the particular curriculum area it is measuring. The result is often a cumbersome, awkward test requiring much clerical work. This is where the computer comes in. The computer, simply as an organizer and record keeper, could assist the test user.

Some criterion-referenced tests commonly in use require from four to eight hours to administer, which is another major problem. Eventually it should be possible to build this type of test into an ICBT system. The ICBT approach seems well suited to handle criterion-referenced tests. The student could take the test by interacting with the computer rather than having it administered on a one-to-one basis by the teacher or educational diagnostician. Both the time problem and the cumbersome aspects of the test would be eliminated. Criterion-referenced testing could then become a much more viable option to educators than at present. The computer could administer certain key items on the criterion-referenced test and use the student's answers to determine which of the remaining test items should be presented.

Diagnostic Simulation

Computer-based simulation is presently being used in a wide variety of situations. Although computer-based simulation has been discussed earlier in this book, it has a specific application in assessment and evaluation. One type of computer-based simulation is diagnostic simulation, the use of the computer to simulate a situation in which a student must consider certain pieces of information and, based on that information, make treatment decisions or make a diagnosis. The emphasis in computer-based diagnostic simulation is on attempting to produce a testing situation which is as lifelike as possible. The primary application of computer-based diagnosis is in situations where something prevents or hinders the opportunities of the student to practice and be evaluated in a real situation. In training a pilot, for example, it is extremely dangerous and expensive to allow the new beginner to learn to make decisions in actual flight. In a flight simulator, which is a sophisticated computer-based simulation apparatus, the pilot trainee can make all the mistakes he or she wants, and the only thing that will be injured is pride and perhaps the pilot's grade or review.

Three other advantages argue for using a computer-based diagnostic simulation over traditional methods in some situations. First, the computer can be programmed so that the process of diagnosis is broken down into its component parts, which enhances both learning and scoring. Second, the time element can be controlled. In the early stages of learning many skills, things often occur too quickly for the student to profit much from practice. The computer could slow the process down in the early stages of training and speed it up, if desirable, in later stages. Third, a variety of diagnostic situations could be assured with computer simulations, whereas, in the real world, the student might be limited to only one or two situations.

An excerpt from a computer-based diagnostic simulation program used with medical students follows:

> *Computer:* IN YOUR JUDGMENT, WHICH PROBLEM SHOULD BE DEALT WITH INITIALLY?
>
> *Student:* POSSIBLE SHOCK
>
> *Computer:* YOUR RECOGNITION OF THE POSSIBLE EXISTENCE OF THIS PROBLEM IS TO BE COMMENDED.
> THE CLINICIAN IDENTIFIED THE PROBLEM SPECIFICALLY AS HYPOVOLEMIC SHOCK.
> WOULD IT BE BEST TO HOSPITALIZE, TREAT AS AN OUTPATIENT, OR PROVIDE NO TREATMENT FOR THIS PROBLEM?

Student: HOSPITALIZE

Computer: YES, HOSPITALIZATION FOR THIS PROBLEM IS WARRANTED.
HOW SHOULD THIS PROBLEM BE RESOLVED?
A) MEDICATION
B) SURGERY
C) EUTHANASIA

(From Christopher and Wilson. "A Computerized Approach to the Teaching of the Clinical Problem-Solving Process." *Biomedical Communications,* Vol. 3, #3, May 1975, 16-18)

The potential of the computer is even greater than illustrated by this brief example. The availability of more sophisticated graphic capabilities and the use of real time simulation offer the opportunity to create situations which closely resemble the real world.

Real time simulation is an important aspect of computer-based simulations. This involves building time elements into the program as they would exist in the real world. The medical student might be asked to make a decision about a patient whose condition is deteriorating even though the lab reports are still being developed. The student may have to go with a best guess and wait for further data. The decision the student makes in such a situation would be an important part of the diagnostic process.

One area in which computer-based diagnostic simulation could be readily applied is in the teaching of science in the public schools. Classification, which is so much a part of science, lends itself very well to computer simulation. The computer would not replace actual practical experience, but it could serve as a way for the student to independently test his or her knowledge of terminology and distinguishing characteristics.

Jonny Smith sits down at the computer as an image of a rock appears on the screen.

The computer presents: YOU NEED TO DECIDE WHETHER THIS ROCK IS SLATE OR OBSIDIAN. YOU MAY ASK FOR THE FOLLOWING INFORMATION:

1. COLOR
2. SHAPE
3. WEIGHT
4. TEXTURE
5. SURFACE
THINK HARD AND TRY TO GET IT RIGHT WITH THE LEAST AMOUNT OF INFORMATION POSSIBLE.
PRESS THE NUMBER OF THE INFORMATION YOU WANT.

Student presses: 1

Computer responds: BLACK
ARE YOU READY TO CHOOSE OR DO YOU WANT MORE INFORMATION?
TYPE "C" FOR CHOOSE AND "I" FOR INFORMATION

Student: I

Computer: WHAT INFORMATION DO YOU WANT?

Student: 2

Computer: SHARP
WILL YOU CHOOSE OR DO YOU NEED MORE INFORMATION?

Student: C

Computer: PRESS "S" FOR SLATE OR "O" FOR OBSIDIAN

Student: O

Computer: CORRECT! THEY ARE BOTH BLACK, BUT ONLY OBSIDIAN IS SHARP

This type of simulated activity has many possiblities in several academic areas.

Computer Scoring

The process of scoring tests and other assessment instruments is one of the easiest and most natural functions for a computer to perform, since it primarily involves data manipulation. The computer can do such work many times faster and more accurately than people can do by hand. Hand scoring is error prone. Time is another problem with hand scoring; it is very time consuming. And this time, which is spent doing clerical tasks, could be put to much better use.

One popular type of computer scoring service is scoring by mail. An assessment instrument which is quite popular in terms of scoring by mail services is the personality inventory. Western Psychological Services (WPS Test Report, P.O. Box 1477, New York, New York 10001) offers this type of service for the Minnesota Multiphasic Personality Inventory (MMPI) and the Personality Inventory for Children (PIC). Personality tests lend themselves well to computer scoring because a large amount of number manipulation is required for a complete analysis of the test results. A second example of scoring by mail is a service offered by Adept, Inc. (Box 11117, L.U. Station, Beaumont, Texas 77710). This service will score the Wechsler Intelligence Scale for Children-Revised (WISC-R) and the Wide Range Achievement Test (WRAT). As Adept puts it, "You need provide us only with the dates of birth and testing, and Wechsler subtest raw scores for your subject." Many services of this nature are available and all indications are that more will become available in the future.

Another way of getting computer scoring services is to purchase a scoring program for your own computer. Psychological Assessment Resources, Incorporated, (P.O. Box 98, Odessa, Florida) sells a computer scoring program for the MMPI and the California Psychological Inventory (CPI) which will run on a TRS-80 or Apple computer. These programs are not as sophisticated as many of the scoring by mail services, but they probably reflect the direction of the future. As the memory and storage capacity of small computers increase, this type of program should come into rather wide use.

Computer-Assisted Diagnostic Report Writing

Although this topic is closely related to computer scoring, there are some additional concerns. When scoring tests the computer is being used primarily to juggle numbers; in report writing there is an attempt to have the computer make decisions which are traditionally seen as requiring human analysis. In this context the critics of computer use in education probably make their strongest point. There is a danger, considering the present state of the art, of exaggerating the potential of the computer for writing diagnostic reports. Present attempts at this often produce rather sterile, mechanical products. Despite this caution there is potential for using the computer as an assistant in writing diagnostic reports. The question of machine intelligence is still unanswered. We have only begun to understand what machines can do. Therefore, the possibility of a computer-generated diagnostic report containing all the nuances of a report created by the most experienced diagnostician may someday be possible.

One way the computer could be brought to the assistance of the report writer is by acting as a quick and efficient record keeper. Information could be stored and organized by diagnostic patterns. When the computer recognizes a specific pattern, it could display or print out various conclusions or recommendations which are consistent with that pattern. The diagnostician could then glean from the display the items which he or she wanted to include in the report. If nothing else, the computer's ideas could serve as stimuli for jogging other ideas.

In this regard, Learning Tools, Inc. (4 Washburn Place, Brookline, MA 02146), has made available a program called Teacher Planning System, which its developers feel is able to "develop IEPs (individualized education plans) or progress reports in draft or final form using the curriculum database of goals, objectives and related instructional information" and to "print IEPs, progress reports and other information with user-defined formatting." This program is available for the Apple, TRS-80, North Star, Commodore, Texas Instruments, Zenith and other small computers.

Two authors of this book (LaMont Johnson and Jerry Willis) are presently in the process of developing a program that will assist in writing a diagnostic report. It will run on the TRS-80 Model III with dual disk drives and 48K memory. This program will accept raw scores from a variety of different instruments, convert all raw scores to standard scores, and perform all of the necessary calculations. It will also print out the format for the diagnostic report with all of the standard information (age, test date, scores) already included. At certain points in the report, space will be provided for comments, observations, and suggestions. At these points the computer will act as a word processor, allowing the user to type in the appropriate information; this will be printed out along with the rest of the report. For example, when a section of the report which involves the WISC-R (an intelligence test) is run, the following appears on the screen:

Name _____   Date of Birth ____/____/____
                         Date Tested   ____/____/____

W I S C - R

VERBAL		PERFORMANCE	
Information	_____	Picture Completion	_____
Similarities	_____	Picture Arrangement	_____
Arithmetic	_____	Block Design	_____
Vocabulary	_____	Object Assembly	_____
Comprehension	_____	Coding	_____
(Digit Span)	_____	(Mazes)	_____

The report writer types in the name, dates, and raw subtest scores. The computer then calculates the chronological age of the subject at the time of testing, finds the corresponding scaled score for each raw score, and then finds the Verbal, Performance, and Full-Scale scores. The printer then prints out all of this information in the desired format. This program should prove to be very efficient since it will perform the same function for nine other assessment instruments in addition to the WISC-R. It is estimated that this process will save about two hours for each report generated as well as provide increased accuracy.

Managing Class Records and Grading

This topic is really part of a broader topic, computer managed instruction (CMI). CMI is discussed elsewhere in this book, but this specific application needs some coverage here. A number of programs allow the educator to use the computer to manage class records and grades. These programs range from those that can be used with a small computer and are relatively simple, to a very sophisticated university-wide system which can handle large classes.

One program (Barnett, B. D. Grading made easy. *Creative Computing*, September 1980, 146-148) consists of only 73 program lines. Written in BASIC, it illustrates what can be done with computer-managed class records and grading with only a small time investment. This easy-to-use program could be adapted very quickly to any small computer equipped with a BASIC language. It will handle scores in three different categories: homework, in-term tests, and final exams. The teacher has to supply the students' names, their raw scores, the maximum score for each assignment or test, and the weighting desired for each of the three categories of scores. The computer will then print out all raw scores by category and by student name. It will also convert each score to a percentage score. It will print each student's average for each of the three categories as both a raw score and a percentage score. The average weighted grade score for each student and the average weighted grade score for the entire class will also be figured. One major advantage of this type of program over the traditional grade book system is that it allows the teacher to use flexible weighting and point values. Instead of always using a nice round number of possible points in order to make calculations easy, the teacher can use 67, 93 or whatever point value fits best with that particular assignment or test. Since the computer does all the math, the teacher may use any number system that seems appropriate. Another advantage is that these calculations could be made periodically during the term in order to determine which students are having trouble.

A more sophisticated grading program (Gates, R.D. *Computer-Assisted Grading. Personal Computing*, October, 1980) performs some basic descriptive statistics and recommends final letter grades. This program computes the appropriate statistics and suggests letter grades based on two different standards. The time saving factor in this program is the fact that the teacher can look at the grading pattern for a class, based on different approaches and using many different standards and cut-off limits, until the pattern that allows for the fairest distribution of grades is found.

A program called *Computerized Gradebook*, a sophisticated record-keeping and grading system, can be easily adapted to most small computers using BASIC (Kaza, K. *Computerized Gradebook*. *Microcomputing*, June 1980, 126-131). The author of the program states that he spends only thirty minutes each week updating the gradebook. The program then allows him to get the latest information when parents or other teachers want to know how a child is doing. Once a week he posts a missing work list which informs students of any assignments they are missing and how many points each assignment is worth.

An example of a large computer system which manages class records and grades is Texas Tech University's Instructional Systems Center in the Department of Psychology. This system administers tests as well as keeps track of scores. There has been an attempt to simplify the use of this system for the student. All technical jargon has been eliminated as well as the use of account numbers, passwords, and other logging-in information ordinarily associated with large systems. All sections of the department's General Psychology course are managed through this system. The student may at any time request and receive all quiz grades for each chapter assigned. The student will also be shown other information such as credit earned through participation in departmental experiments and bonus points earned. An option of the program called *Remark* allows the student to type in comments, questions, and complaints which are then recorded and reviewed by the staff periodically.

For a look at a very large management system, we turn to *Scout*, a system used by the Testing Services Center at Brigham Young University (See also *Proceedings of NECC 1981 National Educational Computing Conference*, June 1981, North Texas State University, Denton, Texas, p. 94-98) to manage the class records and grading of large enrollment courses. The courses managed by this system have a combined enrollment of about 4,000 students who write nearly 35,000 exams in a single semester. This system does not administer the exams. It keeps track of who is in the class, who needs to take which exam, and selects (randomly, if desired) the appropriate exam items to be given. Once the student has completed the exam, the computer scores it and provides the student with a score, a list of items missed, and a list of responses to each question. Scores for specific areas within the test can be obtained in order to indicate explicit areas of student weakness. Scoring, posting, and reporting takes about twelve seconds. Instead of completing their own grade rolls by hand and then having this information transferred to the computer, professors have the option of having *Scout* make all of the necessary calculations and maintain the final grade roll without the professor ever touching it.

Computer-Assisted Training in Test Administration

Two studies (Row, M.H., & Aiken, R.M, A CAI "Simulation Program for Teaching IRI Techniques." *Journal of Computer-Based Instruction*, 1976, 2, 52-56 and Henney, M., & Boysen, V. "The Effect of Computer Simulation Training on Ability to Administer an Informal Reading Inventory." *Journal of Educational Research*, 1979, 72, 265-270) have demonstrated that computer simulation programs can be used effectively in teaching some of the skills required in using individual diagnostic testing instruments.

A typical course in test administration consists of lectures and demonstrations of how the test is given, which are generally followed by practice administrations of the test. These practice sessions may be observed by the professor. In many instances they are not observed because of the time required to observe even one full administration by every student in the class. Finally, some class time is usually spent on the interpretation of the test. A computer simulation program which could put the computer in the role of a student being tested would be a great advantage to the instructor in this type of course. The computer could demand precision in administration and scoring details and could provide immediate feedback. It could also provide a variety of subject responses which the student administrator may not get from live subjects. A printout could be provided to the instructor summarizing the errors each student administrator made. This would insure that the student administrator was practicing correct procedures and would allow the instructor to concentrate on those students who were having the most difficulty. This type of program would not replace the need to administer the instrument to live subjects, because there are some skills that can only be gained through interacting with real people. Yet it could be an effective and efficient method for training those skills which are purely clerical in nature and those which can best be acquired through practice with immediate feedback. The instructor using this method could be freed to spend more time helping students learn the subtle clinical skills which cannot be taught by the computer.

Such a program has been developed at Texas Tech University College of Education for training in administering the WISC-R (Johnson, L. & Willis, J.A., *Comparison of Traditional and Computer-Based Methods of Teaching Students to Administer Individual Intelligence Tests. AEDS Journal,* 1982, 16, 1, 56-64). This program simulates student responses and has built-in checks for appropriate administration and scoring procedures. Essentially the program takes the role of the child being assessed. The student administrator uses the keyboard to tell the computer what decisions have to be made. When the student decides to ask question four on the Block Design test, for example, the computer responds by selecting an answer and displaying it on the screen. In the case of the Block Design subtest, the answer is a graphic pattern of blocks on the screen. The examiner must accurately record the time it took to respond, decide whether the answer is correct, and then decide what to do next (give the same item again, give a less difficult item, give a more difficult item, stop the test). The answer presented by the computer is drawn from a large bank of possible answers. There is an element of randomness in the answer the computer chooses, but the program also considers the age of the child and whether it is simulating a child who is below average, average, or above average in ability. Answers may be clearly correct, incorrect, or marginally correct. Because the program is a relatively accurate simulation of a typical child taking a test, the examiner must deal with most of the types of decisions commonly encountered. The program can be used in two modes—training and testing. In the training mode, the computer monitors each decision and provides immediate feedback. If a student fails to obtain a baseline or ceiling the computer prints a message on the screen which explains the error. It also records the error in its memory and prints out a record of errors for that student at the end of the session. In the testing mode the computer provides no feedback. Instead, it follows the lead of the person administering the test and provides an answer to a question when requested. Every error made is recorded in memory and printed out after the session.

Computer-Managed Test Development

The basic idea in computer-managed test development is this: instead of writing an entirely new test each time a test is needed, a database is created that is read by a standard program. A program can then pull items from the database and develop a different test each time one is needed.

An example of computer generated tests was presented by Bernard Eisenberg ("Final Exams—Let the Computer Write Them." *Creative Computing,* Nov/Dec 1977, 103-106). Due to a change from a two-semester school year to a three-semester school year at Kingsborough Community College, Eisenberg and his colleagues were faced with the task of developing at least four final examinations for certain math courses each academic year. The traditional method for developing these tests was with a five-person committee. One person represented each section of the course and through the committee process, a final version of the test was eventually obtained. If you have ever worked on a college committee you will have some appreciation of how cumbersome this process would be. Because the new semester was viewed as an added burden, the decision was made to look for help. The help came in the form of a computer-generated test system. The resulting program had the following specifications:

1. The questions which made up each test were diverse enough to be representative of that term's work.

2. Even though some questions might have had the same wording from one term to another, the numbers were always different.

3. The randomly selected numbers were appropriate for the type and level of the question.

4. Questions were randomly selected for each version of the test.

5. Students were given choices as to which questions they would answer—a student would not be penalized if a question

or two appeared which covered a concept to which the student had not been exposed.

6. New material could easily be incorporated into the database at any time.

WHAT THE FUTURE HOLDS

The computer has the potential to do much for us in terms of educational assessment and diagnosis. We have probably only begun to realize this potential. Most of the problems and dissatisfactions experienced to date are due to limitations in hardware and software. Trends in these areas are promising, especially in terms of improved hardware at decreased costs. The small computer will provide a very competitive alternative to the large central system. Trends in hardware further suggest that audio and improved video capabilities will soon be incorporated into computer-assisted assessment and diagnostic systems.

Section Four

SOURCES OF INFORMATION

10

Sources of Information

In an era of rapid change it has become fashionable for educators to argue that an educational system should not try to teach everything a student will need to know after graduation. Knowledge has a shorter lifespan today than ever before and new information is appearing too quickly. The goal of education should be to teach students basic or fundamental knowledge, methods of solving problems, and ways of continuing to learn after they graduate.

In the field of small computing the rate of technological development and change is probably several times faster than in other areas. Books, magazine articles, and training curricula which were current and up-to-date when they were written are often out-of-date in months rather than years or decades. The nature of the field, therefore, makes this chapter a particularly important one. It will describe most of the educational computing periodicals, discuss the major organizations which are concerned with educational computing, cover sources of information on educational software, identify relevant indexes, and explain how to use computer databases to find information on a particular topic.

PERIODICALS

There are over twenty publications devoted entirely or primarily to educational computing and many more which deal regularly with the topic. Each of the publications is aimed at a particular audience. *The Computing Teacher* is written for practicing educators concerned with down to earth issues. *Computers and Education* is a research oriented journal with articles of interest primarily to individuals conducting research or writing about the field of computer aided learning. In all likelihood, the subscription lists of these two journals would have very little overlap even though all the articles in both are about educational computing, and both are very good publications.

Educational Computing Publications

The Computing Teacher (Department of Computer and Information Science, University of Oregon, Eugene, Oregon 97403). *The Computing Teacher* (TCT) was created by David Moursund, the editor of TCT, and a respected leader in the field for many years. TCT is practitioner oriented and publishes articles on many topics of interest to educators in public schools and in university and college settings. TCT publishes reviews of significant educational software, reports on new computers and accessories, and publishes quite a few descriptions of projects as well as course descriptions. At $14.50 a year for nine issues, TCT is well worth its price.

Classroom Computer News (P.O. Box 266, Cambridge Massachusetts 02138). CCN began publication in 1980 with six issues a year. Subscriptions are $12.50 per year. Some of the articles in CCN are similar to those found in *The Computing Teacher* but CCN also publishes many short "news" features describing significant happenings (e.g., a conference of educational publishers to discuss how to deal with the software market). A very good publication for the practitioner, we recommend it.

Educational Computer Magazine (P.O. Box 535, Cupertino, California 95015). Begun in 1981 ECM also publishes six issues a year. Subscriptions are $15.00. ECM is another practitioner oriented magazine with articles on everything from preschool software to university computer literacy programs. The emphasis is on articles which provide information to the educator using computers. ECM also publishes listings of some educational programs. If one or two of their programs is useful to you in a year that alone would justify the price of the magazine. This is another excellent magazine.

Electronic Learning (Scholastic Inc., 902 Sylvan Avenue, Box 2001, Englewood Cliffs, New Jersey 07632). A new entry in the Scholastic stable of educational publications, *Electronic Learning* is also a bimonthly magazine. Subscriptions are $15 a year. *Electronic Learning* is very new, begun in the last half of 1981. It tries to cover many areas of technology, not just computers; but early issues have been heavily slanted toward computers and hand held learning aids. Like the three magazines already mentioned, this one is practitioner oriented. Articles published thus far have dealt with topics such as how to select good software, a state by state analysis of funding for educational computing, and an outline of a six-week course on computer literacy. *Electronic Learning* has also published a number of articles about computers and computer-assisted learning which are aimed at the novice who has an interest in the field but little background. (*The Computing Teacher* has also published a number of articles for the uninitiated.) *Electronic Learning* is probably the slickest of the magazines mentioned thus far. It is filled with color pictures, nice artwork and many fancy ads from hardware and software vendors. With the mix of articles, reviews, and columns provided by *Electronic Learning, Educational Computer Magazine,* and *Classroom Computer News* it is difficult to identify one which we would consider better than the others, especially when you consider that all three are new publications. In all likelihood the three magazines will begin to sort out their own special place in the field as they mature.

Electronic Education (P.O. Box 20221, Tallahassee, Florida 32304). *Electronic Education* is smaller than the similar publication from Scholastic and it has less specially designed art. It is, however, a useful publication with many good articles. The March/April, 1982 issue contained articles on selecting a computer system, an article on computer applications for the deaf, and several other up-to-date, relevant articles. Subscriptions are $15 a year for nine issues.

AEDS Journal (Association of Educational Data Systems, 1201 16th Street N.W., Washington, D.C. 20036). The *AEDS Journal* is published four times a year and contains a variety of articles for practitioners and theorists. It publishes more research and conceptual articles than any of the publications previously mentioned. There are fewer articles on using small computers in elementary or high school settings and more on the process of writing and developing educational software.

The AEDS organization also publishes two other quarterlies, the *AEDS Bulletin* and the *AEDS Monitor*, as well as a variety of reports and conference proceedings. Membership is $35 a year ($10 for students) and well worth the investment if you work with computers in an educational setting. The *AEDS Monitor* contains a variety of general articles that would be interesting to people involved in educational computing.

Instructional Innovator (Association for Educational Communications and Technology, 1126 16th Street, N.W., Washington, D.C. 20036). AECT publishes three journals for its members, *Instructional Innovator, Journal of Instructional Development*, and *Educational Communications and Technology Journal*. Computers are not the sole focus of the journals nor is classroom learning. The organization has a membership that includes trainers in industry as well as educators in public school and university settings. All types of instructional media and technology are covered. Many large university libraries carry these journals. You may want to look at current issues to determine whether they publish material relevant to your interests. The same advice applies to *Performance and Instruction*, a journal published by the National Society for Performance and Instruction (1126 16th Street, N.W. Suite 315, Washington, D.C. 20036).

Journal of Computer Based Instruction (Association for the Development of Computer-Based Instructional Systems, Computer Center, Western Washington University, Bellingham, Washington 98225). Similar to the *AEDS Journal*, the *Journal of Computer Based Instruction* has an even stronger focus on research and conceptual articles.

Computers and Education (Pergamon Press, Maxwell House, Fairview Park, Elmsford, New York 10523). *Computers and Education* "sets as its goal the establishment of a forum for communication in the use of digital analog and hybrid computers in all aspects of higher education." The focus is on computer usage at the college and university level; the tone is formal and the articles range from theoretical and conceptual pieces to "how we did it" papers by college professors and administrators. The four issues a year cost $30 to individuals, $83 to libraries.

Computers Reading and Language Arts. (P.O. Box 13039, Oakland, California 94661). This new journal is aimed at readers who are involved in research or teaching in the areas of reading and language arts.
It is edited by Gerald Block and should be a good publication.

Mathematics and Computer Education Journal. (P.O. Box 158, Old Bethpage, New York 11804). This journal was announced as we wrote this chapter. A one year subscription (3 issues) is $13. Although we did not have an issue to preview, it appears to be aimed at classroom teachers who teach math, computer literacy, and programming courses.

T.H.E. Journal (Information Synergy, P.O. Box 992, Acton, Massachusetts 01720). T.H.E. stands for Technological Horizons in Education. This journal publishes articles on many types of technology including computers, videodisks, and audio-visual equipment. *T.H.E. Journal* publishes descriptions of computer projects and computer centers in schools as well as "how to" and "how it should be done" articles. There is as much in this journal about large computers as about small ones and there are many articles on computers in higher education. Three things make this publication a wise choice for many people. First, it contains many advertisements from computer and accessory manufacturers. Second, it has a large new products section; third, it is sent free of charge to individuals in certain positions (such as principals, superintendents, college professors). If you do not qualify for a free subscription the cost is $9.50 a year.

Apple Education News (Apple Computer, 10260 Bandley Drive, Cupertino, California 95014). *Apple Education News* is published irregularly by the manufacturer of the Apple II, one of the most popular computers in educational settings. *Apple Education News* contains product announcements from Apple, descriptions of innovative uses of Apple computers in schools, and short news items of interest to readers. It is a useful publication even for those who do not have Apple II's in their schools. Subscriptions are free.

SIGCUE Bulletin (Association for Computing Machinery, P.O. Box 12105, Church Street Station, New York, New York 10249). SIGCUE stands for Special Interest Group Computer Using Educators. The *SIGCUE Bulletin* is published by ACM through SIGCUE, one of its many special interest groups. It covers the range of educational computing applications and costs $5 a year if you belong to ACM and $12.50 if you do not.

Pipeline (Conduit, P.O. Box 388, Iowa City, Iowa 5224). *Pipeline* is an interesting journal. It focuses on the use of computers in higher education and publishes general articles on that topic. Most of its articles, however, are descriptions and reviews of software packages distributed by Conduit. Several Conduit programs were mentioned in the chapter on Computer-Assisted Instruction. A subscription is $15 a year for two issues.

Educational Technology (140 Sylvan Avenue, Englewood Cliffs, New Jersey 07632). Although *Educational Technology* is not strictly devoted to educational computing it is an established journal with a strong reputation. Many articles, and occasional special issues, are relevant to educational computing. *Educational Technology* has recently made an editorial decision to place even more emphasis on computer technology and to include research articles, software reviews, and conceptual papers. *Educational Technology* is available in most university libraries.

Educational Electronics (One Lincoln Plaza, New York, New York 10023). This monthly periodical covers the broad range of electronic technology which can be used in the school. There are many product review/product announcement articles as well as materials on buying and using both hardware and software.

EDU (Educational Computer Systems Group, 200 Forest Street, Marlboro, Massachusetts 01752). Published three times a year this magazine is supported by one of the established manufacturers of minicomputers, Digital Equipment Corporation. It is free and contains articles on the use of DEC computers in educational settings (primarily colleges and universities).

Perspectives in Computing (International Business Machines Corporation, Corporate Technical Publications, Old Orchard Road, Armonk, New York 10504). Published four times a year by IBM this magazine is "designed to demonstrate a variety of problem-solving computer applications in research and education...intended primarily for the academic community." Subscriptions are complimentary to university faculty.

Journal of Computers in Mathematics and Science Teaching. This is a new journal that has published a number of excellent articles on educational computing recently. Four issues a year are $15 from the Association for Computers in Mathematics and Science Teaching. P.O. Box 4455, Austin, Texas 78765.

The Journal of Special Education Technology regularly carries articles on computers and software used in special education applications. The journal is part of your membership to the Association for Special Education Technology, P.O. Box 152, Allen, Texas 75002. The journal is published quarterly; dues are $25 a year.

Collegiate Microcomputer is a new journal that will cover the use of small computers in colleges and universities. The quarterly journal is $28 per year. The first issue is due in February, 1983. *Collegiate Microcomputer*, Rose-Hulman Institute of Technology, Terre Haute, Indiana 47803.

Access: Microcomputers in Libraries is a quarterly that deals with the use of computers in libraries and media centers. It costs $11 a year. DAC Publications, 76477 LaDuke Street, Oakridge, Oregon 97463.

99er. Although this magazine deals with the TI 99/4A computer, it also includes a section on Logo and another on CAI. At least several articles in each issue are on educational applications. Six issues (one year) are $18. *99er* Magazine, P.O. Box 5537, Eugene, Oregon 97405.

Small Computer Periodicals

The publications described in this section are not concerned specifically with educational applications although many of them regularly devote space to educational applications. Several have even put together special issues with education as the focus. Most of the magazines listed in this section are available at well stocked computer stores.

Byte (P.O. Box 590, Martinsville, New Jersey 08836 – subscription service address – or 70 Main Street, Peterborough, New Hampshire 03458). One of the first small-computer magazines, *Byte* has become very sophisticated and contains articles of interest primarily to the initiated. There are articles on programming languages, many articles that tell you how to build computer equipment, and several regular columns on a variety of topics from education to computer languages. Most beginners will find *Byte* tough sledding. New computer users who already have a strong electronics background, however, may find the construction articles both understandable and interesting. In fact, many consider the series of construction articles written by Steve Ciarcia to be one of *Byte*'s greatest contributions to computer literature.

Almost 70% of *Byte*'s readers are engineers, scientists, or computer programmers and 68% of the readership has at least a bachelor's degree. *Byte* is now a McGraw Hill magazine that is slick, well-edited, and aimed at intermediate and advanced small-computer users. A one year subscription (twelve issues) is $19.

Microcomputing (Peterborough, N.H. 03458). Wayne Green started *Byte* several years ago and lost control of it through a series of conflicts (he put the magazine in his wife's name and she subsequently left him, taking *Byte* with her). Green has always been opinionated, outspoken, and somewhat gruff. He has also frequently been right on the button with his predictions and forecasts. He started *Microcomputing* after *Byte* slipped from his editorial grasp. Green also started a couple of ham radio magazines and has another computer magazine in his stable. His monthly editorial ("Publisher's Remarks") is always interesting to read even if you don't agree with him.

Compared to *Byte*, *Microcomputing* is less cerebral. There are fewer conceptual articles and more "how to do it" articles. A recent issue told how to turn the Exidy Sorcerer computer into a dumb terminal for a time-sharing system, how to build several pieces of computer test equipment, and how to add inexpensive extra memory to the Cosmac Elf computer. The same issue carried general articles on computers in the office, reviews of several new computers, reviews of commercial software packages, and several more construction articles. Since *Microcomputing* always has articles about specific computers, there will probably be many articles in each issue that do not interest you. The ones for the particular computer you use, however, may be worth far more than the cost of the magazine. The articles in *Microcomputing* range from introductory to very advanced, and the topics vary considerably. There are product reviews, how-to-build-it pieces, articles on different types of computer languages, and actual programs you can type into your computer and run. Few people will be intensively interested in every article, but there are likely to be at least ten items in each issue of *Microcomputing* that make it worth its price. That's especially true if you are interested in both software and hardware.

Interface Age (P.O. Box 1234, Cerritos, California 90701). The cover of this magazine says "computing for the home and business." That is, indeed, where *Interface Age* seems to concentrate. Unlike *Microcomputing*, it rarely publishes an article on how to build something. Instead it concentrates on articles of interest to the person who wants to use a computer to do a job. Like *Byte*, *Interface Age* publishes concept or idea articles. *Interface Age* also has several important columns on computers in education, legal issues, and mathematics.

Interface Age is probably the magazine most suitable for the small-business person and the home computer user interested in software but not hardware. By this we mean the person who may be interested in programming the computer, but not in building equipment or repairing sick systems. *Interface Age* has articles on programming and it regularly publishes programs readers can use in their own computers. It has some of the best reviews published, reviews on computers, computer systems, accessory boards, and software packages. *Interface Age* also has a large "New Products Directory" section that includes both hardware and software for small computers. It has to be considered one of the better magazines—the best, in fact, for its target audience. (Subscriptions are $18 a year for twelve issues.)

Popular Computing (70 Main Street, Peterborough, N.H. 03458). The editors of *Byte* correctly surmised that the level of most articles appearing in their magazine is well above the comprehension of most beginners. Not wanting to ignore the needs of a large segment of the market, they created *Popular Computing*. It is a mixture of tutorial articles, product reviews, and application descriptions that seem particularly suited to the needs and interests of relatively inexperienced computer users. Most *Popular Computing* articles can be understood by readers with little or no background. That is not to say the articles talk down to the reader, they just don't assume that you have a Ph.D. in computer science. Subscriptions are $18 per year for twelve issues.

Personal Computing (50 Essex St., Rochelle Park, N.J. 07662). This magazine covers some of the same territory as *Interface Age*. While the format of *Personal Computing* is a bit less formal, it regularly publishes articles of interest to the small-business person. There will probably be more reviews of expensive business computers and software in *Interface Age* and more fun programs in *Personal Computing*. A recent issue of *Personal Computing* included a BASIC program to print price lists for products with a "two-step distribution channel" and another BASIC program that let you be Alice searching for the Rabbit with the mean Queen and dippy Mad Hatter interfering with your efforts. *Personal Computing* also publishes many programs for home and school applications (for instance a grading program for teachers and a program to balance your checkbook). Reviews of new products and listings of programs you can type in and use are *Personal Computing*'s strong points. *Personal Computing* also has regular columns on computer chess, computer bridge, and computer games. It has even been criticized because it devotes so much space to these topics. Perhaps some issues were heavy on chess, but *Personal Computing* has always published articles of general interest. Subscriptions are $18 per year for twelve issues.

Creative Computing (P.O. Box 789-M, Morristown, N.J. 07960). This magazine is similar to *Personal Computing*. It carries articles that can be understood by the beginning and intermediate computer user. Most issues are a mixture of product reviews, tutorial articles, and programs. *Creative Computing* has excellent reviews of computers and computer accessories. It does a good job of reviewing software packages as well. Another strong point of *Creative Computing* is the sophisticated software provided. It has published hundreds of computer games, simulations, and applications programs. Some of their software is just plain fun, but many *Creative Computing* programs are educational (such as a program to teach children to solve math word problems) or applications (e.g., a program to help department heads manage their budgets). Whereas *Personal Computing* has special columns on chess and bridge, *Creative Computing* has monthly columns on the PET, Apple, TRS-80, and Atari computers. These columns are usually only a page or two, but they are extremely helpful to owners of those systems. Subscriptions are $25 per year for twelve issues.

InfoWorld (530 Lytton, Palo Alto, California 94301). *InfoWorld* is different from any of the publications mentioned thus far. To begin with, it is published fifty-two times a year, and it is in a newspaper format. *InfoWorld* concentrates on two types of information—news and product reviews. The news includes anything from a blow-by-blow account of corporate mergers, suits, and countersuits, to in-depth pieces on new areas of application (e.g., computers and satellite communication channels) and descriptions of new products. *InfoWorld* fills a need that no other publication does. Perhaps it's stretching a bit to call it the Wall Street Journal of small computing, but there are similarities.

If you're not interested in news, this publication may still be of interest. It carries some of the most critical reviews in the field. If a new and expensive piece of software is poorly written, if it doesn't do what it claims to do, the *InfoWorld* reviewers say so. They don't mince words. Letters from dissatisfied customers are also published. The letters they published on one manufacturer told such a tale of horror that many potential buyers changed their minds. To be fair, *InfoWorld* also publishes rebuttal letters from the companies involved, but all that butting and rebutting frequently generates quite a bit of heat. If you're likely to be buying a lot of expensive software or if you regularly purchase small-computer equipment for your school, a subscription to *InfoWorld* is well worth its price of $25 a year. *InfoWorld* also offers discount subscriptions to students. If you get ten students to subscribe (at a very attractive price—50% of the regular subscription rate) you get a free subscription.

Product Oriented Publications

A few computer manufacturers publish newsletters or small magazines about their products. Radio Shack, for example, will send *TRS-80 Microcomputer News* free of charge for one year to owners of Radio Shack computers. The price is right and the little newsletter often contains very useful information as well as product announcements from Radio Shack. It also usually contains numerous announcements about bugs discovered in Radio Shack software. Corrections are often supplied.

North Star Computers also has an excellent newsletter devoted to their line and Apple Computers produce *Apple* which is a combination magazine and catalog of Apple computer products. Commodore also began an in-house magazine in 1981 called *Commodore*. If subsequent issues are as good as the first few, this will be one of the best manufacturer supported publications. It contains articles of general interest, descriptions of Commodore products, both new and old, and programs that can be typed in and run on your Commodore computer. Unlike most company publications the Commodore magazine accepts advertising from other companies, even if the product advertised competes with a Commodore product. Subscriptions are $15 per year for six issues.

In addition to the in-house publications mentioned above, there are several other magazines that deal with only one type of computer. A new magazine titled *S-100 Microsystems* (P.O. Box 789, Morristown, New Jersey 07960) covers all the computers which use the S-100 bus. (The S-100 bus is a special pattern for connecting each of the elements in a computer together. Today the S-100 bus is used mainly by the more expensive, business-oriented computers.)

The magazine *Micro* is subtitled "The 6502 Journal." *Micro* (Chelmsford, Massachusetts 01824) contains articles on the computers that use the 6502 microprocessor chip (Apple, PET, Atari, SYM, KIM, AIM, and Ohio Scientific). It publishes a mixture of product reviews, construction articles, and programs written in BASIC and 6502 assembly language. *Micro* has grown from a brief offset newsletter with an amateurish appearance to a professionally typeset magazine filled with useful information for owners of 6502 computers. Many of the articles assume the reader is an intermediate or advanced computer user.

Nibble (Box 325, Lincoln, Massachusetts 01773) is much like *Micro* but concentrates only on the Apple computer. It carries beginners articles but also has many construction articles and program listings for the intermediate and advanced Apple user.

Compute! (Small System Services, P.O. Box 5406, Greensboro, North Carolina 27403) is one of our favorite magazines for computers which use the 6502 computer chip (Apple, VIC, Commodore 64, Atari, OSI, PET, KIM, AIM, SYM). It contains a mix of articles on both hardware and software for beginners as well as advanced users. A strong point of *Compute!* is its articles on the nitty gritty details of how each computer operates. It also publishes lots of programs you can type into your computer and use.

80 Microcomputing is Wayne Green's TRS-80 magazine. Its format is a lot like *Microcomputing* which was described earlier. Every article, however, is relevant to owners of Radio Shack computers. Perhaps the most comprehensive of the special purpose magazines, it publishes many articles of general interest which are slanted to the TRS-80. Virtually every major accesssory available for the TRS-80, and much of its commercial software, is reviewed in *80 Microcomputing*. Many BASIC and machine language programs are also published, as well as beginning and intermediate articles on using the computer in business, home, and educational settings. The magazine also publishes many construction articles. *80 Microcomputing* should be a required purchase if you own a TRS-80 ($19 for a one year subscription of twelve issues). Many people buy a basic computer from Radio Shack and then order accessories and equipment from companies that advertise in this magazine. On a $4,000 system, many people save over $1,000!

If you use an Apple computer or are thinking of buying one, you may want to subscribe to *Apple Orchard*. Published four times a year by the International Apple Corps (a consortium of Apple users groups), it is loaded with useful information about Apple computers. You will find both software and hardware articles. There are also lots of other useful articles and programs. It is available from the International Apple Corps, 910A George Street, Santa Clara, CA 95050. Subscriptions are $10 per year. The publisher of *80 Microcomputing* also publishes an Apple magazine called *InCider*.

PC Magazine (1528 Irving Street, San Francisco, California 94122) is subtitled "the independent guide to IBM Personal Computers." One of the newest of the product oriented magazines *PC Magazine* is a slick, informative, well designed publication. It appeared almost as soon as the IBM PC computer was available in stores, and the magazine has profited from the almost instant popularity of the small computer. Published bimonthly, the magazine costs $14.50 a year. If you own or are considering buying the IBM PC, this magazine should be the number one priority on your reading list.

SOURCES OF EDUCATIONAL SOFTWARE AND SOFTWARE INFORMATION

A particularly frustrating problem for educators is locating good quality software. A reader can thumb through any computer magazine and find hundreds of ads for software with prices ranging from a few dollars to a few thousand dollars. Unfortunately, the quality of educational software varies tremendously and a high price is no guarantee of high quality.

Even with hundreds of ads to peruse, many educators find the search for appropriate software an unrewarding one. There simply is not enough software in the marketplace yet and the software that is available is often difficult to locate. The search for software will be easier if the searcher makes use of some of the resources available. Many of the journals and magazines already mentioned regularly publish reviews of educational software. In addition, there are several software directories. A few organizations have even established software exchanges and software evaluation projects. A software exchange is a way of providing free or inexpensive software to members of the exchange, usually for little more than the cost of the media (i.e., a cassette, diskette, or a photocopy of the program listing.) A software evaluation project, on the other hand, may deal with all sorts of educational programs including expensive commercial packages. The project may run a center or software laboratory where educators can come and actually run software to see how it works, or the project may publish reviews of software it has evaluated. No reputable software exchange or evaluation project should provide you with pirated copies of commercial software. Software pirating is a major problem in every area of small computer applications and is particularly severe in education. If a company knows that many schools will copy rather than buy a potentially useful program that would cost tens of thousands of dollars to produce, the company may decide to spend its money and corporate energy in some other venture. All of education loses then. On the other hand, the company may go ahead and produce the software but write it in such a way that the program cannot be copied even by the original purchaser. Copy protected programs may reduce pirating, but they present major problems for legitimate owners. If the original program, whether it be on a diskette or a cassette, is used over and over, it will eventually develop a flaw that makes it unusable. If it cannot be backed-up you really are not buying a program, you are just leasing it from the company for as long as your original copy lasts.

In the best of all possible worlds software would be sold in unprotected form, educators would make backups for use only by the original purchaser, and everyone would be happy. That is not likely to happen. The best we can hope for is that pirating of unprotected software is not widespread, and protected programs can be backed up five or ten times before the protection inhibits copying.

In the following section, several sources of information about software will be described:

School Courseware Magazine (1341 Bulldog Lane, Suite C, Fresno, California 93710). This, strictly speaking, is not a magazine. Instead it is a publication that will provide subscribers with actual programs which can be used in elementary schools and high schools. The programs are on tape and include teacher manuals when necessary. They can be used on Apple II, TRS-80, or PET computers. Five issues (one year) cost $65.

The Digest of Software Reviews Education. Published by the same group as *School Courseware Magazine* listed above, this magazine is an effort to provide educators with a source of comprehensive reviews of software. It is edited by Ann Lathrop, an experienced and knowledgeable computer oriented educator. Cost is $40 a year for four issues with each issue covering over 50 programs. Lathrop and another well known computer using educator, Bobby Goodson, wrote *Courseware for the Classroom*, a book published by Addison-Wesley.

Softside (6 South Street, Milford, NH 03055). This is another publication which contains programs that can be typed in and run on your computer. Each month the magazine contains several articles of general interest and over ten programs. Most of the programs are games, but they are generally excellent. In addition, there is usually at least one business or home finance program in each issue. *Softside* publishes programs for the Apple, Atari, and Radio Shack computers. For $30 a year you get a lot of programs. This would be a good magazine to use in junior and senior high school programming or computer literacy classes. Students can look through issues, find a program they want to use, type it in, and even make modifications and enhancements. You can also buy the programs in the magazine on tape ($75 for twelve issues of the magazine and accompanying tapes) or on disk ($125). Those who can afford to buy the disk version also receive several bonus programs each year that are not printed in the magazine. The programs in the magazine are as short as eight or nine lines and as long as five or six pages. *Softside* is an excellent magazine.

Commodore Educational Software. Although the Commodore PET is a popular educational computer, many educators are not aware of the software available from Commodore for no charge. The company has several diskettes of software, almost 200 programs, which are available at no cost except the diskettes needed to copy them. Many of these programs are excellent, better in fact than many expensive programs. The free software contains many different types of programs, from drill and practice math programs for elementary school students to sophisticated chemistry simulations. You can't beat the price. Versions are also available for the Commodore 64.

Software Distribution Procedure Booklet (Minnesota Educational Computing Consortium, Publication Office, 2420 Broadway Drive, Lauderdale, Minnesota 55113). This booklet (free in Minnesota, $1 elsewhere) describes a number of educational programs for the Apple II and Atari computers which can be purchased from MECC. MECC also has a number of other publications of interest to educators.

Educational Software Directory, Apple II Edition (Sterling Swift Publishing Company, P.O. Box 188, Manchaca, Texas 78652). This $11.95 book is a directory of educational software indexed by grade level and subject matter for the Apple II computer. It includes short descriptions of the software.

The 1980 edition contained information on more than 700 software packages. This is a well done directory.

Queue (5 Chapel Hill Drive, Fairfield, Connecticut 06432). Queue publishes a number of catalogs and booklets which contain reviews of educational software. The $8.95 Queue IVA Catalog covers software for the Apple, Atari and Compucolor computers. Catalog IVB, also $8.95, deals with PET and TRS-80 educational software as well as the limited number of educational programs for the OSI, Sinclair, and Sol computers. Queue also publishes a monthly newsletter called *Microcomputers in Education* which publishes software reviews as well as news items, book reviews, and general interest articles ($24 a year). Finally this organization publishes a bimonthly newsletter for Atari users ($6 a year) called *Quatar*.

EDSEL (2833 Illinois Avenue, South Gate, California 90281). EDSEL is short for Educational Software Exchange Library. EDSEL founders say their purpose is to "build and maintain a library of computer software relating to all aspects of pre-college level education, and to provide a service whereby you can quickly and inexpensively use the facilities of the library either in person or by mail." Write for more information.

The Book of Apple Software 1983 (The Book Company, 11223 South Hindry Avenue, Los Angeles, California 90045). This book, edited by Jeffrey Stanton, Robert Willis, and Sandra Rochowansky, is excellent. It describes and evaluates many programs in several categories, including education. Editions are planned for the Atari computers. Although the price is $20.00 we feel it is well worth the money.

Foundation for the Advancement of Computer-Aided Education (20863 Stevens Creek Boulevard, Building B-2, Suite a-1, Cupertino, California 95014). The foundation has awarded grants to a number of researchers and program developers. It is also in the process of developing a program evaluation project. In 1981 the first issue of *Journal of Courseware Review* was published. The quarterly publication will contain detailed reviews of software for the Apple II computer. The journal is $5.95 an issue.

MicroSIFT Clearinghouse (Dr. Judy Edwards, Northwest Regional Educational Laboratory, 710 SW Second Avenue, Portland, Oregon 97204). MicroSIFT is an ambitious project originally funded by the National Institute of Education. The basic intent is to evaluate software and software packages and to provide those evaluations to educators who are considering buying educational programs. Write MicroSIFT for information on the current status of the project. Early indications suggest this may be one of the more successful efforts at providing useful information on computer software to practicing educators.

EPIE. In 1981 one of the authors of this book (JW) wrote that there was no "Consumers Union" and no *Consumer Reports* magazine for people who are thinking of buying hardware or software. Since 1981 Consumers Union has undertaken the task of evaluating small computers. The results were published in *Consumer Reports* in 1983. The evaluations cover both hardware and software. In addition, Consumers Union joined forces with EPIE – Educational Products Information Exchange. With funding from the Ford Foundation and others EPIE and Consumers Union set up a project to evaluate hardware and software for the educational market. Copies of their evaluations will only be provided, however, to schools or individuals who pay a fee. For information write EPIE-Consumers Union, P.O. Box 620, Stony Brook, New York 11790.

TRS-80 Educational Software Sourcebook, Volume I. Available at Radio Shack computer centers, this $4.95 book contains a listing of hundreds of educational programs for Radio Shack computers available from many different vendors. Although not complete and not evaluative, the book is a valuable source of information if you use Radio Shack computers. Radio Shack also has a free educational catalog that describes the programs available directly from Radio Shack. The company also has a booklet, *TRS-80 Microcomputer Information Handbook for Educators*, which contains some general information on educational computing. It costs $2.50. Since many Radio Shack salespeople have never heard of this booklet (and tell you it doesn't exist), here is the catalog number: 26-2757.

Educator's Handbook and Software Directory (Vital Information, Inc., 350 Union Station, Kansas City, Missouri 64108). This large book contains several articles on educational computing and a list/description of educational software with an emphasis on software for the Apple computer.

The following five indexes are not exclusively devoted to educational applications but their coverage includes education:

Periodical Guide for Computerists (E. Berg Publications, 14751 112th Avenue NE, Kirkland, Washington 98033). Mr. Berg began the Guide in 1976. The original edition was for 1975-76. It consists of categorized listings of 1,812 articles published in the fifteen magazines and journals most relevant to the small computer user. The $5 guide provides readers with a means of finding articles on a variety of topics. Berg includes all the articles published in the magazines, not just those on software topics. Many of the one hundred categories, however, are software related. Quite a few deal specifically with educational applications.

Belias' Master Index to Computer Programs in BASIC (Falcon Publishing, 140 Riverside Avenue, Ben Lomond, California 95005). The Belias index is a 192 page directory of BASIC programs that have been published in computer magazines. It contains descriptions of 531 programs, all of which can be obtained simply by buying a copy of the magazine in which they appeared. Each program is described in some detail. For $7.95 it is well worth the price.

Schreier Software Index (Schreier Software Index, 4327 E. Grove Street, Phoenix, Arizona 85040). The first edition of this index covered programs published from January to June, 1978. Other issues are also available. Schreier's index covers both machine and higher level language programs which have appeared in magazines and books. The programs are indexed by category and by the type of computer for which they were written. Each edition is $4.96 and is well worth the price.

Applications Software Sourcebook. Available at most Radio Shack stores, this fat publication contains brief descriptions of thousands of programs for the Radio Shack computers. At $2.99 this is virtually a must for anyone who purchases software for the TRS-80 Model I, Model II, Model 16 and Model III computers. The Radio Shack Color Computer and the pocket computer are also covered. There is a section on educational software which contains several hundred descriptions.

Vanloves Apple II/III Software Directory (Vital Information Inc., 350 Union Station, Kansas City, Missouri 64108). This large book is a comprehensive encyclopedia of software for Apple computers. It is somewhat easier to use than the *Applications Software Sourcebook* for the Radio Shack computers. It also costs quite a bit more, $13.00. Several of the categories in this directory are relevant to educational applications. Several people have complained of numerous errors in this relatively comprehensive directory. New editions, however, may correct the problem.

Commodore Software Encyclopedia (Commodore Computer Systems, 681 Moore Road, King of Prussia, Pa. 19406). This $9.95 book lists and describes in detail much of the software for the Commodore computers. The book has a large educational section and also includes descriptions of many accessories available for Commodore machines. The book covers material available from many suppliers in North America as well as Europe.

COMMERCIAL SOFTWARE DISTRIBUTORS

Educational computing has moved quickly from being a rarity in American schools to being a common occurrence. As the market developed, hundreds of large and small companies began advertising all sorts of software for the educational market. Some of the educational computing magazines carry advertisements for hundreds of programs in each issue. The May/June 1982 issue of *Electronic Learning* contained a list of educational software suppliers that included over 200 different companies (from AB Computers to Zweig Associates).

With so many suppliers it is difficult to keep track of what is available, what is good, and what is bad. One alternative to trying to contact every supplier is to get on the mailing list of several of the software distributors. A number of companies publish catalogs that contain descriptions of programs from many different suppliers. In some instances the company has even hired knowledgeable consultants to evaluate software before it is included in their catalog. Instead of ordering software from the developers it is often more efficient to develop one large purchase order for one source than many small purchase orders that go to different companies. Below is a list of some of the better know software distributors:

Scholastic Microcomputer Instructional Materials Catalog (Scholastic Inc., 904 Sylvan Avenue, Englewood Cliffs, N.J. 07632). One of the best catalogs, the programs included in it have been screened by a group of well known consultants. Programs are available for the Apple, PET, TRS-80, ATARI, and TI 99/4A computers. Some books are also listed in the catalog.

Microcomputer Catalog (Microdynamics Educational Systems, Inc., 2360 W. 170th, Beaverton, Oregon 97005). This company sells a number of educational programs for Apple, ATARI, PET, and TRS-80 computers. Their catalog also includes computer supplies such as diskettes, printers, printer ribbons, and dust covers as well as computers such as the Osborne I and the ATARI 800 and 400. A large selection of books from several publishers is also available. Microdynamics Educational Systems has a team of consultants and offers a variety of on-site workshops and seminars on a variety of topics.

MicroMedia Catalog (P.O. Box 17, Valley Cottage, New York 10989). This catalog contains descriptions of reviewed software for the Apple, PET, TRS-80, and ATARI computers. Educational books, some equipment and accessories, and film strips are also available. The catalog includes software from over ninety different suppliers. One of the more comprehensive catalogs.

The MicroCenter Catalog (P.O. Box 6, Pleasantville, New York 10570). Although there are a few books in the catalog, it concentrates on reviewed educational software for the Apple, ATARI, PET, and TRS-80 computers. Marilyn Carson, President of the Micro Center, offers to send evaluation copies of the software they sell free of charge and she also supplies copies of any published evaluations of the software on request.

Selected Microcomputer Software (Opportunities for Learning, Inc., 8950 Lurline Avenue, Chatsworth, California 91311). This catalog contains descriptions of many books, several filmstrip series, and hundreds of educational programs for the Apple, PET, ATARI, and TRS-80 computers. You can also order Atari computers, and accessories such as diskettes from this company.

Microcomputer Software Catalog (Society for Visual Education, Inc., 1345 Diversey Parkway, Chicago, Illinois 60614). This catalog contains descriptions of almost 200 educational programs and a number of books. SVE is an established company in the audio visual field.

American Micro Media (Box 306, Red Hood, New York 12571). Programs for the Apple, ATARI, PET, and TRS-80 computers are marketed by this company. The catalog describes over 500 programs.

Charles Clark Company (168 Express Drive South, Brentwood, New York 11717). In addition to a catalog this company also has sales agents who visit schools in many parts of the country. Clark sells programs for the Apple, ATARI, PET, and TRS-80 computers.

Educational Instructional Systems, Inc. (2225 Grant Road, Suite 3, Los Altos, California 94022). Programs in EISI's catalog were selected by a consultant who evaluated the software for quality and usability. Computers covered include the Apple, ATARI, PET, and TRS-80.

Follett Library Book Company (4506 Northwest Highway, Crystal Lake, Illinois 60014). Follett is well known to many educators. It has distributed products to the educational market for many years. Recently Follett began publishing catalogs of educational software for Apple, ATARI, PET, and Radio Shack computers. Programs included in the catalog were selected by a panel of experts.

GAMCO (Box 310-P, Big Spring, Texas 79720). GAMCO has a very good selection of software for Apple, PET, and TRS-80 computers as well as an extensive list of books of interest to educators.

Educational Activities, Inc. (Box 392, Freeport, N.Y. 11520). Software for Apple, PET, and TRS-80 computers is offered (over 100 programs) as well as supplemental materials.

Sunburst (39 Washington Avenue, Pleasantville, New York 10570). The catalog from Sunburst describes many programs for Apple, ATARI, PET, and TRS-80 computers.

BOOK PUBLISHERS

The field of small computers is growing so rapidly that most publishing companies are rushing to get at least a few books out on the subject. Several publishers, many of them relatively small, have been publishing books about microcomputers for several years. Some of the publishers with books that may be of interest to you are described below:

dilithium Press (P.O. Box 606, Beaverton, Oregon 97075). This publisher has a line of over one hundred books about small computer applications, several of which have won awards. The dilithium Press catalog, *Brain Food*, is a free publication that you may find useful. The company's series on educational computing includes books for classroom use as well as professional books for educators. The company also has a line of educational and business software. dilithium Press has a toll free number for orders and catalog requests (1-800-547-1842). dilithium Press also offers on-site seminars and workshops conducted by the authors of their books.

Addison-Wesley Publishing Company (Reading, Massachusetts 01867). Addison-Wesley has a large number of books about small computers. Its "Microbooks" series contains a number of books of interest to beginning computer users in any field. They also have an educational computing series. The first book in the series, *Practical Guide to Computers in Education*, is very good.

Hayden Book Company (50 Essex Street, Rochelle Park, N.J. 07662). Another important publisher of books on small computers, Hayden publishes a variety of books in the electronics field. Hayden is also an active distributor of computer programs. Two Hayden books, *Stimulating Simulations* by C.W. Engel and *Microcomputers and the 3 Rs* by Christine Doerr, may be of particular interest to educators.

Sterling Swift Publishing Company (P.O. Box 188, Manchaca, Texas 78652). Although relatively small, this publisher has a number of books about educational computing, many of them written by Dr. Jim Poirot who is Chairman of the Department of Computer Science at North Texas State University. The company does not do a great deal of advertising, but will provide a catalog on request.

Osborne/McGraw-Hill (630 Bancroft Way, Berkeley, Ca. 94710). This company concentrates on advanced books for programmers and computer-oriented engineers. It does offer a number of excellent books for beginners as well. Educational computing, however, is not an area of emphasis for the company. Two other publishers, Sybex, Inc., 2344 Sixth Street, Berkeley Ca. 94710) and Scelbi Publishers, (20 Hurlbut Street, Elmwood, Ct 06110) have a line of books similar to Osborne's.

ORGANIZATIONS

Many educational organizations support the use of computers in education. The National Council of Teachers of Mathematics, for example, has a special interest group on computers in education and has been very active in the area of computer literacy. There are also a variety of organizations and interest groups primarily concerned with computers and education. Few people will want to join all of them, but membership in at least one or two is a very good way to keep up with current developments:

Association for the Development of Computer-Based Instructional Systems (Computer Center, Western Washington University, Bellingham, Washington 98225). ADCIS is an active organization involved and interested in many aspects of educational computing. Their annual meeting generally includes workshops and presentations for novices as well as technical presentations on topics of current interest. ADCIS covers both large and small computer applications and has many special interest groups (such as an elementary school interest group, a junior college group, a PLATO user group, a health education group, a music instruction group, and an educators of the handicapped group). ADCIS also publishes the *Journal of Computer-Based Instruction*.

International Council for Computers in Education (Department of Computer and Information Science, University of Oregon, Eugene, Oregon 97403). If you subscribe to *The Computing Teacher* you belong to ICCE. The primary activity of ICCE is the publication of *TCT*. The organization also publishes several booklets which introduce computers to teachers and educational administrators.

Association for Computing Machinery (P.O. Box 12105, Church Street Station, New York, New York 10249). ACM is a very large organization which represents virtually every aspect of computer application and computer research/theory. ACM also has a number of special interest groups including Computer Using Educators, which publishes the SIGCUE Bulletin. ACM has over 50,000 members and is a major force in computing.

Conduit (P.O. Box 388, Iowa City, Iowa 52244). Conduit "reviews, tests, and distributes computer-based instructional materials." It publishes the journal *Pipeline* and distributes over 50 programs written in BASIC or FORTRAN for use in university level courses. Conduit also publishes a series of books on writing educational software which are highly recommended. Conduit was originally primarily concerned with large computers, but in recent years it has taken the lead in promoting the use of small computers in higher education.

Association for Educational Data Systems (1201 16th Street NW, Washington, D.C. 20036). AEDS was founded in 1962 to serve as a forum for the exchange of ideas about the use of computers in all aspects of education. AEDS publishes three journals, holds a very interesting annual convention, and sponsors a number of activities and projects related to computer usage in education. Regular membership dues are $35 a year, students may join for $10 a year.

DATABASES AND INDEXES OF INTEREST

The literature on computer applications in education is spread over several hundred journals and magazines. A person searching for information on a particular topic would find it very time consuming to look through every publication that might have an article or two of interest. Fortunately there are better ways of finding articles on educational computing. Every library reference section contains several indexes, publications that categorize and describe the articles published in journals. A major index in education is *Current Index to Journals in Education* (CIJE). *CIJE* is published monthly with annual editions available for all but the current year. It indexes the contents of hundreds of journals in education and related fields. One section of *CIJE* is a subject index. A user interested in Computer Assisted Instruction can look under that heading in the subject index and find a listing of articles published during that year which are relevant to CAI. Unfortunately, there is no one single subject heading that lists all the articles on educational computing, but a user can look under headings such as educational technology, microprocessors, simulations, and programmed instruction for relevant articles. Once you find the title of an article that might be of interest, you can read an abstract of the article as well as information such as author, institutional affiliation, and source of publication.

CIJE is published by ERIC, Educational Resources Information Center. ERIC also publishes *Resources in Education* (RIE), which indexes unpublished papers and reports as well as articles. The ERIC system includes a series of microfiche documents which are indexed in RIE. Many libraries carry all or most of the ERIC microfiche publications which can be read on a microfiche reader. Large documents such as curriculum guides, manuals, and extended project reports could not be economically published in journals but are easily placed in the ERIC microfiche files since one small microfiche card can hold over 100 pages.

The ERIC indexes do not contain all the literature on educational computing since much of it appears in computer oriented journals and psychology journals. *Psychological Abstracts* is one of the best indexing publications and sorts articles into many different categories, several of which are relevant to educational computing. *Computer and Control Abstracts* plays a similar role in computer science and computer engineering. It has a subject classification entitled computer aided instruction and one called "applications of systems theory to education." Since the ERIC index does not cover many journals in the computer science area an article on computer assisted learning which appeared in a computer journal may not appear in *CIJE*. That means you may want to use several indexes if you want to be sure you locate most of the articles on a specific topic.

The Association for Computing Machinery also publishes an annual index, *Guide to Computing Literature*, which covers some of the same journals as *Computers and Control Abstracts*.

COMPUTER DATABASES

Tracking down relevant articles using an index such as *CIJE* is still a time consuming process. You must look in a thesaurus for the index you are using to identify the specific terms used to categorize articles. Usually there will be several categories that might contain articles of interest. Then you must look through each of the subject categories, note the publication numbers, and look up those numbers in another section where an abstract of the article is printed.

Fortunately there is another way of doing the initial search for relevant articles. There are several computerized information databases which allow a user to search databases such as ERIC or Psychological Abstracts from a computer terminal. One of the most widely used is Lockheed's Dialog system which is based in Palo Alto, California. From our computer terminal at Texas Tech we can call a special number that connects us to the Dialog computer. After giving it our account number we tell it which database we want to search (such as ERIC, or Psychological Abstracts). Then it is possible to tell the computer exactly what we are looking for. We could tell it to find all the articles which deal with teaching reading via computer to elementary school children or articles on Computer Managed Instruction for college level chemistry courses. Dialog then tells the user how many "hits" (the number of relevant articles) it found during each of its searches. Suppose that it found 200 articles on computer based chemistry courses. You can ask Dialog to list some of the abstracts from those articles on the screen. If the abstracts indicate the articles are relevant to your interests, Dialog can be instructed to print the abstracts out on a high speed printer and mail them to you. A printout of 200 abstracts will cost about $20. Each abstract contains a description of the article, the authors, where they work, and where the article was published.

As this section was written Dialog announced plans to offer databases devoted exclusively to microcomputers and software for small computers. By the time you read this section you may be able to dial up Dialog, connect the phone to your computer, and ask Dialog to list on your screen all the software available for a particular model of microcomputer that can be used for a particular purpose (for instance junior high school physics or pupil record keeping).

Most university libraries now have some form of computer search system. A few have contracts that allow them to purchase the databases and put them on their computer systems. The College of Education at the University of British Columbia, for example, accepts search requests at its research center and runs the searches late at night on the UBC mainframe computer. The printouts are available the next morning.

When comprehensive searches are required, using a computer database can save days of work in the library. In some cases the computer search will also be more comprehensive. If you suspect some important articles have been missed because they have not been indexed under the proper subject coding, it is possible (with some databases) to ask the computer to look for keywords in the abstract of the article as well as to find "hits."

SUMMARY

If you have reached this point in the book after having read each of the ten chapters, you have a good foundation of information about educational computing. By subscribing to a few good magazines, joining one or two organizations, and attending some of the very good conventions which are held each year, you can rapidly become a very knowledgeable computer-using educator. Perhaps, in a year or two, we will read an article or book you have written about your use of computers. In any case we hope you will find computers useful additions to your educational armamentarium.

Index

Access: Microcomputers in
  Libraries 231
administrative applications 38
AEDS Journal 228
AEDS Monitor 228
Ahl, D. 15
Aiken, H. 12
Albrecht, B. 15
Algebra Drill and Practice 166
alphanumeric string 100
Altair 17
analogue computer 12
analytical engine 10
Apple Education News 229
Apple Orchard 237
Applications Software Sourcebook 243
arithmetic symbols, BASIC 91
array 108
assembler 87
Association for Computing
  Machinery 248
Association for the Development of Computer Based
  Instructional Systems 248
Author I 190
Autocom 50
Avant-Garde Creations 191

Babbage, C. 10
bar code reader 69

BASIC 15, 88
Belias' Master Index to Computer
  Programs in BASIC 243
Bellingham High School,
  educational computing in 37
Bilingual Math 168
Block, G. 229
Bloom's Taxonomy 196
Book of Apple Software, 1983,
  The 241
bookkeeping 41
Bork, A. 29
branching programmed
  instruction 25
BREAK key 104
British Columbia, educational
  computing in 34
Burroughs, W. 11
Bush, V. 12
buying a computer 54
Byte 231

CAI 27, 159-183
CAIWARE-2D 190
CAL 27, 159
Cannon, S. 176
career counseling 200
cassette recorder 68
cassette storage 77
Chambers, J. 29
Change Agent 181

254 • Computers, Teaching and Learning

characters, BASIC 91
Chatfield, D. 193
CIJE 249
Civil War 180
Classroom Computer News 226
CLOAD 115
CLS 99, 133
CMI 27, 159, 183-203
coexist 181
Collegiate Microcomputers 231
Colossus 12
comma 100
commands 93
Commodore 236
Commodore Educational Software 240
Commodore Software Encyclopedia 244
COMMON PILOT 121
Compete 181
compiler 90
comptometer 11
Compute! 237
Computer and Control Abstracts 250
computer assisted diagnostic report writing 206, 215
computer assisted instruction 27, 159-184
computer assisted learning 27, 159-184
computer managed instruction 27, 159, 185-203
computer stores 74
computer test scoring 214
Computers and Education 228
Computers Reading and Language Arts 229
Computing Teacher, The 226
copy protection 239
Craig, D. 50
Creative Computing 234
cost analysis 205
counters 105
CPU 86

criterion referenced testing 210
CSAVE 115
Cumin 176
Current Index to Journals in Education 249
cursor 96

DEC 14, 15
diagnostic simulation 211
Dialog 251
difference engine 10
Digest of Software Reviews Education, The 239
digital computer 12
DIM 110
dimensioning 110
disk drives 78
Ditmer, R. 166
Doerr, C. 247
dollar sign ($) 102
doomsday key 63
drill and practice 160

Eckert, J. 13
EDSEL 241
EDU 230
Educational Activities 246
educational computing 2
Educational Computing Magazine 226
educational diagnosis 204
Educational Electronics 230
Educational Software Directory, Apple II Edition 240
Educational Technology 230
Educator's Handbook and Software Directory 242
egocentric 142
80 Microcomputing 237
8008 15
8080 15
Electronic Education 227
Electronic Learning 227
ELSE 103

Index • **255**

Engel, C.W.   247
Engle, B.   168
Englemann, S.   140
ENIAC   13, 14
ENTER   94
entry criteria   197
EPIE   242
ERIC   250
ETS   200, 204
Evolut   181
exit criteria   197

false expression   102
Felt, D.   11
Fireside Computing   190
floppy diskettes   78
FOR NEXT   111
4040   14
Foundation for the Advancement of Computer Assisted Education   241

Goodson, B.   239
GOTO   104
grading   217
Grant, G.   11
graphics tablet   67
Guide to Computing Literature   250
Gundach, A.   188
Hallerith, H.   11
handicapped applications   50
hard disk drives   81
hardware   15
Harvard Mark I
history of computers   2, 9
Holcomb, C.   194
Humphrey, M.   191

IBM   11, 13
IC   13
IF THEN   102
Imprinting   181
InCider   237
InfoWorld   235

INPUT   101, 103
input options   65
Institute for Child and Family Studies   38
Instructional Innovator   228
Instructional Systems Center   193
integrated circuit   13
Intel   14
interactive computer-based testing   207
Interface Age   233
International Council for Computers in Education   248
interpreter   90
inventory   41
Ireland, educational computing in   35

Jacquard, J.   11
JEM Research   34
Journal of Computer Based Instruction   228
Journal of Computers in Mathematics and Science Learning   231
Journal of Special Education Technology   231

keyboard   76
key words   93
Kleiman, G.   191

language, assembly   86
language, machine   86
language skills   173
languages, specialized   118
large scale integrated (circuit)   13
Lathrop, A.   239
leasing   72
learning objectives   196
LET   94
Leuhrmann, A.   6
light pen   65

linear programmed instruction 25
LIST 94
Little Professor 162
Logo 136
Loibnitz, G. 10
LOOP 103
LPRNT 115
LSI 13

mail order suppliers 74
mainframe 3
Mallon, M. 168
Mark I 12
Mark-8 16
Mauchley, J. 13
MECC 33
Melmed, A. 30
membrane keyboard 77
Micro 236
Microcomputers in Education 241
microcomputing 223
microprocessor 13
MicroSIFT Clearinghouse 241
Microtype 168
Miller, M. 53
Milliken Math 168
Milton Bradley 173
minicomputer 14
Minnesota Educational Computing Consortium 33
MITS 16
mnemonic 87
mode batch 88
mode, conversational 88
mode, delayed 95
mode, edit 96
mode, immediate 95
mode, interactive 88
Moursund, D. 30, 226
Moynihan, M. 35
music synthesizer 66

Napier, J. 10
nature vs. nurture 139

nested loop 112
networking 7, 22, 65
Nibble 236
Nold, E. 176
numeric 102
numeric information 102

Oregon Trail 181

Papert, S. 137
Pascal, B. 10
PC Magazine 237
PDP-8 14
Periodical Guide for Computerists 243
Personal Computing 234
Perspectives in Computing 230
Piaget, J. 137, 138
PILOT 117
PILOT commands 122, 125
PILOT conditioners 123
PILOT Information Exchange 135
Pipeline 230
pirating 238
plotter 68
Poirot, J. 31, 247
Popular Computing 233
Powell, J. 31
Pressey, S. 23
PRINT 94
program 92
programmed instruction 25
Psychological Abstracts 250
punch cards 11
punctuation marks 92

Quatar 241
question mark 101
Queue 241
Quick Quiz 189
quotation marks 100, 111

READ 112
READY 90, 106
REM 98

Index • 257

repair 71
Resources in Education 250
retail stores 74
RIE 250
Riley, M.T. 38
RND 99, 122
Roberts, H. 16
Rooze, G. 43
RUN 88, 94

S-100 Microsystems 236
safety 70
save 115
scatter 181
schemas 141
School Courseware Magazine 239
Schreier Software Index 243
selecting a computer 54
semiconductor 13
service 71
shock hazard 70
SIGCUE Bulletin 229
SIGI 200
simulations 160, 178-182
Skinner, B.F. 24
Smullen, C. 166
Softside 239
software 15, 85
software selection criteria 182-183
Solomon, L. 17
Speak and Spell 162
speech synthesis 66
sprites 145
SRA 170
statement, matching (PILOT) 124
statements 91
statements (BASIC) 123
statements (PILOT) 92
string 100, 101
string variables 105, 111
subscripted variables 109
SWTPC PILOT v.1.0. 121
syntax 92, 118

T.H.E. Journal 229
Taylor, R. 26, 31
teacher competencies 31
teaching machine 23
telecommunication 41
television display 76
terminal 3
Terrapin, Inc. 144
test administration 220
test development 222
time sharing 4
touch typing 167
transistor 13
Tribbles 131
TRS-80 Educational Software Sourcebook, Volume 1 242
true expression 102
turtle graphics 144-148
TUTORIAL CAI 171-178

usage patterns 45
user's manual 90, 114

Vanlove's Apple II/III Software Directory 243
VIC 14
video display 57, 75
video monitor 76
videodisk 26
Vojack, R. 162

Weir, S. 138
Willis, D.S. 38, 53
Willis, J. 53
word processing 40, 43

Zenith Educational System 191
ZES 191
Zuse, K. 12

Readable Apple® Books

Microbook: Database Management for the Apple II®
Ted Lewis

At last, here is an affordable way for you to have a database management system on your Apple II. Written in Pascal, this program can be used for almost any application involving the storage and retrieval of information. The entire source listing is included if you want to type the programs, or you can buy the diskette with the programs on it.

Book: ISBN 0-88056-072-X
320 pages $19.95

Book & Diskette:
ISBN 0-88056-156-4
$34.95

32 BASIC Programs for the Apple® Computer
Tom Rugg and Phil Feldman

Chock full of programs with practical applications, educational uses, games and graphics. Each chapter fully documents a different program which is ready to run on your Apple computer. You can type the programs in yourself, or buy a diskette for the Apple II, Apple DOS 3.3 with the programs on it.

Book: ISBN 0-918398-34-7
304 pages $19.95

Book & Diskette:
ISBN 0-88056-151-3
$29.95

Basic BASIC-English Dictionary
Larry Noonan

This unique dictionary gives you an alphabetical listing of all commonly used BASIC commands, statements, operators, and special keys, then translates them for use on the Apple, PET, and TRS-80 computers. Translating from one BASIC to another is a breeze, as examples and explanations abound.

ISBN 0-918398-54-1
150 pages $10.95

☐ Please send me the book(s) I have indicated. I understand I may return for a full refund if I am not satisfied.
 __ Microbook — book $19.95   __ Microbook — book & diskette $34.95
 __ Basic BASIC-English   __ 32 BASIC Programs for the
     Dictionary $10.95   Apple Computer — book $19.95
 __ 32 BASIC Programs for the Apple Computer — book & diskette $29.95
☐ Enclosed please find my check which includes $1 to cover handling. $____
Name _____
Address _____   ☐ Please send me
City, State, Zip _____   your FREE catalog
Mail to: dilithium Press, P.O. Box E, Beaverton, OR 97075   BRAINFOOD

dilithium Press
P.O. Box E
Beaverton, OR 97075
(800) 547-1842
(503) 646-2713

✓ Use our toll free number for VISA or M/C orders or to learn the store nearest you that carries our books.

Readable TRS-80® Books

32 BASIC Programs for the TRS-80® Computer
Tom Rugg and Phil Feldman

Here are 32 fully documented programs that are guaranteed to run if entered exactly as shown. Included are practical applications, educational uses, games and graphics. You can type the programs in yourself, or buy a diskette for the TRS-80 model I or model III computers with the programs on it.

Book: ISBN 0-918398-27-4
304 pages $19.95

Book & Diskette:
 Model I $29.95
 Model III $29.95

The Tenderfoot's Guide to Word Processing
Barbara Chirlian

Are you curious about word processing and want some direction? This book gets you started. The first half is a general discussion of word processing, then the rest of the book describes in great detail how to use a specific word processor, *The Executive Assistant*. This gives you a clear idea of what you and a word processor can do.

ISBN 0-918398-58-4
150 pages $10.95

TRS-80® Color Programs
Tom Rugg and Phil Feldman

Chock full of 37 different programs that are ready to run on your TRS-80 color computer, this new book gives you educational uses, practical applications, games and graphics. If entered exactly as shown, the programs are bug-free! Special color section also included showing programs on the computer screen.

ISBN 0-918398-61-4
324 pages $19.95

☐ Please send me the book(s) I have indicated. I understand I may return for a full refund if I am not satisfied.
 __ Tenderfoot's Guide to Word   __ TRS-80® Color Programs 19.95
     Processing 10.95   __ 32 BASIC Programs for the
 __ 32BASIC Programs for the   TRS-80® Computer — book
     TRS-80® Computer — book 19.95   & diskette — Model___ 29.95
☐ Enclosed please find my check which includes $1 to cover handling. $____
Name _____
Address _____   ☐ Please send me
City, State, Zip _____   your FREE catalog
Mail to: dilithium Press, P.O. Box E, Beaverton, OR 97075   BRAINFOOD

dilithium Press
P.O. Box E
Beaverton, OR 97075
(800) 547-1842
(503) 646-2713

✓ Use our toll free number for VISA or M/C orders or to learn the store nearest you that carries our books.

☐ Yes, send me your free catalog, BRAINFOOD, which lists over 90 microcomputer books covering software, hardware, business applications, general computer literacy and programming languages.

NAME _____

ADDRESS _____

CITY, STATE, ZIP _____

☐ Yes, send me your free catalog, BRAINFOOD, which lists over 90 microcomputer books covering software, hardware, business applications, general computer literacy and programming languages.

NAME _____

ADDRESS _____

CITY, STATE, ZIP _____

☐ Yes, send me your free catalog, BRAINFOOD, which lists over 90 microcomputer books covering software, hardware, business applications, general computer literacy and programming languages.

NAME _____

ADDRESS _____

CITY, STATE, ZIP _____

FREE CATALOG FREE CATALOG FREE CATA LOG FREE CATALOG FREE CATALOG FREE CATALOG FREE CATA LOG FREE CATALOG FREE CATALOG FREE CATALOG FREE CATA LOG FREE CATALOG FREE CATALOG FREE CATALOG FREE CATA LOG FREE CATALOG FREE CATALOG FREE CATALOG FREE CATA LOG FREE CATALOG FREE CATALOG FREE CATALOG FREE CATA LOG FREE CATALOG FREE CATALOG FREE CATALOG FREE CATA LOG FREE CATALOG

Mail To:

dilithium Press
P.O. Box E
Beaverton, OR 97075

Or Call:

800-547-1842

FREE CATALOG FREE CATALOG FREE CATA LOG FREE CATALOG FREE CATALOG FREE CATALOG FREE CATA LOG FREE CATALOG FREE CATALOG FREE CATALOG FREE CATA LOG FREE CATALOG FREE CATALOG FREE CATALOG FREE CATA LOG FREE CATALOG FREE CATALOG FREE CATALOG FREE CATA LOG FREE CATALOG FREE CATALOG FREE CATALOG FREE CATA LOG FREE CATALOG FREE CATALOG FREE CATALOG FREE CATA LOG FREE CATALOG FREE CATALOG FREE

About the Authors

Jerry Willis, well-known dilithium Press author, holds a Ph.D. in child clinical psychology. He has 20 years experience in education as a professor of educational psychology and is the director of the Educational Computer Center at Texas Tech University. Dr. Willis is the author of *Nailing Jelly to a Tree*, *Peanut Butter and Jelly Guide to Computers*, and *Computers For Everybody*, all of which were chosen by the Library Journal as outstanding computer publications.

Lamont Johnson is an Associate Professor of Special Education at Texas Tech University. Dr. Johnson specializes in computer applications with children who have learning problems. He is the author of software program, Autowriter, which is designed for school psychologists and special educators who administer and score psychological tests. Dr. Johnson is also the editor of the journal Computers in the Schools.

Paul Dixon, the chairman of the Psychology Department at Texas Tech University, has been involved in educational computing and CMI (computer managed instruction) for the past 12 years. Dr. Dixon has written articles on educational computing for such magazines as Educational Computer Magazine and the Journal of Computer Based Instruction.